WHITEWASHING
UNCLE TOM'S CABIN

Nineteenth-Century Women Novelists
Respond to Stowe

Whitewashing
Uncle Tom's Cabin

Nineteenth-Century Women Novelists
Respond to Stowe

Joy Jordan-Lake

Vanderbilt University Press
Nashville

© 2005 Vanderbilt University Press
All rights reserved
First Edition 2005
09 08 07 06 05   1 2 3 4 5

This book is printed on acid-free paper.
Manufactured in the United States of America
Library of Congress Cataloging-in-Publication Data

Jordan-Lake, Joy, 1963–
Whitewashing Uncle Tom's cabin: nineteenth-century
women novelists respond to Stowe / Joy Jordan-Lake.—
    1st ed.
    p. cm.
Includes bibliographical references and index.
ISBN 0-8265-1475-8 (cloth : alk. paper)
ISBN 0-8265-1476-6 (pbk. : alk. paper)
    1. American fiction—Women authors—History
and criticism. 2. Slavery in literature. 3. Women and
literature—United States—History—19th century.
4. Stowe, Harriet Beecher, 1811–1896. Uncle Tom's
cabin. 5. American fiction—White authors—History
and criticism. 6. American fiction—19th century—History and criticism. 7. Women, White—United States—
Intellectual life. 8. Southern States—In literature.
9. African Americans in literature. 10. Plantation life in
literature. 11. Slaves in literature. I. Title.
PS374.S58J67 2005
813'.3093552—dc22   2004021923

For my family, who asked questions
as if they were genuinely interested,
who cheered me on through many a midnight march,
and who pulled together
to make this possible.

And especially for my son, Justin,
who was born in the midst of this book's creation and
who napped many an hour in my lap
at the computer.

CONTENTS

Acknowledgments

This book began life, quite a few years ago and in a considerably different form, as a dissertation and never would have amounted to anything more than a ream of used paper had it not been for my advisor at Tufts University, Elizabeth Ammons, whose scholarship and social activism I salute. In the midst of teaching, relocating from New England to North Carolina and then to Texas, and having my second child, I was exhausted, disorganized, and desperate to be done with doctoral work. But over and over again, Liz demanded better, deeper, more original thinking—and at least relative to the drivel I probably would have passed off then as good enough, she insisted on something more.

Early on in my graduate school education, Carol Flynn enthusiastically encouraged my wanting to write about literature in relation to issues of poverty and social injustice, while John Fyler actively supported my incorporating feminist theology and regularly stuffed my mailbox with articles he thought might be helpful.

I am indebted to a footnote in Elizabeth Fox-Genovese's *Within the Plantation Household* that probably provided the germ for this research by indicating her frustration that so little study had been done on the antebellum fiction of Southern women.

The interlibrary loan staffs at Wingate University in North Carolina and Baylor University in Texas must have clocked overtime helping me secure obscure antebellum texts from all over the country, and I am grateful.

Teresa Goddu's incisive reading of an early draft of this book proved to be enormously helpful and inspired my adding Chapter 5.

And in this book's final stages, a visit to my university from Catherine Clinton gave me a needed boost of affirmation for the homestretch. Her work, as well as that of Fox-Genovese and Anne Firor Scott, provided essential and fascinating historical background for my reading.

I am grateful for Vanderbilt University Press's support of this book, and particularly for Betsy Phillips's unflagging enthusiasm and wise editorial counsel, as well as for Bobbe Needham's eagle-eyed copyediting.

Throughout the time that I was writing and researching these novels by and about women—and very much having to do with mother-savior and female Christ imagery—the women in my life were monumentally supportive. My mother, Diane Jordan, who then lived a thousand miles away, voluntarily appeared at two critical junctures to help care for children and perform other heroic duties so I could lock myself in my office. My mother-in-law, Gina Lake, who lives even farther away, offered similar help and gave me a birthday gift, *Cane River*, which so perfectly fit my research it found its way into the final chapter. Just before looming deadlines, Susan Lancaster, Christy Somerville, Kay Brinkley, Kelly Shushok, and my sister-in-law, Beth Jackson-Jordan, along with other friends, all busy with their own personal and professional lives, helped out in innumerable practical ways. Ginger Brasher-Cunningham and Laura Singleton sent books and other relevant gifts that often aided research and always gave me a lift.

But this is not to overlook magnificent men. I'm indebted to my father, Moncrief Jordan, and my brother, David Jordan, for their love and affirmation, and for all the ways they share their lives.

And what can I say about my husband? I could not imagine a better friend or conversationalist or co-parent or life partner than Todd Lake. He has been unwavering in his support at every turn and unfailingly generous with his time and hugs and words, and even eagerly, actively pitched in on research. Todd, you are magnificent, and I'm more nuts about you than ever.

And finally, thanks to my children, Julia, Justin, and Jasmine, for who you are, for how you keep the rest of life in perspective, for all the ways you make the smallest, most insignificant thing a wonder. I thank God for you every day.

PREFACE

In the Beginning, a Photograph

Perhaps this book began with a nineteenth-century photograph, grainy and indistinct, handed down in my family from mother to daughter for six generations. The woman in the photo is old, her mouth a thin, determined line, her jaw set stubbornly, and her hair the color of the Birmingham steel-mill smog that would, during the early and mid–twentieth century, smother the land where her farm once stood. Those who told the story to me—my mother and mother's mother—called it a farm. They were good socially progressive Democrats, fans of Martin Luther King Jr., the kind of enlightened white Southerners who did not give money to erect Confederate monuments, did not groom their daughters for Daughters of the Confederacy balls, and avoided using words like "plantation" in relation to their families. The story handed down with the photograph of my great-great-great-grandmother told how she had borne nine children, then lost her husband to the Civil War and—though this was never explicitly mentioned—lost her slaves to the Emancipation Proclamation. She'd never so much as brushed her own hair, the story goes. Yet, left with nine hungry little ones and not a soul who knew how to push a plow, she learned to plant and weed and harvest and haul and barter—and survive; she successfully ran the farm and raised nine children to adulthood. In her old age, she cross-stitched a sampler that read "God doth provide" and hung it over the dining-room table to teach her children and children's children about the difficult years. And so goes the story's lesson to each generation's daughters: you come from a line of women of strength and faith—draw on that strength. Amidst white Southern culture, which, as Lillian Smith has observed, "still pays nice rewards to simple-mindedness in females" (Palmer 455), this story was a gift of courage to me as a little girl from women of courage I admired.

But the story teaches other lessons too—as my grandmothers and my mother and my daughters and I have been learning, generation by generation. Some of the lessons are chilling, to say the least.

I was a graduate student living in New England when I thought of that story for the first time since I was a child. I was reading the recently rediscovered *Iola Leroy*, Frances E. W. Harper's ultimately triumphant tale of a cast of African American characters who, having endured slavery and the Civil War, go on to secure education, material security, and social respectability. Harper concludes her book by assuring the reader of her protagonists' virtuous, useful lives: "Blessed themselves, their lives are a blessing to others" (281).

Staring out a window, I did not see the Boston skyline in the distance but instead wondered about the women who brushed my great-great-great-grandmother's hair. I wondered if they too managed to raise their children to adulthood, if they too survived—even thrived. And I wondered what my own family's story said about the God of the antebellum white South.[1] Did that deity also provide for the former hair brushers and plow pushers? And what did the story say about white Southern men, so conspicuously missing from the strength it celebrated? What did it mean that the white Southern woman of relative privilege discovered her own abilities only in the absence of the white Southern male and of the slaves she had helped oppress? I wondered too if it had ever occurred to anyone—my great-great-great-grandmother, for example—to divide up the "farm" according to who had worked it and for how long. And I wondered whether, had I been in her shoes, it would have occurred to me. "Grief" is the best word I know to describe the journey into and through this book.

In the graduate seminar on American women writers that assigned *Iola Leroy*, I was also reading Harriet Beecher Stowe's *Uncle Tom's Cabin* for the first time. I had almost read it more than fifteen years earlier in an eighth-grade English class in my East Tennessee hometown, Signal Mountain, a lovely, dogwood-studded little community perched two thousand feet above Chattanooga. These days, National Public Radio and the *New York Times* tout Chattanooga as a renaissance city—and deservedly so, with its bustling riverfront and revitalized downtown. But in the late 1970s, plenty of whites my age still belonged to a culture in which the public high school, for which

Harriett Earle Bradford Wood, "Granny," mother of nine children, and the author's great-great-great grandmother. Widowed in Civil War at East Lake, Birmingham, AL. Photo courtesy of the author.

mountain residents had to descend to the valley, boasted giant "rebel" flags flown by frenzied football fans, cheerleaders who choreographed the best pom-pom routines to "Dixie," a spring prom that called for hoop skirts, and prom pictures that featured a Corinthian-columned plantation home as a backdrop. What Faulkner once observed of the South in general held true at that time for us: the past was not even past. Certainly, plenty of whites in my hometown were appropriately appalled when the KKK chapter on our mountain's "back" side appeared in full regalia at a roadblock, where they poked deer rifles in drivers' side windows and collected money in Kentucky Fried Chicken buckets. But I learned as an adult living in Boston that not every American childhood includes the specter of white hoods surrounding one's car. Only as an adult did I learn—and only then while watching the movie *Ghosts of Mississippi*—that black civil rights worker Medgar Evers's assassin, Byron DeLaBeckwith, chose the "back" side of Signal Mountain as his home from 1964, when an all-white hung jury released him, until his 1994 conviction. Those of us who thought we were living in the New South—big on sunshine, flowering trees, and friendly convenience-store clerks, but light on that embarrassing old bigotry of the past—must have paid for our roadside cider and pumped our gas right beside the man and never knew it.

So it was on Signal Mountain in 1977 that I almost read *Uncle Tom's Cabin,* but it was assigned instead to the other eighth-grade English class. And I recall one of my classmates taunting a student across the hall: "You're not really gonna read that nigger-lovers' book, are you?"[2] That in itself should have pointed me to something extraordinarily powerful in its pages.

When at last I did read it more than fifteen years later, I was living in abolition's nineteenth-century hub. (Boston also likes to think of itself generally as the "hub of the universe." And perhaps it is.) By that time I was prepared to recognize the romanticization of the antebellum South in which I had grown up—and participated. By that time I was ready to examine the painful complexities of Southern racism, how it created and was created by slavery, and how that racism still prohibits and excludes, defines and divides.[3]

Reading *Uncle Tom's Cabin* for the first time, I wept—just as Stowe had calculated her readers would do. I was a few months away from having my first child, and Stowe's depictions of slave mothers having their children wrenched from their arms was more than I could bear.

As the following pages reflect, my eighth-grade classmate's reaction to *Uncle Tom's Cabin* and my own response years later echo the polarized national—and international—reactions to the novel in 1852. To this day, the novel provokes lively, often heated, occasionally acrimonious scholarly and political debate—perhaps more than any other single American novel. Stowe strategized literarily to reach her readers at an intellectual and, significantly, at an emotional level: more than 150 years later, her strategy is still at work.

INTRODUCTION

The Personal Becomes the Project

$\mathcal{F}$ew books have had more impact upon the history of the United States and, consequently, on more American lives than Harriet Beecher Stowe's *Uncle Tom's Cabin*. Few books have evoked such powerful emotional responses—and few continue, scores of years later, to do so. One has only to mention *Uncle Tom's Cabin* in a faculty lounge or classroom of any American university to provoke a flurry of strident responses, often from those who have never read it: some will assume that because *Uncle Tom's Cabin* attacked slavery, it must contain no racist elements; some familiar with a particularly disturbing racist caricature or scene in the book will argue that it has no redeeming value socially, historically, or literarily. Both these assumptions would be wrong. Some who have stumbled over its slave characters' dialect or felt swamped by its sentimental, melodramatic tone simply dismiss *Uncle Tom's Cabin* as a "bad book," undeserving of their further reading time. This reaction, too, is regrettably shortsighted.

The first American novel to sell more than a million copies, *Uncle Tom's Cabin* incited an entire reading public to extol it, debate it, berate it, weep over its pages. Some were moved to compassion; others, to violence. One enraged reader sent Stowe the severed ear of one of his slaves. Published soon after the passage of the infamous Compromise of 1850 and its constituent Fugitive Slave Law, *Uncle Tom's Cabin* fanned the firestorm that surrounded slavery. Abolitionists, who had viewed the Compromise as a cowardly capitulation to the South, rightly heralded the novel as a mighty stroke for their cause. Slaveholding Southerners, protesting what they saw as the novel's excesses, inaccuracies, and misunderstandings, took offense at Stowe's portrayal of their way of life. In her scathing review of *Uncle Tom's Cabin*, Louisa McCord, the mid–nineteenth century's leading Southern woman of letters, accused Stowe of both ignorance and inhumanity, since

> it is a cruel task to disturb [the slave] in the enjoyment of that life to which God has destined him. He basks in the sunshine, and is happy. Christian slavery, in its full development, free from fretting arrogance and galling bitterness of abolition interference, is the brightest sunbeam which Omniscience has destined for his existence. (120)

McCord employs here what I define throughout this book a "theology of whiteness," a framework that manipulates religious language and ideology to support the economic interests of a white patriarchal culture, including the creation of a deity in its own image: white, male, indifferent to injustice, and zealous in punishing transgressions across the racial, gender, and class lines it has drawn.[1] Positioning "God" as the chief creator and defender of slavery, and white slaveholders as innocent, McCord suggests that whites do not oppress enslaved blacks; they are not pursuing economic profit but merely obeying what "Omniscience" has "destined" for slaves' "enjoyment." "Arrogan[t]" abolitionists, therefore, challenge divine authority by opposing slavery.

With a few exceptions, particularly in the border states of Kentucky, Tennessee, and North Carolina, regions whose economies did not depend on slavery, the South generally received the book with hostility. Angry townspeople in Mobile, Alabama, harassed a bookseller who dared to display *Uncle Tom's Cabin* in his window and chased him out of town. Students at the University of Virginia in Charlottesville held book burnings. A Maryland court sentenced a free black found with a copy of *Uncle Tom's Cabin* and abolition materials on his person to ten years in prison.[2] Reflecting this acrimony, most reviews of the book in Southern publications could best be classified as tirades, such as George Holmes's assessment in the October 1852 issue of the *Southern Literary Messenger*:

> Every holier purpose of our nature is misguided, every charitable sympathy betrayed, every loftier sympathy polluted . . . and every patriotic feeling outraged by [*Uncle Tom's Cabin's*] criminal prostitution of the high functions of the imagination to the pernicious intrigues of sectional animosity, and to the petty calumnies of willful slander.

Holmes exemplifies here rhetoric that I term "theopolitical," a word I have coined in this book to describe the way in which antebellum proslavery advocates continually weave their interpretations of Judeo-Christian scripture and theology into their political arguments as one of *the* key defenses of slavery, casting it as not only economically necessary but also God ordained.[3] Holmes's argument, for example, links holiness and patriotism with proslavery rhetoric, casting Stowe as a literary slut and a traitor to the cause of national peace. In suggesting that her work has "polluted" and "prostitut[ed]" the "holier purpose of our nature," he couples a Northern woman's antislavery politics with sexual deviance, a pattern frequently repeated in anti–Uncle Tom novels by women. Rather than promoting *toleration,* allegedly a primary goal of anti–Uncle Tom women writers, Stowe has stirred hostility.[4]

Yet, if the South did not like Stowe's book, her opponents would learn from her genius: Southerners and proslavery Northerners fought the fire her novel had sparked with their own fiction, producing nearly three dozen novels in direct response to *Uncle Tom's Cabin.*[5] In addition to the paucity of material written on anti–Uncle Tom novels, several of the scholars who address this genre estimate the number they understand to be—or to once have been—in existence, but proceed to name only a handful of the best-known works. For example, Jane Gardiner's 1975 *Southern Humanities Review* article that describes Southern and Northern proslavery writers addresses only one novel by name. J. V. Ridgely counts fifteen novels written between 1852 and 1854 that responded to *Uncle Tom's Cabin:* six by Northerners, six by native Southerners (one of whom lived in the North twenty years), and three by Northerners who adopted the South as home. Margaret A. Browne focuses on fifteen novels and one poem, though she alludes to the existence of others. In *The History of Southern Women's Literature,* Karen Manners Smith's brief overview of Southern women writers' responses to Stowe does not mention the existence of any anti–Uncle Tom novels by Northern women and includes in its Southern scope Caroline Lee Hentz, who was born and raised and lived her early adult life in the North. While Smith's focus on Southern respondents is understandable given her space limitations and the text for which she is writing, it unfortunately reinscribes a facile dichotomy of antislavery North versus proslavery South, which the anti–Uncle Tom literature complicates significantly. Stephen Railton's superb Web site on *Uncle Tom's Cabin* probably contains the most comprehensive extant list to date of anti–Uncle Tom literature and even includes representative excerpts from the works, and

Thomas Gossett's *Uncle Tom's Cabin and American Culture* has been the most thorough textual examination of them—yet even he concentrates primarily on the texts by men, and his consideration of anti–Uncle Tom literature is limited to a single chapter. Although I have studied the anti–Uncle Tom literature of all genres, I have limited this book's primary scope to fiction to remain consistent with Stowe's chosen literary vehicle for her political persuasion.[6] For reasons I explicate further in Chapter 1, I divide these novels according to the gender of the author. Though such a division might seem arbitrary or contrived, the differences in methodology, characterization, and theopolitical argumentation became increasingly apparent to me and finally demanded separate—and unequal—consideration.

Drawing upon the work of Jean Fagan Yellin, Susan Tracy, Jeanette Reid Tandy, Margaret Browne, Stephen Railton, and Thomas Gossett, as well as my own examination of all the primary texts, I categorize the following as anti–Uncle Tom fiction written by men: Nehemiah Adams, *The Sable Cloud: A Southern Tale, with Northern Comments* (1861); David Brown, *The Planter* (1853); William M. Burwell, *White Acre vs. Black Acre. A Case at Law* (1856); Lucian B. Chase, *English Serfdom and American Slavery* (1854); Robert Criswell, *Uncle Tom's Cabin Contrasted with Buckingham Hall, the Planter's Home* (1852); Matthew Estes, *Tit for Tat; A Novel by a Lady of New Orleans* (1856); Baynard R. Hall, *Frank Freeman's Barber Shop: A Tale* (1852); James W. Hungerford, *The Old Plantation, and What I Gathered There in an Autumn Month* (1857); Joseph Holt Ingraham, *The Sunny South* (1860); Theodore Dehone Mathews, *Old Toney and His Master* (1861); Lawrence ., *Edith Allen* (1855); James M. Smythe's, *Ethel Somers* (1857); John W. Page, *Uncle Robin in His Cabin in Virginia, and Tom without One in Boston* (1853); J. Thornton Randolph, *The Cabin and the Parlor* (1852); William Gilmore Simms, *Woodcraft* (1854); W.L.G. Smith, *Life at the South* (1852); Ebenezer Starnes, *The Slaveholder Abroad* (1860); and Thomas Thorpe, *The Master's House* (1855). Because they fit with the hero-focused model of the anti–Uncle Tom novel by men, I also include in this category Vidi, *Mr. Frank, the Underground Mail-Agent* (1853), and two anonymous novels, *The Olive-Branch* (1857) and *The Yankee Slave-Dealer* (1860).[7]

My list of anti–Uncle Tom novels by women is shorter but, I would argue, more fruitful for intertexual discourse with Stowe and with one another. These novels include Martha Haines Butt, *Antifanaticism* (1853); Mrs. V. G. Cowdin,

Ellen (1860); Mary H. Eastman, *Aunt Phillis' Cabin* (1852); Mrs. G. M. Flanders, *The Ebony Idol* (1860); Sarah Josepha Hale, *Liberia* (1853); Caroline Lee Hentz, *The Planter's Northern Bride* (1854); Maria Jane McIntosh, *The Lofty and the Lowly* (1853); Caroline E. Rush, *The North and South* (1852); and Mary Howard Schoolcraft, *The Black Gauntlet* (1860). While Elizabeth Wormeley Latimer's *Our Cousin Veronica* (1855) cannot be considered technically anti–Uncle Tom, I include it in my discussion of mammy and mistress figures in anti–Uncle Tom fiction for reasons made clear in Chapter 3.[8] I also include Caroline Gilman's *Recollections of a Southern Matron and a New England Bride* (1838) in my discussion because, although it was published earlier, it was reprinted in 1852 as a direct rebuttal to Stowe with the apparent approval of its author, a native Northerner who by the 1850s was residing in Charleston, South Carolina, and had become unwaveringly proslavery.[9]

By my count, the female-authored anti–Uncle Tom novels, including Gilman's, total ten: five Northerners and five Southerners.[10] Given that several of the Southerners moved away from the plantation South as young adults, the majority of these female proslavery novelists were not themselves slaveholders, the implications of which I analyze later in the book. I would emphasize, however, the sometimes blurry distinction between antebellum plantation romances that advocate slavery by sketching it as a gracious, desirable way of life and those that are more polemically proslavery or explicitly anti–Uncle Tom. *Our Cousin Veronica* exemplifies the problem. Initially set among antislavery activists in Great Britain, it often sympathizes with abolition. In the end, however, I argue that it sides against abolition by displaying slavery as an affectionate, paternalistic relationship far preferable to Northern poverty, thus employing—intentionally or not—a common proslavery strategy. I categorize anti–Uncle Tom novels as those that make the defense of slavery the primary purpose for their creation; that were published (or, in Gilman's case, republished) between the 1852 book debut of *Uncle Tom's Cabin* and the onset of the Civil War; and, in most cases, that explicitly indicate within their pages that they are responding to Stowe.

Because only a few scholars have studied the anti–Uncle Tom novels and even fewer have closely examined those written by women, no careful analysis exists to this point of the latter novels as a group and the precise structure of their proslavery polemic. Some scholars have analyzed individual novels such as *The Planter's Northern Bride,* but typically only in relation to other domestic novels and with no particular attention to how an a priori commitment to slavery skews what might appear to be a protofeminist perspective. Minrose Gwin has skillfully contrasted *Aunt Phillis' Cabin* to *Uncle Tom's Cabin,* yet she does not consider *Aunt Phillis' Cabin* in relation to other anti–Uncle Tom texts by women, an investigation which, as I demonstrate in the following pages, reveals the patterns and tropes by which these novels attempt to defend slavery but actually undermine their own and each others' arguments. Historian Catherine Clinton has decried the "New Englandization" of women's studies and the dearth of attention to Southern women's history and writings. As Patricia Morton points out in *Discovering the Women of Slavery,* until recently scholars have neglected white and black Southern women's history and instead upheld the struggle for "manhood" as the central metaphor of slavery. In useful studies of the sexism, racism, and classism found in the literature produced by the antebellum male planter elite and of antebellum Southern women's historical context, both Susan Tracy and Elizabeth Fox-Genovese note the lack of critical attention to antebellum Southern women's fiction.

A number of factors led me to examine Stowe and anti–Uncle Tom women writers: the dearth of research in this area; a lifelong interest in Southern history, literature, and race relations; a more recent interest in liberation theology, which, among other goals, considers the impact of socioeconomic injustice upon both the oppressor and the oppressed; fascination with Stowe's maternal focus in her literary strategy; and hauntings from my own maternal ancestry.[11] Initially intrigued that the gender of the anti–Uncle Tom authors seemed to influence—even determine—the gender of their protagonists, the methodology of their political arguments, and the deployment of their literary strategies, I began analyzing precisely how they construct their arguments and how, I would argue, they later deconstruct them. Throughout my research, I remained intrigued with why white women of privilege would have participated in a system of both slaves' brutal exploitation and their own subjugation. This question led me to examine how the arguments embedded in these novels reflect the intricacy with which racial, class, and gender ideologies supported the construction and protection of whites' economic privileges.

Both within their own pages and in intertextual dialogue, the anti–Uncle Tom novels by women finally implode logically, politically, and theologically. Elizabeth Ammons has highlighted the ways in which Stowe employs images of female Christs, mother-saviors whose nurture, leadership, and example effect transformation. Building upon her work, I demonstrate how, like Stowe, female anti–Uncle Tom novelists attempt to appeal to maternal sensibilities and how, like her too, they offer motherhood as salvific for an admittedly fallen society. Yet I also demonstrate how the narratives destroy their own arguments, as the redeemer-heroines of the proslavery rebuttals finally exercise no real power, provide no effectual solutions to social ills. Contrary to their intent, the proslavery texts' evasions, displacements, and contradictions disrupt their surface narratives, ultimately exposing a profit-driven chattel slavery as savage as anything Stowe envisioned. These texts dismantle themselves and each other to reveal even their most noble women characters—and the writers themselves—to be only pawns in a vast patriarchal game in which the pursuit and maintenance of white society's wealth is made to appear humane, and even holy.

Chapter 1 analyzes, as its subtitle announces, the plantation literary tradition, which reflects the ubiquitous dominance of wealthy white men and demonstrates how white women writers of the emergent anti–Uncle Tom novels import characteristics from sentimental fiction, rendering their own distinctive genre. Contrasting anti–Uncle Tom novels by women with those by men highlights key differences. Certainly, both stockpile arguments from the Bible, the Constitution, and nineteenth-century "scientific" research such as phrenology, and both exhibit similar tropes: the converted abolitionist, the loyal slave who rejects manumission, the miserable fugitive slave who suffers in Northern poverty. How they deploy their arguments, however, divides along gender lines. Insofar as women anti–Uncle Tom novelists emulate Stowe with their female protagonists, particularly their maternal saviors, and with their political issues argued through depictions of women's relationships, their texts are methodologically closer to *Uncle Tom's Cabin* than to those of their male allies. Demonstrating the rigidification of the male plantation literary tradition, I trace the genre's development through several transitional plantation novels and emergent anti–Uncle Tom novels by men, while suggesting the ways in which the novels by women deviate from that pattern.

In the next two chapters, I focus on the women-authored anti–Uncle Tom novels themselves and pay particular attention to the writers' female Christ imagery, their perspectives on women's rights and sufferings, and their use of a theology of whiteness, which I demonstrate is employed by these women writers far more than by their male counterparts. Concentrating particularly on the novels set in the North, Chapter 2 shows how Rush's *North and South,* Cowdin's *Ellen,* and Flanders's *Ebony Idol* follow sentimental fiction's pattern of challenging male dominion and appearing to promote female independence. Ultimately, though, they shy away from threats to any of slavery's three primary buttresses: racial, gender, and economic oppression. By narrative's end, each of these attacks on patriarchy collapses under its own proslavery social agenda. Unlike the male-authored anti–Uncle Tom narratives, whose male protagonists debate and soliloquize on slavery, Rush, Flanders, and Cowdin advance their arguments through relationships, primarily between mothers and daughters and between Northern and Southern mothers. In contrast to Stowe's female Christs, though, these would-be redeemers "save" by reenslaving and by promoting submission to white male authority.

Chapter 3 focuses on selected novels that feature a plantation setting: Eastman's *Aunt Phillis' Cabin*, Hale's *Liberia*, Schoolcraft's *Black Gauntlet*, Hentz's *Planter's Northern Bride*, McIntosh's *The Lofty and the Lowly*, Latimer's *Our Cousin Veronica*, and the Stowe-induced reprint, Gilman's *Recollections of a Southern Matron and a Northern Bride*. In these texts, key mammy and mistress figures defend slavery through their alleged cross-racial affection and their appearing to revel in "belonging" to the white male planter. Together, these two complementary maternal images portray plantation life as one big happy biracial family, presided over by the omniscient white male planter–god. On closer examination, however, these narratives themselves represent plantation patriarchs as potential tyrants and predators, and expose how the plantation South brutalizes enslaved black women and debilitates wealthy white women. Revealing their anxiety that their support of slavery appear to follow Judeo-Christian teachings, the anti–Uncle Tom women writers use proof-texts to support their position, that is, biblical verses taken out of context, and routinely blame an apparently capricious, sadistic God for slaves' sufferings. In trying so hard to demonstrate their religious orthodoxy and the antislavery industrial North's godlessness, these writers commit their own heresies, positioning the wealthy white male as plantation society's god of gods and advocating white economic security as the ultimate good.

As a background upon which to juxtapose the women-authored anti–Uncle Tom novels and their depictions of slavery, Chapter 4 analyzes the historical and literary context of antebellum planter-class and slave women. Based on their journals and letters, as well as a few slave narratives and oral histories, this chapter primarily explores the complex relationship of white planter-class women to their slave-based society and attempts to discover why, by my count, the majority of women anti–Uncle Tom novelists would be nonslaveholders without an obvious and direct political and economic stake in slavery's perpetuation.[12] As Helen Papashivly asserts, the antebellum South "was full of literary ladies articulate, not to say garrulous, on a variety of subjects," yet "when it came to defending slavery as an institution, the native-born and -bred Southern women kept discreetly quiet and let those with less firsthand knowledge, less real experience answer Mrs. Stowe" (77). As my fourth chapter demonstrates, planter-class women, while highly motivated by hierarchical subjugation and economic self-interest not to protest slavery publicly, were likely to acknowledge slavery's atrocities privately. Loath to attack the "peculiar institution," they proved just as loath to defend it.[13] After sketching a grim historical context for slaveholding and enslaved women, I argue that it was precisely the narration of plantation life *from a distance* that enabled nonslaveholding women to present the plantation South as a fantasyland of impeccable estates and unfailingly harmonious race relations.

Chapter 5 considers a free Northern black writer, Harriet Wilson, and her fairly recently rediscovered novel, *Our Nig*, which Henry Louis Gates Jr. has described as, in many ways, an anti–Uncle Tom though also antislavery text.[14] I contend, however, that while Wilson's novel exhibits striking similarities to several anti–Uncle Tom novels by women, including the exposure of a phony fugitive slave, Wilson emulates Stowe's political strategies and, literarily, several of her key scenes of persuasion. Then Wilson performs a revision to Stowe, ultimately offering a more damning critique of American society, North and South.

The sixth and concluding chapter examines four novels that span the twentieth century—*Uncle Tom's Cabin of Today*, *Gone with the Wind*, *Savannah*, and *Beloved*—and two in the twenty-first, *Cane River* and *Wind Done Gone*. I show how the first three reinscribe the plantation tradition with its consequent impact on American cultural ideas of the South and on the white South's image of itself and how, in contrast, Toni Morrison's *Beloved* refutes the romanticizations by subverting the plantation myth and resurrecting Stowe's mother-savior ideology. Demonstrating that, like *Uncle Tom's Cabin* and its rebuttals, *Cane River* relies upon mother-daughter relationships for its persuasive power, I also examine the poignant biracial mother-daughter dynamics of *Wind Done Gone*. Like the anti–Uncle Tom novels by women, particularly those covered in Chapter 3, *Wind Done Gone* centers its narrative on the plantation South's two-mother, mammy-mistress system, but author Alice Randall reproduces the myth only to annihilate its glorification. Randall also addresses what I have termed a theology of whiteness, and she exposes its worship of the Confederate male as a stand-in for the white South's God, and the trap, even for a relatively independent black woman, represented by this misguided racial reverence. Finally, I speculate briefly on the current presence of the plantation myth in the South, and its impact on twenty-first-century political and social issues.

Throughout this study, I emphasize the complexity of antebellum racism. For example, though I use terms such as "the plantation South" and "the antebellum white South" to mean Southern defenders of slavery, I also try to disrupt any simplistic equation of all white Southerners with a single unvarying proslavery political stance or all white Northerners with abolition. As I show, neither South nor North was politically unified, and individual cases illustrate the pitfalls of facile generalizations. Hinton Rowan Helper of North Carolina offers a prime example. The author of *The Impending Crisis of the South*, which argued for the eradication of Southern slavery for economic reasons, Helper proved a mixed blessing to Northern abolitionists when he evinced an abiding detestation for persons of color and refused even to sit next to any African American at antislavery rallies. Cassius Clay of Kentucky praised *Uncle Tom's Cabin* for its accurate portrayal of slavery but, after donating the land for Berea College, founded in 1858, later declined to serve as a trustee because the school accepted blacks and whites on an equal basis.

My conclusions rest primarily upon close readings of the novels themselves, as well as readings of the novels in relation to each other and *Uncle Tom's Cabin*. Methodologically, I employ feminist theory together with socio-historical analyses of racism and of the construction of white hegemony, in which such scholars of language and history as Henry Louis Gates Jr., Ronald Takaki, and Thomas Gossett prove invaluable, as do critical race theorists such as Ian Haney-Lopez and Cheryl Harris. Toni Morrison's *Playing in the Dark: Whiteness and the Literary Imagination* became foundational to my observing how what Morrison terms the "Africanist presence" disrupts surface narratives. Liberation theology, as seen in the works of Gustavo Gutierez, provides reminders that perpetrators of social injustice not only cause suffering to their victims, but also, ultimately, damage themselves.[15] In opposition to such theories as Carl Degler's in *The Other South*, which assert that race and class should be separated in considering the complex social forces that supported slavery, I maintain that we cannot omit race, class, or gender in any complete understanding, so inextricably linked are they in antebellum Southern society.

Although I concur with Degler on the bewildering complexity of pro- and antislavery perspectives, I insist on a decided political rigidification of the white South as its slave-based economy became increasingly threatened. That the moneyed classes led this shift seems to me irrefutable. In arguing that support for slavery did not fall neatly along class lines, Degler marshals evidence that includes Governor John Floyd, who in 1831 confided to his diary that he wanted slavery abolished in Virginia, and Congressman Robert Reid of Georgia, who labeled slavery both unnatural and evil. The former, however, was silenced after the 1832 Virginia slavery debates, and the latter concluded that emancipation was not in the best interest of *all* citizens. Granted, William Gaston, a superior-court judge in North Carolina, ruled in 1834 that a slave could resist a white man to save his own life, and Gaston insisted that slavery was holding the South back from progress. But such voices faded after the 1830s beneath a well-orchestrated roar of proslavery unanimity. By the late antebellum period, historian Garry Wills has observed, Southerners "had decided that a slave society cannot afford the luxury of free speech" and began employing verbal intimidation and vigilantism as legitimate means to social conformity—that is, proslavery unanimity among whites (201). Proslavery rhetoric became increasingly histrionic, so that petitioners to end slavery in the District of Columbia were labeled "murderers of Southern women and children" by livid slaveholding legislators (204).

Insisting on the diversity of opinion among Southern whites regarding slavery during the early nineteenth century, Degler notes that in 1827 the South could boast 106 antislavery societies, as opposed to the North's 24. He concedes, however, that many of the South's antislavery factions resulted from fears of amalgamation and miscegenation, and I would add that these Southern societies disappeared by the 1850s—illustrating an astoundingly rapid shift toward a univocally proslavery message. Meanwhile, in either North or South, as Degler confirms, few abolitionists based their convictions primarily on the welfare of the slave.[16]

Trying to address these ambiguities, I show how the defense of slavery bound anti–Uncle Tom women novelists to subscribe not only to a particular racial caste system, but also to a rigid economic and gender hierarchy, always accompanied by elaborate theological embellishments. Examining precisely how these constructions support and protect one another—and how they finally deconstruct—helps illuminate how racism both creates and is created by socioeconomic structures such as slavery, and how it impacts both oppressed and oppressor. I hope, too, that this analysis of fiction composed by white women who defended the enslavement of black women, men, and children sheds light on the ethical and moral disaster of privileging any single social group's economic strength over other groups' access to dignity, compassion, and fundamental justice.

Whitewashing
UNCLE TOM'S CABIN

CHAPTER 1

"To Woman . . . I Say Depart!"

The Plantation Literary Tradition, the Emergent
Anti–Uncle Tom Novel, and Gender

*I*n writing *Uncle Tom's Cabin,* Harriet Beecher Stowe herself, whether consciously or not, was writing both within and against the plantation-romance tradition—as were the writers who attempted to rebut her.[1] Consequently, it is important to examine first the plantation literary tradition and its evolution into anti–Uncle Tom novels. Laid out by such popular Southern novelists as John Pendleton Kennedy, William Gilmore Simms, and Nathaniel Beverley Tucker, the plantation literary tradition's inception, usually dated to the 1832 publication of Kennedy's *Swallow Barn,* coincided with the white South's political rigidification. Although before the 1830s the South's antislavery groups actually outnumbered those in the North, in the years that followed slaveholding states increasingly silenced or forced out dissenting voices.[2] In the wake of the Denmark Vesey plot, Nat Turner's rebellion, the Virginia slavery debates, and mounting opposition from abolitionist forces, the white South became increasingly sectional, defensive, and conservative. Significantly, the process of romanticizing the plantation South began with political stockading, including an absolute insistence upon white society's univocal support of slavery.

The early roots of anti–Uncle Tom fiction reveal significant ambivalence regarding slavery. Though slightly pre-dating the generally accepted commencement of the plantation literary tradition, the life and writings of George Tucker exemplify the early nineteenth-century white South's political oscillations. In 1800, when Tucker was twenty-six years old, he published a pamphlet that argued against the South's "peculiar institution" (Yellin, *Intri-*

1

cate Knot 19). Sixteen years later, the anonymously published *Letters from Virginia, Translated from the French,* now attributed to Tucker, includes not only trenchant criticism of the racism evident in Thomas Jefferson's *Notes,* but also a strident attack on slavery itself (ibid.). Yet in 1824 Tucker published *Valley of the Shenandoah,* one of the earliest nineteenth-century novels to employ a plantation as romantic backdrop and to include a lengthy defense of slavery. Though the protagonist admits that slavery "is repugnant to its [the country's] justice . . . and dangerous to its peace" (1:63), the narrative ultimately frames slavery as economically expedient in the short run, and colonization, unpromising. "We . . . find domestic slavery," observes main character Edward Grayson, "established among us, and the evil, for I freely admit it to be an evil, both moral and political, admits of no remedy that is not worse than the disease" (1:61). According to the narrative, chattel slavery should be operated as beneficently as possible, with an eye toward its gradual demise.

Tucker's increasing tolerance of race-based slavery may be explained, at least in part, by economic self-interest, which, as Henry Louis Gates Jr. argues in his introduction to *"Race," Writing, and Difference,* consistently serves as a powerful catalyst behind the arbitrarily applied trope of "race." Financial scandal had forced Tucker to leave Richmond before the writing of his first novel. In serious debt, he moved to Woodbridge, Virginia, bought slaves, and attempted to remake himself as a Tidewater planter. Yet Tucker's depiction of the planter-class patriarch, a role he had begun to play, exposes not entirely positive characteristics:

> a nice sense of honour; a hatred of all that was little or mean; more fond of hospitality than show; great epicures at table; great lovers of Madeira wine, of horses and dogs; free at a jest, particularly after dinner, with a goodly store of family pride, and a moderate portion of learning; never disputing a bill, and seldom paying a debt, until like their Madeira, it had acquired age; scrupulously neat in their persons, but affecting plainness and simplicity in their dress; kind and indulgent rather than faithful husbands, deeming some variety essential in all gratifications of appetite. . . . The luxurious and social habits in which they were educated, gave them all that polished and easy grace, which is possessed by the highest classes in Europe. (*Valley of the Shenandoah* 2:105–6)

Aristocratic though this depiction is, there is nothing here of the planter-god image, the stern, morally upright, all-powerful Southern white male who comes to dominate later novels bent on theopolitical aims. As Susan Tracy notes, such forthright confessions of planter profligacy and infidelity as Tucker's would not be repeated after the late 1820s, as white men of privilege suppressed all intimations of moral or ethical flaws in the antebellum South's socioeconomic structure (53). While *Valley of the Shenandoah* concedes—or at least stops short of denying—the white South's responsibility for slavery, it also warns that emancipation might unleash another Santo Domingo revolution and argues that colonization could never provide a practical solution. Characters in the novel defend slavery as necessary and inevitable. Tucker apparently retains some slivers of his former doubts: he glorifies Southern culture's beauty and grace, yet he criticizes planter society and while he inveighs against abolitionist rhetoric, he insists upon black humanity.[3] Having opposed Southern secession from the Union and predicted the abolition of slavery but the perpetuation of the United States as a "white man's country," Tucker died the day before the firing on Fort Sumpter when, on a visit to Mobile, Alabama, he was struck—as if by poetic justice—by a falling cotton bale (Tracy 48–49).

Novelist John Pendleton Kennedy's ideology presents similar complexity. During the final days of 1831, just after Nat Turner's rebellion and just before the Virginia slavery debates in which abolition was narrowly defeated in a 68–65 legislative vote, Kennedy confessed to his journal his reservations regarding slavery and his resolve to free his own slave—though a few entries later he records having sold the slave because he suspected him of stealing (Yellin, *Intricate Knot* 50). In 1831, Kennedy also completed *Swallow Barn*, often cited as the first plantation novel. From it, a familiar line of stock characters marches into the twentieth century, including, as I examine in my final chapter, key figures in Margaret Mitchell's *Gone with the Wind*, published a century later: the hospitable, if occasionally silly, slaveholder; the lovely, capricious Southern belle; and the faithful, domineering mammy. Published in 1832, *Swallow Barn* depicts plantation society as simultaneously provincial and charming, pretentious yet abounding in hospitality. Observing how Kennedy flatters the Virginia aristocracy, then pulls back "smilingly," William Taylor notes that satire and sentimentality coexist within the novel's pages (162–64). Both lovable and laughable, the planter aristocracy presumes to view itself as feudal nobility, parodied in the character Bel Tracy, who attempts to train a marsh hawk as if it were a falcon.

Presumably representing a Northern perspective, the novel's narrator, New Yorker Mark Littleton, describes planter society with both humor and admiration. Though admitting initial apprehensions on visiting the South, before long Littleton is musing that "a thousand acres of good land, an old manor-house, on a pleasant site, [and] a hundred negroes [would] be sufficient to make him happy" (452–53).

Still, slavery in the 1832 edition of *Swallow Barn* serves only as a backdrop, never as an institution to be defended unequivocally.[4] Country squire Frank Meriwether confesses to Littleton he believes slavery to be morally wrong, though ineradicable, and reveals his plan for manumitting all male slaves as they reach their forty-fifth year, when he will retrain them as tenant farmers. This, he states proudly, would not only encourage good conduct but also relieve him of supporting elderly slaves. In addition to the protagonist's confessions of slavery's immorality, *Swallow Barn* contains decided forebodings. As Jean Fagan Yellin has noted, an impenetrable swamp surrounds the sunny, cheery plantation, and the slave Abe appears as a heroic young rebel (*Intricate Knot* 56). In this first edition of his book, Kennedy equivocates on slavery.

By the second edition, in 1851, however, *Swallow Barn* has become far less satirical, as well as far more adamant in its defense of white-controlled Southern society.[5] As MacKethan has observed, for the 1851 edition Kennedy elaborates on the education of Meriwether's daughters and lauds their being cloistered from the sullying influences of the world outside the plantation: "Kennedy quite simply locks the southern white woman in a domesticated bower and throws away the key" (229). Consequently, Kennedy emphasizes domestic ideology and the crucial slavery-supporting role of the sweet and sequestered planter-class woman. The slaves, too, appear even more content than in the earlier edition.[6] Touring the picturesque slave quarters, Yankee Mark Littleton now observes: "The contrast between my preconceptions of their [the slaves'] conditions and the reality which I have witnessed, has brought me a most agreeable surprise" (452). The text now insists upon slavery as an issue that pertains only to the white South, which should consider not abolishing the institution but reforming it by legalizing slave marriage and preserving slave family units. Meanwhile, the North should not intervene. Yet

Kennedy, a staunch Unionist, was the only one of the prominent plantation tradition writers to eventually free his own slaves (Tracy 23).

In the two decades that followed the 1832 publication of *Swallow Barn,* the white South's reigning power structure began recasting the institution no longer as an agrarian society's regrettable necessity, but rather as an indisputable social good to both master and slave. The year 1850 saw the acrimonious legislative debates over the Compromise, which admitted California as a free state but also included the infamous Fugitive Slave Law, which allowed slaveholders to reclaim their "property" above the Mason-Dixon Line and motivated Harriet Beecher Stowe to write *Uncle Tom's Cabin.* Stowe's novel, coupled with the white South's already defensive stance, prompted immediate, often belligerent, responses from the region's established novelists.

Nothing inherent in the plantation setting predetermined a proslavery message, as *Uncle Tom's Cabin* best exemplifies. In fact, antislavery activists who chose fiction as a form of social protest sometimes created Southern settings equally as lush as those of their proslavery counterparts. For the latter, romanticized visions of the planter family's gracious manners, lavishly appointed mansion, elegant clothing, and blooded horses justified what white writers termed the "Southern way of life"; antislavery writers painted equally enviable homes, gardens, evening repasts, and wardrobes to juxtapose planter opulence and the wretchedness of the slave quarters (Gaines 30). As Gaines points out, abolitionists were writing plantation novels as early as 1688.[7] While Harriet Beecher Stowe did not pioneer abolitionist plantation fiction, *Uncle Tom's Cabin* was the first novel to show female characters working for social transformation in quintessentially antebellum Southern settings: a Kentucky farm, slave quarters, a Mississippi River paddlewheeler, semi-tropical gardens, and two mansions, one as decadently gorgeous as the other is dilapidated. Some of the novelists who learned from Stowe imitated her formula for similar abolition goals. Others, the anti–Uncle Tom women novelists in particular, emulated Stowe in order to refute her, typically acknowledging that combat as their raison d'être.

Contrasting the anti–Uncle Tom novels by men with both their stated antagonist, *Uncle Tom's Cabin,* and the anti–Uncle Tom novels by women shows striking differences in their portrayals of female characters and their persuasive methods.[8] Provided with no real agency of their own, white planter-class women in the male-authored novels do not attempt to improve society except in its physical beautification. Female slaves may exhibit more assertiveness than do their mistresses, but even this ultimately serves the masters' interests, as when slave wives discourage their husbands from attempting escape or participate in the safe return of runaways. Though the plots of the male-authored books differ considerably, some involving the courting of fair maidens, others the reeducating of abolitionists, all action revolves around white male characters. Consistently, wives, mothers, vassals, and damsels in distress represent devotion, loyalty, and, occasionally, silent suffering. Female characters, white and black, become mere recipients of the hero-master's munificence and never rise above secondary significance to the narrative, which, as Sara Evans asserts, "reveal[s] more about the needs of white planters than about lives of women, white or black" (1353). As in the early plantation romances from which these novels developed, only white male protagonists provide the narrative drive and, just as *Swallow Barn*'s Meriwether lectured his Northern guest on slavery's merits, their proslavery arguments proceed via men's soliloquies and contentious debates.

Though William Gilmore Simms has typically been grouped squarely among proslavery novelists, his life if not his work belongs more appropriately to the transitional period between the political ambivalence of the early plantation tradition and the belligerent confidence of the antislavery and anti-Stowe novels after 1852.[9] Like Kennedy, in his younger years Simms did not subscribe to an unequivocally proslavery, states' rights agenda, even though as a native of Charleston, South Carolina, he had inherited two homes in the city and approximately two dozen slaves from his mother. As editor of Charleston's *Gazette* in 1830, Simms publicly professed both Unionist and antinullification views, positions which not only provoked a mob attack but eventually caused him to flee north. Returning from New England, he married Chevilette Roach, whose father gave the newlyweds one of his plantations, Woodlands, situated on the Edisto River. As Simms's economic situation shifted, his political ideology followed, so that just before the outbreak of the Civil War, he would write to John William Bockee:

> The Southern states are welded together by the institution of African slavery—an institution which has done more for philanthropy and humanity in one year than ever has been achieved by all the professed philanthropists of Europe and America in 100 years: and this labor, in our genial climate, can be applied to all the industrial arts—the construction

of railroads—to the working of mills. . . . Our water power never freezes, and it is abundant, our labor never times itself to short or long hours, and never *strikes* impatient to share largely in the profits of the capitals. (*Letters IV* 302)

Having once found the "peculiar institution" morally dubious, Simms the planter now lauds it. Writing his economic treatises in London even as Simms penned his fiction, Karl Marx would have predicted just such an ideological shift.

By 1835, Simms had begun publishing his Revolutionary War novels, all set in a romanticized South.[10] In the first of seven of these works, *Yemassee* (1835), whites and subjugated blacks defend an English colony against assailing Indians. In Simms's *Woodcraft*, originally titled *The Sword and the Distaff* and published the same year as *Uncle Tom's Cabin*, Revolutionary War patriot Captain Porgy defends his plantation as the British retreat. Though *Woodcraft* contains no explicit proslavery arguments, it communicates clearly, if indirectly: slaves are delighted to serve a cultivated planter elite. The contentment of Simms's fictional Southern blacks belies his familiarity with the Denmark Vesey affair, a vast Charleston slave insurrection crushed in its final planning stages by city leaders. In *Woodcraft*, however, Simms envisions a planter aristocracy certain of its subordinates' happiness and unwavering devotion. Porgy crows that "his" Tom would " 'rather die my slave, than live a thousand years under another owner' " (113) and even suggests that Tom commit suicide rather than switch masters. Though Tom appears decidedly less eager to prove such loyalty, he does obligingly refuse his freedom: " 'You b'longs to *me* Tom, jes' as much as me Tom b'long to *you;* and you nebber guine get *you* free paper from me long as you lib,' " (509). (This is a trope common in anti–Uncle Tom fiction—an affectionate slave choosing to remain captive—that assuages the white South's guilt.[11] Theodore Dehone Mathews's *Old Toney and His Master*, for example, employs this trope, portraying abolitionists either as unfeeling for wanting to separate a devoted vassal from a benevolent master, or as charlatans; the novel's full title is *Old Toney and His Master; or, The Abolitionist and the Land-Pirate, Founded on Facts: A Tale of 1824–1827.*) Accordingly, Simms attacks the motives of antislavery forces, as exemplified in his character Mrs. Eveleigh's confronting British hypocrisy as she tries to regain her slaves: "South Carolina [by the close of the Revolutionary War] had already lost 25,000 [slaves], which British philanthropy had transferred from the rice-fields of Carolina, to the sugar estates of the West India Islands" (6). *Woodcraft* repeatedly depicts Great Britain, which by this time had outlawed slavery throughout its empire, as conniving and unscrupulous. In pillorying Britain for the existence of slavery and for abolitionist agitation, *Woodcraft* sets a precedent enthusiastically followed in other anti–Uncle Tom novels by men, such as *English Serfdom and American Slavery; Uncle Robin in His Cabin in Virginia and Tom without One in Boston; The Planter; The Slave-holder Abroad;* and *White Acre vs. Black Acre.* In these texts, in fact, the white women of the "mother country" as well as white women of the United States, both susceptible to sensationalized tales of human suffering, bear the blame for American unrest over slavery and regional fragmentation.[12]

Like the anti–Uncle Tom fiction that would follow, *Woodcraft* positions the South as the Edenic paradise that remained after the fall of an uncouth, industrialized North. As J. V. Ridgeley notes in *Nineteenth-Century Southern Literature*, from the early 1830s on the South increasingly withdrew from all things beyond its own borders, including literary trends: over the ensuing three decades, the historical romance, the Gothic tale, and sentimental fiction advanced little in technique below the Mason-Dixon Line (75), with Samuel Richardson and Sir Walter Scott remaining not only favorites but also literary models.[13] Plantation romances that glorified a neofeudal society helped salve whites' uneasiness over socioeconomic inequities and reassure planter-class males of their nobility: in the literary "cult of chivalry," cavaliers kneel before the altar of Southern femininity and familial devotion (Taylor 148).[14] Male protagonists struggle heroically not only against fictive antagonists, therefore, but also for the hegemony of their class, race, and gender.

Romanticizing the plantation South necessitated elevating white Southern women, as Francis Pendleton Gaines observes, insisting that the plantation literary tradition

> did not so much unreasonably glorify the plantation women as remain strongly silent about certain . . . exceedingly important phases of her existence. . . . Honored with . . . a peculiar reverence, the boast and idol of masculine society, she was, nevertheless, the pathetic victim of that society. . . . In all the romance there is a conspicuous absence of the psychology of lovely young girls who married young sports and found that matrimony locked a door and threw away the key, locked a door so

thick that not even a cry of pain could ever penetrate to the outer world. (180)

In naming white women as *"the* pathetic victim[s] of that society" (italics mine), Gaines both elides the primary victims of plantation society and overstates the helplessness of white women. Yet he does pinpoint what the private writings of white antebellum Southern women make abundantly clear: whether managing their own households or exercising their own judgment, they lived under the constant scrutiny and economic control of white men with a political stake in the plantation South's appearing lovely, happy, and harmonious (see Chapter 4).

In both the early plantation literary tradition and the emergent male-authored anti–Uncle Tom novels, one solution to handling the white Southern female was to omit her from the page. In many of these texts, such as *The Yankee Slave-Dealer, The Olive-Branch, Old Toney and His Master, English Serfdom and American Slavery*, and *Frank Freeman's Barber Shop,* women function marginally, if at all, in the plots. And where female characters appear, they typically exist solely to perform touching tableaux of plantation harmony, such as two scenes depicted in *The Sable Cloud*: the grieving slave mother with her dying child, her white mistress by her side; and the planter's wife holding a Maternal Association meeting in which she is educating fifteen slave mothers. Or, as in *Mr. Frank, the Underground Mail-Agent,* white women characters walk on only as vulgar flirts, such as the buxom Mrs. Burton, who makes passes at men in front of her husband, or as helpless victims, such as two young women who are sexually assaulted, one by a gullible but harmless slave, Tom, duped by an abolitionist. In *Woodcraft,* Simms does include the feisty widow Mrs. Eveleigh, who is savvy about firearms as well as her own property rights.[15] Yet in admiring her, the protagonist, Captain Porgy, particularly notes her more traditional feminine behavior as she kneels at her son's feet in a "sweet picture of maternal love; of all the forms of love, perhaps the most pure, the least selfish, the longest lived!" (138). Furthermore, in rejecting Porgy's marriage proposal, the widow highlights white Southern culture's hierarchical model of marriage: " 'I have been too long my own mistress to submit to authority. I have a certain spice of independence in my temper, which would argue no security for the ruler which seeks to restrain me' " (513). After Porgy's rejection by yet another widow, Simms achieves an all-male pastoral paradise in which Porgy, his friends Dr. Oakenburg and Sergeant Millhouse, and his slave Tom congratulate themselves on the absence of females. When informed of the near desecration of Porgy's bachelorhood, the doctor is horrified:

> "A wife!" cried Oakenburg,—"the Lord deliver us!"
>
> "Maussa better widout 'em," quoth Tom; "I nebber kin 'tan for to be happy in house whar woman's is de maussa." (518)

Representing the contented subservient class, a slave here affirms Southern patriarchy's gender, racial, and class control. Porgy, meanwhile, declares his fealty to his comrades in near-nuptial vows:

> "But for your sakes I renounce [the temptations of the flesh]. I shall live for you only. . . . You shall be mine always—I shall be yours. To woman, except as friend or companion, I say depart! I renounce ye! . . . For your sakes, dear comrades, there shall be no mistress, while I live at Glen-Eberley." (518)

To assure male security and requited love, women must be excluded. In matrimonial language, Porgy pledges fealty to his male comrades and shields their masculinity and his own by prohibiting contact with the feminine Other.

Unlike the female protagonists of the female-authored anti–Uncle Tom novels analyzed in the following chapters, white women characters in these male-authored texts are rarely central to the plot, and even the secondary female characters who exhibit any traditionally masculine trait—financial savvy, political activity, strong personal opinions—elicit the narrator's immediate derision. In William M. Burwell's *White Acre vs. Black Acre: A Case at Law*, for example, the author is never subtle in his misogyny, or in this genre's attempts to establish punitive control over white women's behavior. Of the very few women even mentioned in the narrative, Miss Lizzie Bull is "very rich, very stingy," and, the narrator sneers, "the milk of Miss Lizzie's maidenhood stood so long that it curdled and grew sour then became still more cross, pernicious and revengeful" (28). In the same novel, the eminently undesirable, independent Miss Maria Mule edits the *Emancipator*, which, the narrator scornfully reports, attempts "to liberate women and black people from servitude" through its journalistically unreliable habits of "spinning yarns" (98).[16] Miss Mistress Clam, a member of the White Acre community, which freed its slaves and now must perform its own labor, represents that portion of "the milder sex [that] has forgotten its timidity in the ferocious pursuit of an obnoxious opinion" (218). Repeatedly, these novels link proper female submission with a slaveholding society.

Also refortifying gender divisions, Thomas Bangs Thorpe's *The Master's House* begins with a gathering of men at a New England college, journeys through various male-guided transactions of Virginia land and slaves, involves political elections, and concludes in a duel. Men rule markets, property, families, and community relations. And though they do not always handle their areas of control wisely or well, as portrayed in the novel's climactic duel, they nonetheless retain unquestioned autocratic power. Though personally ambivalent toward slavery, Thorpe, who later fought for the Union army, in some ways portrays the plantation South as his fellow proslavery novelists do: since the economic system was imposed upon them, the argument goes, slaveholders themselves bear little or no guilt. And though Thorpe's protagonist may find owning human laborers morally distasteful, the narrative also depicts slaves as often sullen and stupid, therefore deserving of servitude (e.g., 158).

Elements of *The Master's House*, however, do suggest anti-plantation-South sentiments. After the protagonist Mildmay's wife, Annie, has died of a broken heart and of "the enervating influences of a Southern climate" (381), he sits alone, brooding: "The sun that had for some moments been struggling upon the horizon, and in flickering gleams illuminated the landscape, now rapidly disappeared; and as there is no twilight in a Southern sky, the thick darkness of a starless night enshrouded the form of Graham Mildmay" (391). Such a passage marks the novel's liminal position, distinguishing itself from the public relations propaganda of the unambiguously anti–Uncle Tom fiction.

The anti–Uncle Tom novels by women in particular admit no flaws in the South's sky or in its climate, while disease, poverty, and moral turpitude occur only above the Mason-Dixon Line. Describing the South, female proslavery writers detail nothing but sunny days, salubrious country air, friendly neighbors, and flowering trees. Even more important, unlike the rancorous feuding and violence of *The Master's House*, the woman-authored texts depict wealthy, white Anglo-Saxon Protestant Southerners dwelling in a perpetual peace disrupted only by outside agitators, usually a Northerner but occasionally a Southern Jew or Italian Catholic.

The Master's House offers a somewhat more realistic picture. Yet, while often negative toward the white South, Thorpe's novel ultimately earns its place among anti–Uncle Tom fiction. Throughout its pages, white men observe codes of honor that ultimately prove self-aggrandizing: for example, their care for slaves' basic physical needs actually protects the masters' economic investments.[17] White women perform only as supporting cast: mothers, housekeepers, and objects of desire. In one scene that confirms historical planter-class women's complaints, the secondary character Mrs. Moreton informs native Northerner Annie Mildmay: " 'You will find . . . that a planter's wife is the greatest slave that exists. If I don't see to everything, all goes wrong' " (158).[18] Echoing the Yankee ethnocentricity of Stowe's Miss Ophelia, Annie confesses: " 'I cannot overcome my repugnance to the blacks enough, to bear with comfort the necessary presence of my servants' " (159).[19]

Though contributing little narrative interest, female characters' psychological fragility contrasts sharply in *The Master's House* with male stoicism and initially seems to promote the slave-based South's hierarchical agenda: men rule women because men are better equipped mentally and emotionally, the same logic that applies to whites' domination of blacks. While the protagonist, Graham Mildmay, returns home snarling manfully after having killed his opponent, Mr. Moreton, in the duel, Mildmay's wife sobs like a child (378). Swiftly descending into madness, the widowed Mrs. Moreton is "carried raving into the house" (371). Later, shrieking and in disheveled—even seductive—attire, she appears before her husband's friends, then swoons; thus the author links female sexuality with social deviance and psychic collapse. Before she disappears from the narrative, Mrs. Moreton does ferociously attack those who goaded her husband into dueling: " 'May the scalding tears you have seen shed to-day burn your craven hearts! may all mothers and wives spurn and despise you' " (375).[20] Yet even here, she frames her curse in traditionally feminine terms. Thorpe's message is complex: while clearing the narrative's ending of women, as Simms did in *Woodcraft*, the author of *The Master's House* leaves his male protagonist alone and miserable.[21] While Thorpe reinforces white Southern males' right to rule, he questions their judgment; while he portrays women as weak, sickly, and only marginally important, his narrative implies that Annie Mildmay's broken-hearted death and Mrs. Moreton's madness are reasonable responses to a white male–controlled slaveocracy. Like Stowe's black female characters such as alcoholic Prue and crazed Cassy, Thorpe's white female characters ultimately reveal the omnipotent, destructive power of the patriarchal South.

W.L.G. Smith's view of the plantation South is far less nuanced. Also set in Virginia, Smith's anti–Uncle Tom novel *Life at the South; or, "Uncle Tom's Cabin" as It Is: Being Narratives, Scenes, and Incidents in the Real "Life of the Lowly"* advances its unabashedly proslavery arguments through white and black male soliloquies, as well as its reconfigurations of *Uncle Tom's Cabin*. Visiting Washington, D. C., refined planter Mr. Erskine observes the national legislative debate on slavery, which for him illustrates the vacuousness of abolition, as Congressman Pettibone addresses fast-emptying congressional seats with "an ass's load of pamphlets and periodicals, . . . some of them giving an account of the adventures and hair-breadth escapes of the friends of the colored man, and others containing graphical descriptions of slavery and its evil tendencies" (21–22). Believing Pettibone merely misinformed and "actuated solely by the impulses of genuine philanthropy, [Erskine] does not anticipate much difficulty in undeceiving him" (23). When Erskine's speeches fail to persuade, however, he retreats to Virginia disillusioned. His return to his plantation echoes the feudal lord's greeting by devoted subjects: "Pleased with his condescension and affability, they respected, if not loved him more than ever; and, after he walked on, chatted his praise to each other" (42). Like *Woodcraft's* Tom, this novel's Hector refuses his freedom in a homily that extols the beneficence of slavery. Initially bewildered, the master assumes that Hector must be hesitant to leave his wife, Philisee, behind in bondage. Even with Philisee's freedom granted, though, Hector dutifully responds according to the proslavery script:

> "I dam to hell, mass, if I guine to be free!" roared the adhesive black, in a tone of unrestrainable determination. "I can't loss you' company; and who work for you like Hector? 'Tis unpossible, massa, and dere's no use to talk about it. De ting ain't right; and enty I know wha' kind of ting freedom is wid black man. Ha! you make Hector free, 'come wuss more nor poor buckrah; he tief out of de shop—he get drunk and lie in de ditch; den, if sick come, he roll, he toss in de wet grass of de stable: you come in

de morning—Hector dead! . . . No, massa you berry good company for
Hector; I tank God he so good! I no want any better." (47)

Employing theopolitical strategies, Smith connects damnation with freedom
for slaves, and credits God with the wisdom and benevolence for placing Hector in servitude to a master who is such "berry good company." By forcibly
keeping slaves sober and honest, Hector testifies, slaveholders actually protect
blacks' best interest. However, despite the narrative's insistence that liberty,
always accompanied by responsibility, is overrated, the master's astonishment
at Hector's refusal highlights the value of human freedom.

Although Hector "tank[s] God he so good" in this passage, most anti–
Uncle Tom novels by men take their theological justifications for slavery
lightly—a stark difference from the highly pietistic novels by their female
counterparts, as I show beginning in Chapter 2. More typical of the male
authors is the callously practical philosophizing of Nehemiah Adams, a Boston clergyman whose anti–Uncle Tom novel *The Sable Cloud* includes this
passage:

> **SLAVERY MADE UNCLE TOM.** Had it not been for slavery, he
> would have been a savage in Africa, a brutish slave to his fetishes, living
> in a jungle, perhaps; and had you stumbled upon him he would very likely
> have roasted you and picked your bones. A system which makes Uncle
> Toms out of African savages is not an unmixed evil. (135)

Echoing Smith's primary strategy, Adams justifies slavery based on the alleged welfare of would-be Africans, without any pretense of invoking divine
favor.[22]

Just as in *The Master's House* and *Woodcraft,* the female characters of
Life at the South merely flit like shadows through the primary action, yet
even as secondary figures two of them valorize slaveholding males by recasting *Uncle Tom's Cabin.* White women matter little to Smith's plot or to his
proslavery argument: not until page eighty-six does the reader learn anything of Erskine's wife, who is dead, or children, including a daughter. Black
women, however, provide Smith with a direct rebuttal to Stowe. Although
Yankee schoolteacher Mr. Bates—whose Yale diplomas baffle rather than
impress Erskine—is terrified of contracting disease from close contact with
"negroes," he nevertheless sexually assaults Cassy, a female slave.[23] Erskine

leaps to the rescue, instructing the weeping Cassy: " 'Go, my honest woman, to your quarters, and keep your own counsel. I have always been a father to you; I will protect you now. So, hush! dry up your tears; and if the scamp again approaches you, slap him in the face—he is too white-livered to resent the insult' " (271). A pointed revision of Stowe's Cassy, whose life story highlights white men's brutality, Smith's Cassy frames white men's ownership of and access to slave women as paternalistic protection. Meanwhile, the faithful slave Dinah unsuccessfully entreats her husband, the Uncle Tom of *Life at the South,* to ignore abolitionists' enticements to escape. When Dinah later finds Tom cold and starving in his Northern freedom, she dutifully returns him to the plantation fold—for which he is delighted. In the pattern of male-authored anti–Uncle Tom texts, a black woman supports the patriarchal cast and proslavery message from her position in the narrative wings.

Similarly, in *The Cabin and the Parlor; or, Slaves and Masters,* J. Thornton Randolph, using the pseudonym Charles Jacobs Peterson, creates a female slave character as enthusiastic about slavery as is Dinah of *Life at the South.* After Randolph's Cora begs her husband, Charles, not to attempt escaping, she reluctantly accompanies him, all the while feeling, the narrator insists, "like Eve when our first mother left paradise for ever" (49). Again, Randolph puts theopolitical allusions to work, linking the loss of the biblical Eden to a slave's "loss" of her own bondage, which Randolph would configure as security and safety: paradise for childlike Africans too simple to function on their own. Unlike Stowe's invoking Eve as a progenitor of faith through the Christlike character Eva, Randolph's allusion evokes an Eve guilty of rebellion and depravity. In the pitiless urban North, Cora gives birth in a hideous tenement and is nearly murdered, together with her child, by a rioting mob, which, she calculates, would be just punishment for betraying her mistress, Isabel. A white man, the fearless Walworth, rescues the penitent, then carries mother and child back into the dubious security of slavery, according to Cora's pleas and Charles's dying wishes. Through the cowering of a secondary black female character and the posturing of a central white male, Randolph communicates clearly that the antislavery North offers only unfulfilled promises and bodily harm, while the slave-based South offers the "paradise" of protection by wealthy white males and by an appeased patriarchal God.

Although *The Cabin and the Parlor* follows a white female character more closely than does the typical male-authored proslavery novel, it adheres to the paradigm of the white woman as weak, selfless, proslavery, and finally unnecessary. Randolph's hothouse beauty, Isabel, though more self-reliant than her ineffectual, hypochondriac mother, finds the northern winter too ferocious and teaching school too arduous: she sickens under the strain. Devoted to patriarchy in all its forms, just like other white and black female characters in male-authored proslavery novels, Isabel Courtenay mouths feminine compassion as a safeguard against "misfortunes" in slavery. When Dr. Worthington announces her family's bankruptcy, the young woman first expresses concern for her bound dependents:

> "Oh! this is terrible," she said finally. "They love us so, and are so helpless. I could bear my own misfortunes, doctor, but to think of them!"
>
> "The neighbors won't allow any of the families to be separated."
>
> "Of course not. We read of such things in novels sometimes. But I have yet to see it in real life." (39)

Taking an unmistakable stab at *Uncle Tom's Cabin,* published only months earlier, Isabel faithfully parrots wealthy white Southern males' paternalistic defense of slavery: because the slaves " 'love us so, and are so helpless,' " the Courtenays have not been coercing black labor for profit but instead caring altruistically for devoted, defenseless creatures.[24] Also portrayed as ill prepared for independence, Isabel in her flagging strength and waning courage affirms slavery's gender hierarchy. "Self-reliance," the narrator attests, "is the peculiar characteristic of the Anglo-Saxon" (110). By this he means, however, the Anglo-Saxon monied male, for the white Isabel Courtenay fails to support herself successfully without the help of two wealthy white men and a toadying slave, Uncle Peter, who predictably refuses his freedom. With even more limited autonomy, the central black female character can only plead with dominant black and white men and then, when their machinations have left her in mortal danger, await rescue by a scion of the plantation South. Despite its more significant female characters, *The Cabin and the Parlor* ends where most other male-authored anti–Uncle Tom novels begin, with its focus on a wealthy white Southern male: in a happily-ever-after conclusion, the hero Walworth restores the Courtenay family fortune and, not unrelatedly, marries the heiress.

In place of male characters' extended proslavery speeches and debates as modeled in other anti–Uncle Tom novels by men, *The Cabin and the*

Parlor's narrator lectures the reader on slavery's benefits. As if responding to the reader's rebuttals, he targets Northern hypocrisy and, while admitting the slave-based South could stand reforming, he hastens to add: "If there is one truth more true than others, it is that social systems cannot be safely changed in a day" (3, 6). Repeatedly, the narrator argues for slaves' unalloyed contentment and seems unaware that even these assurances hint otherwise: "At all times [the slaves] are a happier people than we are. Their merry faces show this. Yet, like every race in a rude state, their mirth finds its food as well as expression, in music that to more advanced races is almost mournful" (78). Repeatedly, the narrative cites masters who sacrifice their own comfort rather than separate a slave family. Yet in acknowledging the tribulations of planter's daughter Isabel Courtenay, Dr. Worthington indirectly reveals a less beneficent system: " 'Even the slave, sold to a sugar plantation, and torn from his family at that, doesn't endure a quarter of what you've gone through, this last year!' " (317). Glossing over the characters' admissions of slave families' separations and of the infamous brutality of Deep South sugar plantations, the narrator continues to pummel the reader with arguments that defend slavery and finally resorts to a belligerent "but they did it first" rhetoric, implicating Europe and the northeastern United States while exonerating the white South.

Offering even fewer significant female roles, J. W. Page's *Uncle Robin in His Cabin in Virginia and Tom without One in Boston* deploys the converted-abolitionist plot and preaches slavery through its male protagonist's incessant sermons. Set in Virginia like so many other anti–Uncle Tom novels by men, the novel's Arcadia is Selma, home to approximately fifty slaves, a stone mansion, and stuccoed slave cabins. Protagonist Dr. Boswell's new wife, Northerner Ann Stephens, becomes the potter's clay, ready to have her mind molded by her husband's superior faculties. She admits that, having been reared by abolitionists:

"I have come to Virginia entertaining a strong feeling against slavery; indeed almost with a horror at the thought of being in its midst; but, as I am doomed, you know, to wear the harness all my life, I must wear it, and obey my husband in all things, even should it be to tolerate slavery. It may be, that when I have become familiar with all its incidents I may pull tolerably well in that harness." (17)

Though Ann's references to being "doomed" and "harness[ed]" suggest re-
luctance, the narrative casts her as speaking good-naturedly. Indeed, Page,
like other male anti–Uncle Tom novelists, typically portrays white women as
willing—even eager—to have their convictions, passions, and energies controlled by a husband at the reins. For these writers, a woman unharnessed is
as dangerous—and useless—as a wild horse unbridled. Like Ann Boswell, a
good wife must be shown "who is boss" and sacrifice her own ethical sensibilities in the name of harmonious matrimony. Page here inserts furrow-browed
religiosity unusual in anti–Uncle Tom novels by men—although significantly,
even here the fervent concern for divine approval belongs solely to female
characters. Dr. Boswell begins patterning his wife after his mother, who
"having consulted her Bible . . . had come to the conclusion that it [slavery]
was not sinful in the sight of her Heavenly Father . . . but that there were
duties and responsibilities growing out of it the neglect of which was highly
sinful" (27). In his own defense of slavery, Dr. Boswell wields his mother's
piety as his best weapon. Waging theopolitical war, Page carefully aligns his
female proslavery characters with true religion, with meticulous concern for
biblical mandates and divine opinions on slavery. With her interpretation of
the Bible and "her Heavenly Father" in accordance with her owning slaves,
Dr. Boswell's mother alleviates her own guilt and that of her son—and consequently, as Page would have it, of all well-meaning slaveholders.

Repeatedly alluding to Stowe and women social reformers in general,
Page depicts female judgment as dangerously susceptible, while human compassion and ethical outrage become mere infections of a weak intellect. Page
stages the new Mrs. Boswell facing her first test when two young slaves, Tom
and Dick, commit a theft for which they must be either hanged or sold. Elect-
ing to sell the slaves, Dr. Boswell shuns his wife's entreaties not to separate
the boys from their parents. A paragon of female slaves' loyalty, young Tom's
mother justifies the master's decision to the weeping mistress: " 'Well, missis,
tain't wufwhile, madam, to grieve so much. To be sure, I does feel might bad
at partin' wid Tom, but he bring it all 'pon heself, madam. . . . 'Twas he own
fault, missis' " (47). Similarly, another faithful female slave, Mammy Betty,
serves as confessor to a repentant young Tom, who dies of consumption in
Boston. Initially scolding his wife—" 'It will perhaps be necessary to harden
that little heart of yours, as our friends the Abolitionists may make frequent
drafts upon it' " (49)—Dr. Boswell soon avows: " 'I have the very best soil to

operate upon; and if Ann does not resemble my dear mother in all things, it will be the fault of her instructor' " (63). Eventually, the "soil" so beautifully responds to the master's design that she assists in proselytizing her parents. Ann's mother, Mrs. Stephens, represents the duplicitous antislavery Northerner, sighing over "the poor creatures" in bondage while abusing her own young white servants. Finally embracing slavery, Mrs. Stephens converts not because her ethical evaluations change but because, as the narrator points out, blacks make better servants than do poor whites. In Page's narrative, black and white women who think and act autonomously threaten to topple a carefully constructed patriarchal paradise, as Dr. Boswell observes to his father-in-law: " 'It does seem to me, Mr. Stephens, that this whole abolition feeling has originated in, and is kept up by the diseased, sickly sensibilities of females' " (104). *Uncle Tom's Cabin's* having been published the previous year, Page no doubt means to discount its author, among others, as unreliable. Like the raving and heartbroken females in Thorpe's *Master's House,* in Page's tale all women inherently possess unstable emotional health and unsound judgment, and any impassioned idea beyond domestic concerns inevitably unbalances them. No woman is to be trusted, and particularly not one whose own ideas have rendered her unwilling to wear "the harness" of silent submission.

Also following the converted-abolitionist model, the proslavery argument of Robert Criswell's *Uncle Tom's Cabin Contrasted with Buckingham Hall, the Planter's Home; or, A Fair View of Both Sides of the Slavery Question,* maps its proslavery argument through two white men's debates, mostly in letters, and employs female characters only as pasteboard representatives of a wealthy white male's ideal. The plot's romance tracks the attraction of wealthy Charleston, South Carolina, planter's son Eugene Buckingham to New Yorker Julia Tennyson, who asserts no independence and speaks few words of her own. When Julia relinquishes her free will to her father, an ardent antislavery activist, the remainder of the book primarily becomes an epistolary volley between Eugene and Dr. Tennyson, both vying for rhetorical victory and for Julia's ultimate allegiance. His slaves entailed to him and therefore ineligible for manumission, Eugene defends himself with a cry of helplessness common in proslavery novels. Yet Eugene regales an audience with the story of an abolitionist tricked into marrying a fair-skinned female slave, whom he promptly abandons upon discovering her lineage. Even in attempting to win one woman by successfully arguing his moral innocence,

Eugene highlights—and laughs at—another woman's victimization by the very social structure he defends. Significantly, the anti–Uncle Tom novels by women contain nothing like this.

Back at Buckingham Hall, Eugene's sister Cora provides further gender instruction. Tall, graceful, blonde, and blue-eyed, Cora is weak-minded and indolent, distinguishing her sharply from most female protagonists the women anti–Uncle Tom authors create. Cora exhibits "a lady-like softness of manner, and a sweet insinuating smile, that were to the enthusiastic Southerners, irresistible" (12). Neighbor Susanna Jones, on the other hand, while possessing a striking face and figure, also rides fearlessly, hunts flawlessly, and generally asserts herself—to her own detriment. Repulsed by all she represents, Eugene demands of his father: " 'Am I a *slave?* I *will not* submit to such *tyranny!* I *will not* be *forced* to marry against my will!' " (76). Though he has admired Julia's sweetly feminine submission to paternal authority, the planter-class male rebels against that same authority, and the narrative applauds him. Similarly, the subjugation he has called benevolent when applied to slaves becomes intolerable tyranny when applied to himself. Toward the novel's conclusion, Criswell presents Susanna as a warning to women:

> [She] still rode, raced and hunted with the young men who visited her father's mansion, but never could get any farther than a flirtation with any of them. She was destined to remain in a state of single blessedness, for her unladylike and disagreeable qualities rendering her unloved, unrespected and unapproached. (119)

Refusing to be harnessed like Ann Boswell but instead handling the reins herself, Susanna has refused a hierarchical mandate that would position her beneath men. Rather, she insists on remaining on top and in control, which, the narrative teaches, indicates something revoltingly wrong with her feminine nature. Failing in the skills of successful flirtation, which require in the patriarchal model at least the illusion of the woman's willingness to be hunted, Susanna herself remains a hunter. Too much like the idealized Southern cavalier in her courage, physical prowess, and aggression, the masculinized woman must be shunned according to the white antebellum South's social code.[25] Her "strong-minded" nature renders her, like Criswell's Susanna, disagreeable to the point of repugnancy (292). Consistently, the male-authored anti–Uncle

Tom texts will not stand for even the marginal success of an assertive, accomplished woman.

The white male combatants of *Uncle Tom's Cabin Contrasted with Buckingham Hall, the Planter's Home,* meanwhile, fire rhetorical shots at one another up through the very last chapter, when both sides can finally concur on slavery's general beneficence because they have tacitly agreed on the insignificance of black females' sexual vulnerability. Representing the ideal Southern gentleman, Eugene's father, Colonel Buckingham, points the visiting Tennysons to his slaves' good fortune: " 'You see,' said Buckingham, throwing some coppers among them, 'how I spoil these creatures' " (128). In this gesture, Buckingham mimics Stowe's gentleman-planter Mr. Shelby, who "snap[s] a bunch of raisins" toward Jim Crow, yet while Stowe paints Shelby as foolish in thinking himself munificent, Criswell depicts Buckingham as genuinely indulgent and generous, just as he sees himself.

Typical of proslavery novels by men, paternalism lightly sheaths the machete edge of patriarchal oppression—yet even the sheath sometimes falls away, revealing slavery's cruelest edges.[26] Colonel Buckingham's showing Dr. Tennyson Charleston's slave market is a prime example. In a scene that presumably spotlights the planter's magnanimity, the narrative vividly discloses slavery's horrors, as the "item" for sale, a slave named Maria, stands alone on the platform:

> And then he [the auctioneer] continued, "If she gets lazy give a touch or two with the whip, and I'll engage she'll do your work." He then began some indecent jokes concerning her appearance, observing that whoever bought her, would have an increase of stock before long.
>
> Col. Buckingham, out of pity for her forlorn condition, made a bid for her, and she was knocked down to him for $365. (*Uncle Tom's Cabin Contrasted* 136–37)[27]

Motherhood, theoretically worshipped in Southern white women, becomes for black women merely the space of sexual violation and economic profit by white men. Immediately following this raw reminder of the atrocities that lurked just behind magnolia and mint julep, white male characters decry the inaccuracies and exaggerations in *Uncle Tom's Cabin.* In fact, Dr. Tennyson, the target of Colonel Buckingham's missionary efforts, concludes the discussion by conceding that " 'I shall not go home as strong an abolitionist as I came hither' " (145). Witnessing the complete sexual vulnerability of a black female already stripped of dignity fails to prejudice him against the institution he has now seen firsthand. In staging an imminent sexual assault nearly as horrific as the violations recounted by Stowe's Cassy and then following it with white men's calmly agreeing on Stowe's unreliability as a social commentator, Criswell makes clear one thing: rape of black females, to whom white males have legal access, does not even count as an argument against slavery. In purchasing the slave, Buckingham has merely responded to a pitiful, ill-treated creature, not to a woman whose body is her own threatened by predators.

The mere inclusion of such a scene as Criswell's slave auction distinguishes male- from female-authored anti–Uncle Tom novels. Nothing like this explicit admission of slavery's allowing—even encouraging—Southern white rape of black women and its consequent increase of "stock" exists anywhere in the women's narratives. Similarly, in *Frank Freeman's Barber Shop,* a white overseer, Mr. Hecky, brutally flogs a young pregnant slave and kicks her viciously in the side, an act that a group of whites witness and protest but neither prevent nor punish. Apparently, even the sacredness of motherhood proves easily ignored when the mother is black, overpowered by the wrath of white male authority challenged. Another male-authored anti–Uncle Tom novel, Burwell's *White Acre vs. Black Acre,* concedes the barbarity of the slave trade, depicting captured Africans crammed into the hold of a slave ship and crawling over one another " 'like so many black beetles' " (29). Passages that briefly admit to the atrocities of the slave trade do appear very infrequently in female-authored anti–Uncle Tom fiction, but only in the context of blaming slavery's existence on Europe, particularly Great Britain, as *White Acre vs. Black Acre* does. Blatant violence perpetrated by Southern slaveholding whites—and the tolerance of this violence—simply does not appear in anti–Uncle Tom novels by women.

While black women represent only faceless possessions subject at any moment to assault, white women in Criswell's novel represent no more than trophies. As a final affirmation of the Northerners' new toleration for slavery, the concluding chapter depicts a wedding for which the slave community is "permitted" a festival by munificent whites: "Blythe and happy, the slaves retired to their quarters, chattering about their pleasant holiday" (150). Meanwhile, the properly submissive white woman, Julia Tennyson, plays first a blushing bridesmaid, then a bride, provoking envy among the men toward Eugene, "who alone would *possess* the brilliant prize" (147, italics mine).

Even those male-authored anti–Uncle Tom novels that bear a white woman's or a slave's name in the title center on white men and retrace the pattern of women and blacks in roles of only marginal importance to the narrative and, by implication, to the plantation South. *Edith Allen, or Sketches of Life in Virginia,* by Lawrence Neville, for example, follows a white male protagonist, Briscoe Letaré, as he falls in love with one woman but eventually marries another for money, thereby regaining the fortune lost during his improvident college days. In James Smythe's *Ethel Somers; or, the Fate of the Union. By a Southerner,* white male characters discuss the eponymous secondary character, labeling her "a rich prize," "an object to admire," and one whose love "any man might be proud to possess" (9). By contrast, the protagonist, Edward Clinton, evinces "honor and principle," "exalted intellectual faculties, a highly cultivated taste, and an amiable, elevated and glowing heart" (15). Providing a paradigm for male-authored anti–Uncle Tom novels and deliberately borrowing names from Stowe's novel to countermand Stowe's message, the final scene of Joseph Holt Ingraham's *Sunny South: or, The Southerner at Home: Embracing Five Years' Experience of a Northern Governess in the Land of the Sugar and the Cotton,* depicts a planter's new bride writing of her toddler, Harry: "He knocked over a little wooly-crowned black baby, Chloe's grandson, which had crawled near him," to which the slave Chloe responds, " 'Mass Harry make little nigga know hi' place!' " (416). The planter's wife, a former governess from the North, observes of her newly adopted culture: "I could not help laughing at the old woman's remark; at the same time could not but feel its truth. The white infant on a plantation very early understands as if by instinct, its superiority; while the African child tacitly recognizes it" (417). The heir to a patriarchal utopia, Harry is just beginning to discover a whole world of nonwhites and nonmales, his for the knocking down.

Like the governess wife and the female slave of Joseph Holt Ingraham's imagination, black and white women characters of the male-authored plantation romances acknowledge white male superiority and shrink obligingly into narrative shadows. As Susan Tracy observes, to reach manhood, the white male protagonists of these novels must escape the shelter of the maternal wing, where, should they linger too long, they risk becoming emasculated, infantilized, and far too gentle. While "mother love" potentially disables, the narratives illustrate, "father love" toughens, preparing the way for independence and success (Tracy 106). In this antebellum culture where rulers establish and maintain superiority by knocking down—economically, socially, and literally—the politically weaker Other, plantations become synonymous with paradise. Taking its form from a patriarchal reading of the second biblical creation account, in which the guilty Eve is condemned to be ruled over by her husband, this paradise enshrines a male-controlled hierarchy and imposes its invariable structure over all aspects of life.

In a sweeping judgment of the antebellum plantation romances by men, which she too often assumes encompass all significant plantation romances, Susan Tracy accurately evaluates the entire genre to be more valuable "as cultural artifacts of a defeated planter class than as works of art" (5). As art, many of these novels fail miserably even to sustain a coherent narrative, and most of them do not merit preserving; as artifacts, however, they are invaluable, representing a world carefully established and policed to benefit the social, political, and economic concerns of planter-class males. In portraying white women as physically, mentally, and emotionally weak, the male-authored anti–Uncle Tom novels create scenarios in which all deviations from the passive, submissive patriarchal ideal can be construed as sick. In depicting black women as eager adherents of slavery and, at the same time, figures of little narrative interest, the novels excuse slavery's sexual violence. And by presenting their proslavery arguments primarily through wealthy white male characters' speeches and debates, the novels confirm exactly who is in control of the narrative and of antebellum Southern society.

Shunning this male protagonist–centered, debate-driven, generally secularized model, both Northern and Southern women writers created their own hybridization of the plantation literary genre in which hearth, home, and fervent religious devotion are central. While anti–Uncle Tom novels by women show many of the same technical faults as those by men—pasteboard characters, for example, and convoluted plots awkwardly interrupted by proslavery invectives—they also include some of the more literarily proficient texts, all the more chilling for their sophisticated brand of racial bigotry.[28] Far from mere dusty museum pieces, these woman-authored narratives, like their counterparts by men, offer fertile ground for feminist and socioeconomic analysis of racism's inevitable, ongoing collusion with gender and class oppression.

CHAPTER 2

Sanctified by Wealth and Whiteness

Mother-Saviors—and Not—in the Urban North

*Q*nd you, mothers of America," Harriet Beecher Stowe implores the audience of *Uncle Tom's Cabin,* "by the *sacred* love you bear your child, . . . I beseech you" (384, italics mine). Plantation romances and anti–Uncle Tom novels by women commonly employ similar direct appeals, one mother to another. Like Stowe, too, her fictive detractors consistently modify maternal love as sacred, holy, and divine, reflecting a trend among nineteenth-century domestic novels.[1] In *Douglass Farm,* for example, popular domestic novelist Mary E. Bradley's main character invokes her dead mother as divine mediator for the fragmented family: " 'We must . . . keep her spirit so present with us always that he [their father] shall . . . be won by our likeness to her. I do believe . . . that if we watch and pray, and strive to act always as she would wish, . . . there will be peace and love amongst us once more' " (38–39). Stowe assigns black and white mothers to powerful messianic roles in which they comfort, teach, protect, and redeem others from slavery and from spiritual pitfalls. Stowe's respondents also employ theopolitical strategies in their fictive rebuttals, rhetorically linking religious dogma and imagery with specific legal, social, and economic aims; like Stowe, too, they depict central mother figures with christological imagery. I contend that contrary to their intent, however, the proslavery texts, with their evasions, displacements, and contradictions, disrupt the surface narratives, ultimately exposing a profit-driven chattel slavery as savage as that on Simon Legree's plantation.

Particularly in the novels set in the North—Caroline Rush's *North and South,* Mrs. G. M. Flanders's *Ebony Idol,* and Mrs. V. G. Cowdin's *Ellen*—anti–Uncle Tom women writers follow sentimental fiction's pattern of lionizing white women and often demeaning white men, the seeming antithesis of the male-authored anti–Uncle Tom novels; yet by their narrative's end, each of these female-authored attacks on patriarchal domination collapses under its own proslavery social masonry.[2] Like Stowe and distinct from the male anti–Uncle Tom novelists, Rush, Flanders, and Cowdin propel their arguments through relationships between mothers and daughters, between Northern and Southern mothers, and between white women and black men. In contrast to Stowe's mother-saviors, however, these would-be female protectors further endanger the weak; rather than rescue others from oppression, they "save" by reenslaving; rather than advocate freedom, they teach submission to white male authority, including a hypermasculinized deity; rather than address social systems, they focus only on the security of their immediate families—and even then, a brutal, industrialized North usually defeats them.

The cultural context of sentimental fiction, including *Uncle Tom's Cabin* and its respondents, promoted matrifocal themes. In seventeenth- and eighteenth-century America, with fathers often working near home and mothers necessarily engaged in labor outside child rearing, Ruth Bloch asserts, cultural forces emphasized proper parenting with little regard to any polarized sexual differentiation (102–13). When nineteenth-century industrialization pulled men out of the home to factories, mills, mines, and urban business hubs, women became the primary child-care givers and keepers of the hearth, a role Victorian ideals embellished as gender specific. As Mary Kelley notes: "The family, glorified as a source of virtue and as a sacred refuge from an increasingly competitive, fragmented and transitory society, was regarded as the arena in which woman would fulfill her exemplary, anointed role" ("The Sentimentalists" 437). While such polarization may have led to romanticizing the home setting, it also allowed many women to perceive themselves as *the* principal actors in propagating personal ethics and, consequently, societal justice. For many antebellum American women, motherhood became a unifying and emboldening experience, illustrating Adrienne Rich's observation that the cultural concept of "mothering" can vary from "acute vulnerability" to "a space invested with power" (102).

At the 1837 Anti-Slavery Convention of American Women, for example, the nation's first interracial gathering on such a large scale, mothers claimed authority for social transformation. An initial resolution contended that "there is no class to whom the antislavery cause makes so direct and powerful an appeal as to *mothers*," and another enjoined women to "lift up their hearts to God on behalf of the captive, as often as they pour them out over their own children in joy with which no stranger may intermeddle," and to "guard with jealous care the minds of their children from the ruining influences of the spirit of proslavery and prejudice, let those influences come in what name, or through what connections they may" (Sterling, *Turning* 17). The conveners thus positioned themselves as a unified class of citizens perfectly prepared to countermand cultural forces and to chart their own societal course. Far from recommending female subservience, inferiority, or dependence, their shared experience of maternity drove their resolve to change the world.

Although such appeals to "lift up their hearts to God on behalf of the captive" seem to exemplify what Barbara Welter terms the "cult of true womanhood," characterized by piety, purity, submission, and dedication to domesticity, her much-cited analysis is inadequate. In demonstrating that mid-nineteenth-century culture portrayed religion as "the core of woman's virtue, the source of her strength," Welter attempts to show how societal expectations encouraged women to prioritize prayer over intellectual inquiry and self-sacrifice over demands for justice.[3] Her assertions, however, fail to encompass the complexities of antebellum free women's worlds, including either the Anti-Slavery Convention women, whose domesticity and piety spurred their attack on injustice, or Stowe, who credited *Uncle Tom's Cabin* to her own maternal affections and a divine calling.[4] Although Welter's analysis is not new, it most clearly represents one extreme of a much-debated spectrum on which Jane Tompkins, among others, places herself at the opposite end, arguing that in sentimental novels literate women found a vehicle for assert-ing themselves, "reorganiz[ing] culture from the woman's point of view," and "offer[ing] a critique of American society far more devastating than any deliv-ered by better known critics such as Hawthorne and Melville" (*"UTC"* 81).[5] Tompkins contends that sentimental fiction should be viewed as a "political enterprise, halfway between sermon and social theory, that both codifies and attempts to mold the values of its time" (*Sensational Designs* 126), and the work of anti–Uncle Tom women writers illustrates this point. Caroline Rush, Mrs. G. M. Flanders, and Mary Eastman inveigh against wives' mindless sub-servience to their husbands, while Mary Howard Schoolcraft berates society's valuing a pretty face above female erudition. In anti–Uncle Tom fiction, as in other sentimental fiction, plots continually push men into narrative margins, leaving female protagonists to dominate the page. And just as Stowe depicts the root evil of slavery as "the displacement of life-giving maternal values by a profit-hungry masculine ethic . . . [in which] mothers and motherless children show the human cost of the system" (Ammons, "Heroines" 156), anti–Uncle Tom women portray a relentlessly money-hungry industrialism that sullies female innocence and snaps family ties. So convincing is the progressive women's rights rhetoric of these narratives' surfaces, in fact, that some recent domestic-novel scholars have failed to see the racialized undercurrents that pull these novels toward ever more oppressive conclusions.[6]

The proslavery sentimentalists oscillate wildly in their willingness to rebel, even subtly, against what historian Catherine Clinton has labeled the Southern penarchy.[7] Welter's contentions prove more accurate for Southern and proslavery Northern sentimentalists, who, subscribing to an intricately interwoven racialized and gendered hierarchy, limit feminine power to the domestic realm. As South Carolinian Maria McIntosh, author of the anti–Uncle Tom novel *The Lofty and the Lowly,* maintained, the home should provide "the nursery of pure and high thoughts"; and a woman's overstepping the boundary of her own hearth, Georgia writer Augusta Evans Wilson feared, risked "rendering the throne unsteady, and subverting God's law of order" (Kelley 438–42).[8] In her *Recollections of a Southern Matron,* first published in 1837 but so directly rebutting Stowe it was reissued in 1852, Caroline Gilman, a Northerner comfortably reestablished in Charleston, South Carolina, had made clear her position on female submission:

> To repress a harsh answer, to confess a fault, and to stop (right or wrong) in the midst of a self-defense, in gentle submission, sometimes requires a struggle like life and death; but these three efforts are the golden threads with which domestic happiness is woven. . . .
>
> [A woman's] first study must be self-control, almost to hypocrisy. A good wife must smile amid a thousand perplexities, and clear her voice to tones of cheerfulness when her frame is drooping with disease or else languish alone. (256)

In the midst of portraying a Southern plantation's domestic bliss, Gilman invokes spinsterhood and social isolation as the ultimate punishment for a woman's deviating from this model of "good wife." Because it threatened white male dominion, female self-assertion, including self-defense, invited exile. With this, Gilman begins laying the foundational gender standards for proslavery fiction's battlements.

Stowe's work would concur with Gilman, and with others of the domestic novelists, on presenting women as primarily hearth and family-centered creatures—yet Stowe deftly transforms this role from a limitation to a source of empowerment. As Elizabeth Ammons has said: "Harriet Beecher Stowe displays in *Uncle Tom's Cabin* a facility for converting essentially repressive concepts of femininity into a positive (and activist) alternative system of values in which woman figures not merely as the moral superior of man, his inspirer, but as the model for him in the new millennium about to dawn" ("Heroines" 163). While Stowe's agreeing that home was "the appointed sphere for woman" classifies her as traditionalist by twenty-first-century standards, she grants women ecclesiastical authority that extends beyond the sweet, diminutive, passive household angel: "more holy than cloister, more saintly and pure than church and altar. . . . Priestess, wife, and mother, there she ministers daily in holy works of household peace" (*The Minister's Wooing* 567–68). In contrast to proslavery sentimentalists, the female characters of *Uncle Tom's Cabin* do not hesitate to defy husbands, fathers, and slave masters when their own ethics clash with socially prescribed submission, and are presented as or in some cases evolve into mother-saviors: Eliza physically saves her child through superhuman feats and saves her husband's soul through what Stowe presents as the young woman's steadfast faith; Rachel Halliday assists in redeeming fugitive slaves, even as she serves as her Quaker community's center of comfort and instruction; Mrs. Bird opposes her husband's domestic authority and federal law in harboring fugitives; Mrs. Shelby and Chloe conspire to protect Eliza; and the child Eva, whose name derives from the biblical Eve, which in Hebrew means "mother of all living," comforts and catechizes her father's slaves and attempts to secure their freedom. Even Tom, though male and physically powerful, becomes, in Stowe's paradigm, a feminine-identified Christ figure who prioritizes relationships with the divine and other human beings over his own freedom, who exemplifies nurture and gentleness, who unashamedly weeps, and who embraces weakness over strength to the point of death to secure the "salvation," physical and spiritual, of others.

Tom's identification with the maternal is intentional: Stowe crafted her best-selling novel with the goal of showing "how Jesus Christ . . . has still a mother's love for the poor and lowly" (C. E. Stowe, *Life* 154), and in doing so, she was not the first to feminize the nature of Christian divinity. Stowe knew her Bible well, and feminist theologian Phyllis Trible has examined the substantial number of Hebrew and Christian biblical texts that employ maternal imagery for God. Only a partial listing includes: "The Rock who gave you birth you forgot, and you lost remembrance of the God who writhed in labor pains with you" (Deut. 32:18); Shall I bring to the birth and not cause to bring forth says Yahweh; shall I, causing to bring forth, shut the womb?" (Isa. 66:13); "God chose to give us birth through the word of truth" (James 1:18); and the "Holy Spirit must give birth to [human] spirit" (John 3:6). Medieval mystics as early as the twelfth century but even more frequently during the two centuries that followed wrote of the second person of the trinity as a mother.[9] This trend reaches its culmination in the fourteenth-century female mystic Julian of Norwich, who insists, in one of many such passages: "The Saviour himself is our Mother for we are forever being born of him and shall never be delivered" and "The human mother will suckle her child with her milk, but our beloved mother, Jesus, feeds us with himself" (164). Relative to the conservatism of her culture, Stowe's endowing her novel's male and female Christ figures with maternal attributes certainly appears radical; however, given her particularly thorough knowledge of Hebrew and Christian scriptures, many of which celebrate the mothering of God, her technique becomes, perhaps, less surprising.[10]

Even Stowe's secondary characters who portray negative maternal images do so to underscore the centrality of motherhood: the slave Prue, for example, has become an alcoholic precisely *because* of being forced to hear her infant wail as it starved to death; Northern abolitionist Ophelia, who is frightened to touch black skin, becomes a sympathetic character only once she begins to function as priest and parent toward Topsy; Cassy's redemption begins when she is able to act as a mother and protector toward Emmeline, a kind of black Evangeline; and Marie's self-absorbed obsessions become substantially more monstrous, as Stowe has framed it, when juxtaposed with the mother of Christ, from which her name derives, and contrasted with the self-sacrificial redemptive power of the book's other mothers. Plantation-romance and anti–Uncle Tom writers also attempt to display mother figures as the salvation for personal and societal ills—yet with very different results, as I demonstrate.

Some of the sentimentalists who set their narratives in the slaveholding South never explicitly defend the "peculiar institution" yet ultimately promote its agenda. Throughout the 1850s, for example, such writers as Lizzie Petit Cutler, Eliza Ann Dupuy, Mary E. Bradley, Judith Page Walker, Augusta Jane Evans Wilson, E.D.E.N. (Emma Dorothy Eliza Nevitte) Southworth, and Mary J. Holmes combined the sentimental novel's formula with the backdrop of gracious plantation living. Many of their female protagonists exhibit considerable courage and self-reliance—at least until a suitably strong, pious male arrives on the scene. While certainly glamorizing the lives of white planter-class women, these writers did not necessarily intend to advocate chattel slavery as a just, viable social and economic system. Some, like the prolific Eliza Ann Dupuy, born in Petersburg, Virginia, did voice fierce regional loyalties; Dupuy avowed: "As a Southern woman, I would sooner have thrust my hand in a blazing fire, as the Roman youth did, than have taken a pen in it, to throw discredit on my own people."[11] But others such as E.D.E.N. Southworth privately opposed slavery. Similar to Stowe's focus upon the sacred power of motherhood, Southworth's *Virginia and Magdalene* commences with the homeward struggle of a sixteen-year-old mother, recently widowed, to the doorstep of her own mother, whom she trusts will, godlike, forgive past misunderstandings. Providing the narrative with a nearly virginal conception, one maternal character, Mary, finds herself pregnant after her husband Joseph's demise: Mary names her daughter, significantly, Virginia. Typical of Southworth's work, the novel spotlights white women of intelligence and strength. " 'Call on God and be a woman!' " cries one character to another, admonishing her to be as courageous as, the narrative implies, white women inherently are (13). Slavery in this novel and most of Southworth's other fiction serves only as a stage set that features aristocratic planter families and well-bred steeds.[12] Yet the set's very glamor recommends the plantation as a desirable way of life and ignores the workers upon whose backs the system rests. Though Southworth was personally antislavery, her fiction favors the interests of the planter elite.

Similarly, setting *Household Mysteries* on Virginia plantations, Lizzie Petit Cutler showcases noble Southerners who cherish fine homes and horses.[13] Like other domestic romances, *Household Mysteries* features paeans to and models of ideal motherhood, as in its final scene where the protagonist, Ida, teaches, frolics, nurtures, and prays with her young. As in Southworth, slavery is never explicitly advocated but simply assumed as part of gracious Southern living. Despite *Household Mysteries'* including a shuffling, sycophantic Uncle Tom character, its overall inattention to slavery places it outside the ranks of explicit anti–Uncle Tom fiction. Nevertheless, while neither *Virginia and Magdalene* nor *Household Mysteries* could be considered intentionally political, their idealization of the planter lifestyle ultimately condones the socioeconomic system that finances it.

Anti–Uncle Tom novels move past these ideological borderlands by mimicking Stowe's mother-savior ideology, privileging proslavery concerns over everything else, including plot and characterization, and typically referring directly to Stowe and *Uncle Tom's Cabin*. A world away from the stinging social criticisms aimed at the South of Thomas Thorpe's *Master's House*, female authored anti–Uncle Tom novels present only positive views of the plantation South, countering what the archival evidence reveals of antebellum white Southern women's lives and suggesting the authors' distance from the day-to-day realities of chattel slavery (see Chapter 4).

In her tale of intense maternal suffering, *The North and South*, anti–Uncle Tom writer Caroline Rush strategically emulates Stowe in calling for compassion based on a distinctly matrifocal conception of love and justice.[14] In *Uncle Tom's Cabin*, Stowe had directly addressed mothers as part of her persuasive technique:

> You, who have learned, by the cradles of your own children, to love and feel for all mankind, . . . by your joy in his beautiful, spotless infancy, . . . by the desolation of that empty cradle, that silent nursery, . . . pity those mothers who are constantly made childless by the American slave-trade! And say, mothers of America, is this a thing to be defended, sympathized with, passed over in silence? (2:316)

Defending Southern slavery as benign relative to Northern poverty's "white slavery," Rush's response attempts a similar strategy:

> O! mother, thou who lovest so fondly the little cherub that lies in thy arms, or sleeps in its crib beside thee, roseate with health and beauty, how canst thou tell but that adversity may come, and doom thine innocent to such a life of hardship? . . . Can you read your bible, pray, go to church, dress, give parties and be happy, while thousands are around you, lost

in degradation, fallen so low that they are even loathsome to the sight? (128–30)

While echoing Stowe, Rush here misdirects her readers toward Northern white children in urban misery.[15] Targeting religiously conservative white Southerners appalled by New England Christianity's trend toward Unitarianism since the turn of the nineteenth century, Rush inserts the words "bible, pray, go to church" into her pietistic appeal: she will, the author implicitly announces, not only take up arms against Stowe's abolitionism, but also outdo the religious fervency of *Uncle Tom's Cabin*.[16] As in this passage, Rush often alludes to "degradation[s]" and intimates sexual "fallen[ness]," ranking white females' sexual vulnerability among the most horrific of Northern cities' myriad dangers. Indeed, the social construct of "whiteness" at the heart of race-based slavery relies upon the reproductive white female's sexual purity and inaccessibility—yet incessant desirability—by the black Other. As Rush's novel demonstrates, exposing white femininity to the promiscuity, violence, and temptations of urban life threatens the clarity of racial demarcations and therefore of peace and freedom from violence.

Bent on exposing Northern hypocrisy and highlighting Southern benevolence, Rush extends the matrifocal trope, presenting herself in a maternal relationship with her novel, positioned to help save the fractious Union: "Go forth, little book, and do your humble work in the world. . . . If you will perform, Oh! child of my brain, the duties I require of you then indeed, I shall be blessed and happy" (vi–vii). From the beginning, Rush casts herself as mother-savior of the nation's peace. "I feel that I have right on my side," she interrupts her narrative, "and that I have only to handle my subject with skill, to turn the tide of sympathy from imaginary evils at the South, to those abuses which exist in our midst" (43). Though never denying that slavery might separate black mothers from their children, Rush appeals to her white readers' social assumptions of white privilege and protection from commodification, so that relative to the outrage of a white family's sufferings, a black family's fragmentation matters little.[17] Rush takes for granted what Toni Morrison calls the slave's "natal isolation": slave women are not real mothers and slave children have no real emotional attachment to the women who bear them (*Playing in the Dark* 21).

Juxtaposing Stowe's Uncle Tom against her own Gazella Harley, Rush intimates the threat of black men to white women:

We shall see whether "the broad-chested, powerful negro," or the fragile, delicate girl, with her pure white face, is most entitled to your sympathy and tears. God forbid that you should waste your sympathies on the slaves of the South. . . . Why takest thou the mote out of thy brother's eye and seest not the beam that is in thine own? (128–30)

Invoking late eighteenth- and mid-nineteenth-century scientific "research," which reflected and exacerbated dominant whites' sexualized fabrications of race, Rush's juxtaposition of the " 'broad-chested, powerful negro' " against the "fragile, delicate [white] girl" suggests a subtext: the predatory black male overpowering a helpless white female. The dominant culture's fetishization of white females' sexual purity had been fueled by renowned English surgeon Dr. Charles White, who promoted the theory of polygenics, or the multiple origin of races.[18] In his 1799 *Account of the Regular Gradation of Man*, White argues that Negroes occupy an intermediate position between apes and white humans. Claiming that "every anatomical school in London" had "the *Penis* of an African" in its museum, as did he, White maintained that Negroes possess larger sexual organs and smaller brains than whites; yet he insisted that he did not wish "to give the smallest countenance to the pernicious practice of enslaving mankind," and he promoted abolition.[19] Reflecting White's theories and white culture's racialized anxieties, Rush hypersexualizes black males in her narrative, while her primary white female protagonist bears nine children apparently conceived out of nothing but wifely submission. In Rush's world, white reproductivity has nothing to do with female desire.

Rush applies a theology of whiteness with a heavy hand, never subtle in connecting divine favor and spiritual acceptability with one race and its social entitlement. Associating skin pigmentation with female sexual innocence in the "pure white face," the text discloses the vulnerability of whiteness as a social construct: since whiteness arises from erecting boundaries of "not black," attempts to transgress those boundaries and "sully" its fabricated purity threaten its very existence.[20] Having admonished her imagined readers, presumably white Northern women, Rush directly attacks their hypocrisy and, in pointedly formalized King James rhetoric, again assumes the role of national redeemer and divine judge, mimicking Christ's condemnation of self-righteousness: "Why takest thou the mote out of thy brother's eye?" Consistently, Rush evades questions of slavery's benevolence or cruelty by going on the offensive, typically with just such theopolitical moves that challenge the North's moral superiority. Framing sympathy spent on slaves as "waste," Rush reflects the Constitution's assessment of slaves' humanity: because a slave is only three-fifths of a person, white society's concerns always supersede those of slaves.[21]

Just as she follows Stowe in offering herself as a cultural prophet regarding slavery, Rush also challenges gender constraints—to a point. With striking candor, Rush protests the inequity of men's and women's roles. Often, she goes beyond the protofeminism of the typical domestic novel and dares to connect domestic duties with confinement, frustration, and subservience. In marriage, for example,

> men have decidedly the advantage over women. Women must be docile, and subject themselves unto their husbands. They must be obedient and tractable as lambs. (I suppose I shall be accused of high treason against my country, but I don't care if I am; I will say, in this parenthesis, where our masters can't see it, Oh! fellow women, stand up for your rights, and don't obey: don't yield up every thought to your owners.) The laws of society are all formed for the man and against the woman. She must stay at home and darn stockings, and nurse the baby, while he, happy creature, walks abroad in all his majesty, and shines at the club, the theatre, and the ball-room. He spends, of course, a large amount of money in these pleasures; but then, be it remembered it comes off his wife's allowance for marketing and shopping; and who ever heard of a dutiful wife making complaints. . . . Now mind, I don't say that women ought not to darn stockings and nurse babies and such little nick-nacks, but I think there is a time for all things and that she needs relaxation from her duties, as well as lordly man. (165)

In defining women as the property of their "owners," Rush frames mid-nineteenth-century marriage as a form of slavery, and even in conceding "there is a time" for nursing and darning, she categorizes domestic and maternal obligation, "such little nick-nacks," as essentially trivial relative to the "lordly" man's access to social centers and monetary control. Like many nineteenth-century white advocates of women's rights, Rush rallies white women to resist subjugation, while she ignores black oppression. But there is more going on in this text than another Northern white woman's overlooking the rights of the impoverished and nonwhite. Rush's lament replicates what this book's fourth chapter demonstrates as a standard proslavery evasion: Southern white women's framing themselves as victims. Russ Castronovo rightly argues that "the Southern refutation of Stowe was itself indebted to black articulations, especially in its narrativization of gender," and Rush provides a paradigmatic example, as throughout her novel she borrows from abolitionist and slave narratives the images and rhetoric of imprisonment, bondage, and suffering.[22] Detailing their own onerous duties and bemoaning their husbands' access to female slaves, whom Mary Chestnut labels "prostitutes," white planter-class women displace responsibility by depicting themselves as slaves.[23] White-defined assumptions of racial and class privilege enlist the reader's sympathies for any white woman of considerable wealth—since her husband's social circuit includes "the club, the theatre, and the ball-room"—who would ever be constricted by domestic duty. Self-pity and selective perception about victimization deflect attention from questions of social justice.

While *The North and South*'s mother-protagonist, Mrs. Harley, catechizes her daughter on abject submission to one's husband, regardless of circumstances, the plot shows Mrs. Harley rejecting her husband's alleged authority. The narrator insists that

> Gazella [the daughter] had been reared in a different school; her mother, who was a tender and dutiful wife, had taught by her example the duties of her position; and her precepts of affection, her devoted love, and above all, the uncomplaining submissiveness of her life, became in turn the heritage of her daughter. (36)

Despite the narrator's persistent didacticism, Mrs. Harley fails to follow her own instruction. When her husband responds to the family's bankruptcy by suggesting that both parents and children lie down by the fire and starve, Mrs. Harley ignores his instructions, and his weak resignation enrages her. The text contradicts itself, rendering her neither "uncomplaining" nor "submissive":

> "As long as I have hands to work, and strength to drag myself about, I will make every exertion to provide for the helpless creatures I have brought into the world: and when I am prostrated upon my sick bed, and

my unborn child sees the light, I will trust in God who, though he has seemed to forsake me, will not, I am sure, desert me at my utmost need." (54)

While the text dismisses Northern white males as ineffectual and irrelevant, Southern white males remain in the narrative wings. Though in the absence of male support, the white Northern female risks masculinizing herself, the text allows Mrs. Harley limited agency because she acts not for herself but for her children: her domestic concerns remain paramount. With unflagging perseverance, Rush's female messiah sets out to save those she has "brought into the world." Though like Christ on the cross she admits feeling forsaken by God, she nevertheless testifies to her faith in divine assistance, reassuring the reader of the text's religious commitments and placing the assertive woman under the authority of a patriarchal deity. Struggling to earn the family's living, she is limited by social position and skill to needlework, but labors with formidable energy from four in the morning to midnight and enlists her eldest daughter's assistance. Searching hostile city venues for work, Mrs. Harley is "armed with a desperate courage, for she remembered her poor sick daughter and her starving children at home: she felt that every sentiment of pride must be sacrificed to her duty, and with an inward aspiration to God, she awaited the opening of the door" (244); thus she trudges on. The text applauds white female courage, so long as it operates for domestic goals.

Contrary to the author's rallying cry for white women's rights, her narrative teaches the inevitability of feminine compliance to the power of wealthy white men: all dissenters in the novel are punished. Vividly demonstrating that protection and support of a family cannot be trusted to women, particularly not poor women who have no significant political or economic power, Mrs. Harley fails. In the end, the most fervent mother love cannot compete with—or survive—the grinding inhumanity of male-driven industrialization. Whereas in Stowe, divine mother love successfully combats the political and marital status quo, defying federal laws, husbands' instructions, and social mores, Rush's principal mother-savior circumvents her husband's authority only to witness the decimation of her family. The subtext of *The North and South* suggests both the woeful inadequacy of men and the impossibility of women's autonomy.

Although Mrs. Harley does initially rebel against her husband's authority just as Rush's invocation to wives encourages, her refusal to submit and her determination to support her family financially result in dissolution, assault, disease, abuse, deprivation, and eventually deaths: the family's misery has only been prolonged. And though Rush depicts all her white male characters as spineless and insignificant, offering a resounding denunciation of the male-authored, male-focused anti–Uncle Tom novels, nevertheless, racial, gender, and class privilege allows them to prey upon the sexual and economic vulnerability of poor women. Disrupting the narrative's protofeminist surface, the financial and social power of white men ultimately undermines women's attempts to survive. Negating her advocacy for women's rights, Rush's pro-slavery commitments position her as a buttress for wealthy white men and their chokehold on antebellum Southern society.

Though decrying urban social ills, Rush scorns the women who combat them:

> Such persons belong to that class who neglect all duties of home, in order to make a great noise in the world, and create for themselves the representatives of philanthropy. These persons are generally small and mean in all their operations. The sight of a widow struggling through the world with her fatherless children cannot awaken their pity. (13)

Rush attempts to present herself as defender of the poor and outcast, yet she castigates those who give a political voice to the poor, and she offers a protagonist who is a social and economic aristocrat fallen on hard times. Setting up a series of binary oppositions, Rush pits "representatives of philanthropy" against Mrs. Harley, a true practitioner of submissive faith; "noise" against Mrs. Harley's silent suffering; social protesters against uncomplaining docility; "operations"—the industrialized, commercial world—against the Harleys' home; "neglect" against Mrs. Harley's domestic focus; and people "for themselves" against her selflessness. Rush goes on at length, delineating the sufferings of child workers and factory girls, the "white slaves" of the North, "tortured, goaded, and lashed until every refined sensibility is totally destroyed" (13). Yet never are the white female "slaves" subject to being stripped, raped, or sexually violated in any way: whiteness alone, the text suggests, precludes any blurring of racial demarcations. Always juxtaposed against an invisible but nonetheless present background of Southern slavery, white women remain their own decision makers; though limited in their choices, they retain free will; though beleaguered by white male power, they die noble, romanticized deaths. The daughter Gazella Harley, for example, dies of consumption with an adoring lover by her side. Despite the text's intent to privilege white urban suffering, its foundational contrasts of black and white worlds ultimately highlight black female slaves' sexual vulnerabilities.

Over and over, Rush's ideology dismantles itself: while calling for white women to soften their hearts toward Northern social injustice, Rush demeans a white woman whose time is divided by family and the broader social good; while inveighing against husbands as tyrants and their wives as pathetically helpless, she lauds young Gazella Harley, the epitome of sweet, feminine submission; while eliciting compassion for "fatherless" children in the foregoing passage, she composes a narrative in which the *presence* of a father causes bankruptcy, near–mass suicide, and continued degradation as he drinks away the family's meager income.

In *Recollections of a Southern Matron,* Caroline Gilman had set the precedent for proslavery views of women social reformers.[24] Her narrator presents the ideal mother-teacher as one who models inaction and disengagement from social issues. Praising the mother's "passive virtues," the narrator applauds her having never "interfered" with her children's education, attending instead only to the family's dress and manners. Further, the narrator, a mother herself, scolds the kind of woman who neglects combing her children's hair because she is "busy sewing for children in Burmah!" (32). Both Gilman's and Rush's tirades against women who engage in social action typify anti–Uncle Tom novelists who, like Harriet Beecher Stowe, idealize mother-saviors as teachers but, unlike her, confine maternal instruction to domestic realms.

When Rush's persevering Mrs. Harley, singularly devoted to her own domestic circle, teaches piety to her starving children, she repeatedly couples all her admonitions to trust God with the pronouncement that "it is all for the best" (e.g., *The North and South* 70), passively promoting the status quo. After the deaths of three Harley children and the irreparable damage to and permanent departure of more, the mother's continued Panglossian clichés become perverse parodies of religious instruction. As part of this mother-savior's strategy to save the family, thirteen-year-old Harry Harley is apprenticed to Mr. Hardgripe, who whips him and squeezes lemons into his wounds. A stark contrast with Stowe's young Harry, who escapes in his mother's arms from victimization, when Rush's Harry escapes, Mrs. Harley censures her son both for having left and for having finally struck back. Harry initially attempts to defend his behavior, insisting that he had tried to receive the abuse passively, but that

> as I grew older, the kicks and cuffs I received began to awaken in my mind feelings of revenge and retaliation. My spirit rebelled against the indignity with which I was treated, and I not unfrequently spoke very freely in my own defence, but alas, I soon found I was but riveting my own chains. (252)

Casting him as a slave, the proslavery text relies upon the reader's finding articulate whiteness coupled with "chains" intolerable. Teresa Goddu examines the ways in which Stowe invokes gothic horrors of torture and imprisonment to enlist her readers' sympathies, and Rush, not to be out-gothicized, once again borrows from the methodology of the author she is attempting to discredit.[25] Yet Rush's commitment to the boundaries of whiteness often prevents her going as far in her descriptions of white characters' sufferings: unlike Stowe's slave character Cassy, for example, who is repeatedly misused by white men and finally forced to function as Legree's mistress, Rush allows no white female character in *The North and South* to be raped. Although some twenty-first-century scholars have argued that sentimental texts such as Stowe's buttress rather than demolish the bondage of blacks by presenting scenes of slave abuse and torture for the voyeuristic pleasure of whites, Rush's employment of gothic horrors similar to Stowe's suggests the opposite conclusion: that both authors, while strategically appealing to nineteenth-century tastes for the melodramatic—and, yes, the gothic—also relied upon the gothic to heighten readers' sociopolitical sensitivities, not merely to provide a means of entertainment and escape.[26]

Harry describes having struggled, after one of his beatings, to abide by his mother's religious instruction:

> I writhed in agony, and in that hour I remembered the prayer you had taught me, oh! my mother! I remembered that you told me there was a God who was a friend of the friendless and destitute. . . . I called upon his name so long forgotten, and prayed that he would help me in this hour of sore distress. But my help was not yet. (*The North and South* 253)

Once again, the text shows a Northern white male to be helpless and, contrary to its intent, also suggests the impotence of the white-imaged "Father" God, who fails to act anywhere in the narrative. Despite Rush's insistence upon her novel's religious groundedness, the text enervates the South's patriarchal deity. Yet when a Southern white woman stands in for the unresponsive deity by finally answering Harry's prayers, the text resists any feminist assertion. Rather, the redeeming mother-savior represents and reinforces the omnipotence of Southern wealth and whiteness, which is repeatedly cloaked in a religiosity that hides the absence of any real deity: what is being worshipped is whiteness itself.

By having Mrs. Norton, a planter-class mother of six children, "save" Harry by helping him become a sailor on a China-bound vessel, Rush attempts to glorify plantation mistresses and Southern society. Yet the boy is forever lost to his mother and to the narrative. Although the text positions Mrs. Harley's separation from her son as akin to—and because they are white, far worse than—slave-family separations, the subtext resists: Harry's Southern "savior" is the instigator of the family's fragmentation. Her slave-based society has taught her to weigh nonwealthy or nonwhite human life and family relationships lightly. Exposing the text's underlying racial and class assumptions, she deems the Harleys worthy of help because they are white and socially refined, yet because they are of a lower economic class, she allows the family's dismemberment, despite her having the financial means to keep its members together.[27] That the rich Southerner watches and allows the Harleys' separation and starvation makes her—and her culture—appear grostequely inhumane rather than generous and benevolent. In a pattern repeated throughout *The North and South*, a Southern mother-savior effectively "redeems" an individual by cleaving him from his family and securing new cords of subservience: what the surface text presents as heroic, the subtext reveals as monstrous.

Rush's frequent authorial asides trumpet her admiration of white Southern women, who exhibit almost preternatural perfection:

> I should like to see an instance of cruelty like this [Northern treatment of Mrs. Harley] in the Southern country. The Southern ladies are the very soul and essence of kindness. 'Tis true they may not, as a general thing, have as much energy of character as our ladies of the North but that is owing to their climate. I have never met a class of beings so lovely, so

kind-hearted, so gentle. . . . God bless the ladies of the South, for they
seem indeed nearer akin to angels than to men. (64)

Invoking divine approval, Rush compares white Southern women with angels,
a common trope in the domestic tradition. Yet in the other half of the comparison, "men," the text suggests not only humankind but also white Southern
males, commonly disparaged by antislavery activists as anything but angelic.
Even white Southern women loyal to the "peculiar institution" privately
chronicled—and attributed to slavery—rampant sexual license among planter-
class males.[28] While the surface message praises white Southern women,
the subtext evokes less flattering images of white Southern men. In contrast
with Stowe's beautiful but self-absorbed Marie St. Clare, Rush follows the
proslavery writers' pattern of connecting white Southern female beauty with
compassion. Although Stowe does link Eva's beauty with her goodness, she
distinguishes her from Rush's female angels. Eva issues instructions to her
elders, reprimands planter-class males, including her father and her cousin,
and positions herself as a source of divine authority.

Despite Rush's valorization of Southern culture, her central Northern
mother exhibits tireless determination against insurmountable odds, while
Southern mothers appear lazy and spoiled, suggesting slavery's perversion of
maternal love. The kindness, too, that Rush celebrates in Southern women
appears narrow and self-interested in her narrative. Mrs. Dunlap, a pious
young planter's wife from Mississippi whose own child recently died, "assists"
the starving Harley family by essentially purchasing one of their children, Ida.
For a ten-dollar gold piece and a promise that the child will eventually receive
ten thousand dollars a year, Mrs. Dunlap plays the mother-savior-extortion-
ist, blithely "saving" Ida and leaving the other Harleys desolate, hungry, and
despairing. Soliciting maternal sympathy, the narrator bemoans Mrs. Harley's
tragic dilemma: "Let those imagine, who have the feelings of a mother, how
agonized she was when she had spoken the word that had given her darling to
another" (235). Yet the narrative rewards the wealthy, slaveholding Southern
mother with continued material security and the addition of a devoted daughter. As Mrs. Harley's selfless mother love sacrifices itself to Mrs. Dunlap's
mercenary self-interest, the indigent mother relinquishes all claims to her
child and never sees her again.

Although Rush stages the scene to portray the brutalities of Northern
industrialism relative to gracious Southern plantation culture, the text's de-

piction of Mrs. Dunlap's charity also reveals slavery's corrupting influence: systematically commodifying human bodies, slave-based culture assumes that even the ties of human affection are for sale. For a price, a slaveholder's fiscal power can secure anything, even the sacred status of motherhood. Further, while slave women are victims of external, profit-driven transactions that sell their children away from them, this text presents two white women agreeing upon the sale of a child who belongs to one of them, which renders whiteness itself heartless and acquisitive. Rather than evoking horror that a white, once-rich family could be so abused by urban poverty, the text's comparisons with the invisible slave presence continually point toward slavery as the root corruption of Southern *and* Northern social systems that allow market forces to determine family relationships and human value. The way in which Mrs. Dunlap acquires a daughter replicates white Southern patriarchy's purchasing white women's compliance: both have been bought with material security. Redeemed from poverty but wrenched from her family, the child, Ida, grows up to marry a rich half-Italian, foreign enough to represent exoticism and a titillating opportunity for taming wildness beyond domestic borders, but no real threat to whiteness.[29] Living happily ever after in isolated, undisturbed ease, Ida apparently never attempts to alleviate her biological family's misery: white privilege allows—even encourages—such detachment from external suffering. Unlike Stowe's mother-saviors, who actively engage societal ills through radical civil disobedience, daring escapes, and collaborative efforts, Rush's successful mother-saviors insulate themselves and, when they confront personal loss, purchase their way out of grief.

Creating another maternal figure who redeems by fragmenting, Rush refutes Stowe's Quaker matron Rachel Halliday with her own Quaker, Mrs. Atlee. In *Uncle Tom's Cabin,* Rachel Halliday administers comfort and healing:

> For twenty years or more, nothing but loving words, and gentle moralities, and motherly loving kindness, had come from that chair; head-aches and heart-aches innumerable had been cured there,—difficulties spiritual and temporal solved there,—all by one good, loving woman, God bless her! (116–17)

Stowe chooses her words with theological care, positioning the Quaker's "motherly loving kindness" as central to her function within the community, and the phrase carries layers of meaning. Throughout Hebrew scripture or the Old Testament, biblical writers repeatedly image the power, intensity, and depth of God's love by employing a word that means "womb love," typically translated as "loving kindness." In all of Hebrew and Christian scripture, in fact, the only gender-specific bodily organ mentioned in relation to God is the womb. Stowe enlists this potent term, "loving kindness," and strategically, almost redundantly, couples it with "motherly" in the service of depicting one of her key mother-saviors.

Rachel Halliday's form of comfort extends beyond mere caresses: in harboring fugitives, a patently illegal act by 1850, she provides material, emotional, and physical comfort for the oppressed at the risk of her own safety. For Rush's Quaker, however, personal interests remain paramount. Rather than assist the entire Harley family, numbering eleven before they begin dying and leaving, Mrs. Atlee gradually adopts the loveliest of the little girls. Not long before Mrs. Atlee completes the transfer of little Rose's affections and physical presence from biological to adoptive mother, the child asks permission to attend her father's deathbed. Drawing the grieving child onto her lap, Mrs. Atlee smooths her curls in gestures that initially appear to emulate Rachel Halliday's healing strokes. But Rush's Quaker whispers not comfort but self-serving theopolitical rhetoric: that she hopes "her little Rose would act like a woman and remember it was God who gave life, and he therefore had a right to take it, and that she would not cry, or do anything to vex or worry her poor mother, but try to think that God knows what is best for us, and afflicts us for our own good" (142). As Toni Morrison argues that the Africanist presence complicates and often contradicts a white text's expressed intentions (*Playing in the Dark* 66), so here proslavery gender and theological anxieties sabotage the surface text: Rose must "act like a woman," meaning not the liberated autonomy Rush advocates earlier in the novel, but the pious submission of "true womanhood," best exemplified by Southern planter femininity. Rush's theological framework for Mrs. Atlee's God exactly parallels the male planter, who also has a "right to take [life]," "knows what is best," and "afflicts" enslaved blacks for their own "good." Earlier in the narrative, Rush's God never answers young Harry's pleas for deliverance, and this passage reveals why: that deity acts only to afflict, not comfort, protect, strengthen, or redeem. The God that Rush constructs to show her solidarity with Southern slaveholders appears just as petty, inept, and tyrannical as her Northern white men, and as aloof as her male Southerners. Though unequivocally positioned as a heroine, Mrs. Atlee promotes a deity who willfully inflicts suffering upon innocent devotees.

Unlike the Quaker women of *Uncle Tom's Cabin*, who calm, comfort, and reassure the frightened, the Quaker woman of *The North and South* intentionally instills fear. Coaching Rose on feminine delicacy, Mrs. Atlee warns:

> Remember, my child, that the soul of a young girl is like a mirror, which reflects even the breath that sullies it; or like a sheet of white paper, upon which should be inscribed nothing but the purest characters. It is of so fine, so sensitive a nature, that even the breath of impurity contaminates it. (93)

With the obvious metaphor of a sheet of *white* paper that must not be sullied, Rush leaves lurking behind Mrs. Atlee's speech the hint of sexual threat to white female innocence. Using the term "soul" to represent the dominant culture's fetishization of its females' sexual purity and its fears of the sexually aggressive, sullying black Other, Rush reflects a stereotype prevalent among whites in the United States since its colonial beginnings.[30]

As if to reinforce—even test—her theology of whiteness, Mrs. Atlee has purchased "contamination" by hiring nonwhite household servants. Like the stereotype of black male sexual aggression, the association of blacks with disease was nothing new by 1852. A friend of Thomas Jefferson and a respected scientist, Benjamin Rush (to my knowledge, unrelated to Caroline Rush) argued that "the Black Color (as it is called) of the Negroes is derived from **LEPROSY**" and could be cured to return to its natural white state (see Gossett, *Race* 41). Yet he argued that both his theory and the biblical accounts of creation prove the innate equality of blacks and whites. A staunch opponent of slavery, Benjamin Rush insisted that this "leprosy," which he diagnosed as not contagious, be treated with compassion rather than oppression. Proslavery advocates, however, latched on only to the idea of contamination, using it as another buttress for racial walls. Mrs. Atlee demonstrates whiteness's obsession with boundaries:

> "If I permitted thee to go into my kitchen, and sit down with Dinah and Andy [black servants], I should expect to hear thee repeat all the sayings

and negro talk thou wouldst learn there; and I should not consider this so pretty or becoming as the simple words with which thou now expressest thyself." (*The North and South* 94)

As Amy Kaplan observes, traditional allusions by whites to Africa displaced their own preconceptions onto it and thus helped define "whiteness" as "not them," that is, not black; in the same way, Mrs. Atlee distinguishes proper behavior for a white female as "not what they do" and thus inculcates racial and class superiority in Rose.[31] In elaborate King James diction, Mrs. Atlee praises Rose's "simple words," by which she means "not how they talk." The servants' dialect defines language outside that dialect's grammatical, syntactical, and pronunciation patterns as "white"—and therefore, the narrative implies, desirable. Under the tutelage of the woman she comes to call "Mamma," Rose grows cultivated enough to become a Southern planter family's governess, marries a wealthy planter's son, and bears many children.[32] Yet in Rose's development from child to blissful matron, the text contradicts two of its messages: that whiteness is entirely natural—much anxiety and energy are expended in establishing whiteness and maintaining its boundaries—and that slavery is a compassionate system. Coercing human property to labor for her comfort apparently teaches Rose insensitivity to human suffering: nowhere in the narrative does the privileged planter's wife remember her own starving biological mother or siblings. The Quaker mother Mrs. Atlee, cast as a mother-savior but performing as a usurper of family affection, teaches her lessons well: Rose holds herself and her happiness apart from anyone outside the South's rarefied social, racial, and economic rulers. Rush's theology of whiteness not only permits but spiritualizes, lauds, and rewards such behavior.

Bad mothers also prove effective teachers in *The North and South*, though the narrator condemns their lessons, in part by detailing their ugliness. Mrs. Anson, for example, is

tall and slender, with a waist the same width as her shoulders. . . . Her complexion was somewhere between a well-used copper cent, and a piece of untanned leather, and had something of the consistency of the latter. . . . Her hair, if hair it could be called, who hair had none, save what was her's by purchase, was of a raven's blackness: her nose was hooked, considerably, . . . but her eyes [had an] owl-like roundness. (161)

With darker skin always linked in *The North and South* to depravity, the text images this mother's body to represent other moral flaws. In the proslavery tradition of signaling degradation, Mrs. Anson's thick waist and baldness masculinize her, while the "hooked" nose suggests her foreign extraction. The antithesis of Rush's angelic Southern "ladies," this "mother's vanity taught [her daughter Julia] to believe that the adornment of the body could make up for the absence of jewels of the heart" (166). Lacking spiritual beauty herself and having hired Rose Harley's twin, Lily, as a servant, Mrs. Anson attempts to set off Julia's talents against the once-beautiful Harley child, while Mrs. Harley, though aware of the abuse of her child, does nothing to stop Lily's physical and emotional destruction. Rather than valorizing slavery in contrast to Northern inhumanity, however, Mrs. Harley's passively allowing her daughter's and her own suffering replicates the self-assisted subjugation of wealthy white Southern women. By accepting the material and social advantages offered by the ruling patriarchy, planter-class women tacitly agreed to conspire with a system that constricted their own freedom, damaged their own families, and brutalized slaves.[33]

In contrast to Mrs. Harley's relative calm toward her children's beatings, exile, and hunger, she responds with unprecedented ferocity when a local merchant sexually harasses her daughter Gazella, highlighting proslavery's fixation on the undefiled reproductive white female. With the sacredness of white virginity threatened, Rush's Mrs. Harley leaps into action: "the smothered fire burst forth and found the vent that is necessary for a mother's insulted feelings, when the honor of a beloved daughter is at stake" (187). But what is "at stake," the text suggests, is less Gazella's physical safety than maternal pride, family reputation, and the preservation of class boundaries: having once been wealthy, the Harley family would not have allowed intimate association with the working class. The text praises only those daughters who offer themselves for the use of Southern slaveholders. Rush calls upon maternal sympathies that she frames as universal, but that the text makes clear exclude all but refined white motherhood: "Oh! there was a madness in the thought that you, oh! mother, who have been blessed with daughters, can imagine, but which my pen is weak and impotent to describe" (185). Inscribing authorship as masculine, she underscores her theme of male ineffectuality. When Mrs. Harley's rage challenges the mercantile male power structure, she lands in jail and is finally rescued by a wealthy, proslavery female, Mrs. Atlee. Despite Mrs. Harley's commitments to wifely submission and faith in a patriarchal deity, neither a white male nor a white-privileging male God attempts to help liberate her. [34] Contrary to its surface message, the text frames masculine whiteness and the divinity created in its image as ultimately imprisoners of status quo challengers.

Midnarrative, Rush inserts herself into the text, heralding her role as mother-protector—but for whites only:

> I have sympathy with sorrow, wherever it may be found; but I love, far more, to expend upon the poor destitute white children, who are lashed and goaded all through that season of their lives, which should be so happy, than for the pampered, well-fed lazy negro children of the South, whose most horrid task consists in taking off and putting on the shoes and stockings of their mistress and children. (100)

Immediately reversing herself, the protector of children becomes the attacker of slave children. Moving from a scene of gothic horror, which in this text plagues only whites, to one of domestic indolence, which here characterizes only blacks, Rush's "sympathy" degenerates even before the end of the sentence into rank bigotry. In her associating blackness with "pampered, well-fed laz[iness]," Rush perpetuates a pattern in U.S. racism that reappeared in the twentieth century with the metonymic identification of blacks with welfare.[35] Alluding to Stowe in citing "trump[ed-] up stories of imaginary cruelty practised upon the blacks" (192), Rush not only dismisses antislavery propaganda but also reflects late eighteenth-century and antebellum white culture's assumptions that blacks had less well developed nervous systems than whites had and therefore were less sensitive to pain. The physician Charles White, for example, quotes a fellow surgeon who claimed to have "amputated the legs of many negroes who have held the upper part of the limb themselves" (qtd. in Gossett, *Race* 48–49). As if responding directly to Mrs. Shelby's exclamation in *Uncle Tom's Cabin* that she would as soon have one of her own children sold as Eliza's little Harry, Rush counters with this portrait of a white woman's arrest for her dead husband's debts:

> A mother, still young and lovely, and endowed with all the virtues that make woman so honored and so dear, pressing to her snowy bosom an infant just six weeks old, that infant's father sleeping in the grave, with

an arm powerless to avenge her children, one a cripple, kneeling before two drunken, profane, worthless vagabonds, armed with the authority of the law, to tear the mother from her children, and leave her home unguarded, and take her, all helpless and innocent as she was, to the loathsome confines of a prison. . . . In [God's] own good time let us hope that he will defend the innocent. Talk about the abuses of slavery, indeed. (192)

By invoking God as defender of the innocent, Rush displaces guilt for social oppression from the dominant culture to divine whim. In language that stems from a theology of whiteness, Rush positions the young mother as worthy of the deity's protection, presumably because of her "snowy" bosom and its concomitant connection with spiritual innocence. She evokes the contrast of Eliza's dark skin by stressing this white mother's "snowy bosom" and relies upon her readers' assumptions of white privilege to make her maternal figure's danger appear more horrific. Though designing her character's situation after that of Stowe's Eliza, Rush aligns her ideology with Robert Criswell's *Uncle Tom's Cabin Contrasted with Buckingham Hall, the Planter's Home,* whose Charleston slave-auction scene reveals that even the clear, undisputed victimization of black females fails to discredit slavery. In a pointed revision of *Uncle Tom's Cabin,* Rush relates: "The [white] mother pressed her child to her bosom, and went forth, not to leap over fragments of floating ice on the Ohio river, but to walk between two drunken men to prison, where herded infamy and vice in every phrase" (196). According to the proslavery agenda, the exposure of a white female to "infamy and vice" ranks as more intolerable than physical threats to the lives of a black female and her son.

Rush highlights the fragility of young Gazella Harley, modelled on Stowe's Eva, and links it with her sexual and spiritual purity. But unlike Eva, Gazella represents nothing but the patriarchal Southern ideal of unsullied white feminine delicacy and silent selflessness. At first glance, Rush's Gazella and Stowe's Eva do seem cast from similar molds, both frail, fair, unearthly, beautiful girls. One-dimensionally good, both characters function more as allegorical types than as fully developed characters.[36] Like the "deep spiritual gravity of [Eva's] violet blue eyes" (*Uncle Tom's Cabin* 1:126), Gazella Harley's "dark blue eyes [are] filled with . . . a holy light (*The North and South* 30); like Eva too, the young Gazella lives and dies in virginal purity. Eva, however, speaks forthrightly, to the point of contradicting and instructing both parents and, despite her youth, consistently functions as the household's spiritual leader, while Gazella epitomizes unquestioning obedience to parental authority.

A teacher and preacher, little Eva, who dons a crown of tuberoses (*Uncle Tom's Cabin* 1:189) analogous to a crown of thorns and dresses entirely in white, is the "dear, little, blessed lamb" (2:240), patterned on the christological Lamb of God. Most clearly in her sermon to the St. Clare slaves just before her death, Evangeline speaks as Christ approaching the crucifixion.[37] In contrast, Rush's Gazella Harley offers a wan imitation: rather than a Christ figure, Gazella's "devoted love for her parents so shadowed forth in their [her eyes'] depths, that one might imagine them not unlike those beauteous orbs of the virgin mother of God, as she gazed upon her divine son" (124–25). Shying away from a direct analogy to Christ, Rush conforms to Southern patriarchy's constricted role for women and settles for a less radical comparison of Gazella to another mortal female. In Stowe's naming her character after Eve (Hebrew for "mother of all living"), she suggests Eva's spiritual maternity, while rejecting any patristic overlay of Eve as the instigator of all sin: Stowe upholds Eva as a mother-redeemer.[38] Though sketched as gentleness personified, she wields considerable influence. In opposition to her mother, Marie, a perversion of Christ's mother, Mary, Eva redirects individual lives and the course of events within the St. Clare household. Rush's Gazella, on the other hand, merely stitches hour by hour, silently assisting her mother in needlework, an appropriately "feminine" occupation, according to patriarchal definitions. But again the text disrupts itself: the same gender, class, and racial prescriptions that uphold Southern slavery limit the Harley women's occupational choices to delicate "women's work," that, even with sixteen-hour workdays, fails to secure them a subsistence income. Although Rush attempts to convey Gazella's dying as a Christlike self-sacrifice, the narrative has already positioned Gazella as entirely a victim, the virgin sacrifice to the gods of Northern avarice, and the Harleys sink deeper into their morass of poverty and grief. Mother and daughter are both defeated by Northern society's callousness toward *white* human suffering. The text teaches that because white Southern society desensitizes itself only to *blacks'* well-being, it is not equally culpable.

Caroline Rush arranges her hermeneutic pieces to polarize motherhood, South and North. Secure on Mrs. Dunlap's plantation, Ida thrives on her ten thousand dollars a year, while Northern Mrs. Harley's most heroic efforts cannot save Gazella; with proslavery Quaker Mrs. Atlee, Rose flourishes, while Lily, in the clutches of Mrs. Anson's Northern industrial maternity, shrivels and eventually perishes. According to the subtext, mother love is a quixotic affection, available for purchase, subject to regional alterations, and always vulnerable to the machinations of men. Mother-saviors who sacrifice themselves for their young fail miserably to protect or maintain the family, while the self-interested succeed. In the end, the violent, bottom-line ethics of both Northern industrial and Southern agrarian empires triumph over maternal protection and nurture: a mother's love proves no match for the money controlled by men.

Like Mrs. Harley of *The North and South*, the mother-savior of Mrs. G. M. Flanders's *Ebony Idol* suffers from the antislavery hypocrisy of her hardened Northern neighbors. In Minden, a small Northern town with many of the same social dynamics as Rush's unfeeling urban center, a white woman, the Widow Wellman, struggles to sustain her invalid son. A townsman of Minden, the Squire, demands to know why Minden prioritizes abolitionist concerns above the needs of the worthy widow: "Who of us have not seen her, in our own hours of sorrow, . . . forgetting her own afflictions in those of her fellow creatures?" (37). In explicit christological imagery, the narrator testifies to her "never [having] . . . swerved from the path of duty or rectitude, though often and again her weary feet have been pierced by thorns. . . . She has borne her cross of heart crucifixion down her stairway of adversity" (37). Yet, ultimately, the widow's messianic strength collapses in mortal weakness: when her son dies, she remains as nothing but a maudlin reminder of the town's choice to worship abolition rather than "Christ," the struggling white mother in their midst.

Like *The North and South*, Flanders's *Ebony Idol* follows domestic novels' pattern of elevating women and disparaging men.[39] The narrator sneers, for example, at Reverend Cary's "conviction of his personal infallibility of judgement and action" (3). Just back from a denominational convention, the cleric bombastically airs his newly formed abolitionism, then berates his wife for challenging his positions: " 'Women,' he muttered contemptuously, 'never should try to argue; however good you may be at heart, you are terribly deficient in logic. Knit, Madam, but don't argue! You remember the advice of St. Paul in regard to your own sex?' " In seemingly protofeminist fashion, Mrs. Cary counters: " 'St. Paul was a bachelor, and possibly had been disappointed, as most bachelors have' " (17), then, significantly, serves her husband apples and observes that " 'it has occurred to me that God created woman for some higher and nobler purpose, than to administer to the animal wants of Adam' " (69). When she further contends that " 'men . . . do not hesitate to exercise this . . . oppressive vigilance, and many an active, high-spirited girl degenerates into a hackneyed, hum-drum housekeeper," her husband accuses her of being " 'a little tainted with "woman's rights"' " (69), a marital exchange in striking contrast to those in the anti–Uncle Tom novels by men, in which only acquiescent wives and omniscient husbands exist. Throughout the novel, while Reverend Cary represents foolish fanaticism, his wife displays levelheaded wisdom as she rises above male censure.

However, the racialized subtext disrupts and constricts Flanders's seeming advocacy for women's rights. With a myopia that has plagued twentieth- and twenty-first-century white feminism, Flanders promotes only the liberation of privileged, properly domestic white women—and the narrative's conclusion problematizes even that; the oppression of black women concerns her not in the least.[40]

Interestingly, much of current feminist scholarship on *Uncle Tom's Cabin* seems to assume that Stowe's attack on slavery grew out of her critique of the patriarchy's oppression of middle-class women, or that her concern is primarily the liberation of women and only secondarily the plight of slaves.[41] But not only do these assumptions unintentionally replicate the mistakes of many early women's rights activists, they also fail to recognize the inextricable way in which race, gender, and class oppression functioned as a three-sided fortress to protect slavery. Scholars troubled by Stowe's laying white maternal care as the foundation for her racial restructuring would be rightly disturbed about how this might imply proprietary ownership by whites, but Stowe's vision of maternal care not simply includes but features black mothers who refuse to accept the slave-based society as it is, and refuse to accept whites as ontologically superior: Eliza, Chloe, Prue, Cassy, the slave mother who jumps from the riverboat, and so on.[42]

Despite Stowe's admittedly chilling depictions of black grotesques such as the young Topsy, she understands, whether consciously or not, the many-faceted complexity of the racism that made American slavery possible, and that to attack any part of the fortress is to attack the entire system; to undermine patriarchy is to yank the scaffolding from black bondage; to elevate lower-class white characters is to suggest the intellectual potential of slaves; to empower maternal redeemer figures is to discredit an unfeeling, mechanistic industrial society controlled by men. Thus Stowe's two primary Christ figures are an upper-class but economically powerless, physically weak white female child and an enslaved, feminine-identified, physically powerful black man: proslavery's sacralizations of race, class, and gender, all three, get disrupted.

Flanders's concern for the rights of women, however, goes only so far. As she capitulates to the plantation South's extreme gender and racial polarization, Flanders's protofeminism terminates altogether, and she denounces women abolitionists. In scorning "would-be orators, sighing for Ciceronic laurels, like Rachel weeping for her children, [who] lifted up their maiden voices and mourned over the wrongs of their injured country!" (82), the narrator alludes to a grisly New Testament narrative, Matthew 2:13–18, in which mothers "refus[e] to be comforted" because their infant sons have been slaughtered by Herod.[43] Though her handling of that biblical allusion seems to contradict the novel's sacralizing of motherhood, Rush reestablishes her position by setting up binary oppositions between the abolitionists' "maiden voices," impassioned by social injustice, and "genuine" biological mothers, focused solely upon domestic concerns. The mourning of abolitionist spinsters and black mothers falls into the same category as the sexual safety of black women: insignificant concerns. Because these white women plead for blacks, the subtext suggests, they become black themselves and unsexed, unworthy of their status as women. To Sojourner Truth's question "Ar'n't I a Woman?" Flanders's novel responds with a resounding *no*.[44] Yet despite the surface text's scorning all but proslavery white women, the subtext ironically links the pain of Hebrew mothers whose children are wrenched from their arms with the plight of slave mothers and, contrary to its author's intent, evokes the reader's compassion toward slaves.

In the absence of black females, Flanders targets the brunt of her misogyny at the leader of the ladies' Carean African Aid Society, Miss Dickey, "one of those sentimental demi-intellectual personages, who seem to have been born with a book in their hand" (88). Playing on antebellum denotations of this female abolitionist's surname, Rush economically characterizes her as a male jackass (Dickass or Dicky-ass), something peculiar or in unsound condition (dickey), and a man who uses fine words without much meaning, or a "know-it-all" (a "clever Dick"). Miss Dickey's intellectual and political activity has disqualified her from the humility, purity, and submission required of women: she has forfeited her claim to womanhood and to the respect of "polite" society. A confirmed old maid at thirty-five, Miss Dickey imagines herself surrounded by distraught lovers and replaces her involuntary celibacy with a fanatical affection for animals. Political activity and sexual dormancy have warped her desires toward bestiality, the text implies. Further, just as Stowe signifies black characters' "civilization" by presenting positive images of their housekeeping, as Lori Merish points out, so Flanders depicts Miss Dickey as barbaric, her home overtaken by dander, fur, feathers, and stench.

In Miss Dickey, self-appointed redeemer of the oppressed, messianic activity degenerates to nothing more than desperate, frustrated sexuality, supporting the patriarchal South's classification of women who hold strong political opinions or shirk the marital harness as sick and deviant. Fanning Minden's abolitionist fervor, Flanders's Miss Dickey leaps at the opportunity to protect a fugitive slave: " 'We, that is, the Society, wish to open our arms (figuratively, of course), and clasp him to our bosom!' " (102–3). Suggesting that an abolitionist woman's passion stems from sexual sublimation rather than desire for social reform, the narrator dismisses Miss Dickey's "principles of freedom and equality" as the inevitable products of frustrated depravity: the abolitionist woman becomes a white inversion of the stereotypical "Jezebel," white society's imaging of female slaves' overt, unbridled lusts, since here the sexual desire is covert. Playing off white antebellum Southern society's obsession with the racial "purity" essential for one race to maintain absolute hegemony, Flanders features Miss Dickey's flirtations. In announcing she wants to "embody" principles of freedom and equality (103) and in placing a wreath of black and white roses on the newly arrived fugitive's head, Miss Dickey suggests the abolitionist's openness to racial amalgamation, particularly if it provides her a lover.[45] Throughout Caesar's boarding with her, the social reformer's concern for him manifests itself as both maternal and romantic, until the fugitive's mistreatment of her beloved menagerie—that is, his own beastly behavior—causes his eviction. Repeatedly, *The Ebony Idol* demonstrates Ronald Takaki's assertion that white male–prescribed stereotypes of both the black "child/savage" and the angelic, unsullied "true woman" create the iron cage which racism and sexism conspire to keep locked.

In addition to amalgamation, the text links abolition with religious heresy and emasculation of black males, yet here too it ultimately upsets its own correlations.[46] Rather than Christ in a crown of thorns, Minden gathers around its "ebony idol" in a wreath of roses; rather than worshipping the shepherd who lays down his life for his sheep, Minden's citizens fete their fugitive slave with a pork dinner: the pig has laid down his life for Caesar. Working within a theology-of-whiteness paradigm, the text's readers are supposed to understand that a Christ figure cannot possibly be black, that this must therefore be a farce, that its players must be committing sacrilege—and that, not insignificantly, Harriet Beecher Stowe apostatized when she created a black Christ figure in Tom.

Although the novel plays with the stereotype of the spoiled planter's son by depicting the only Southern male character, Frank Stanton, as profligate and effeminate, always dressed in slippers, dainty waistcoats, and immaculate linens, it quickly attempts to redeem him by having him marry and become serious about his profession. Having been sent North by his Alabama planter father to study law, Frank is feminized not by any inherent character flaw, the text tries to insist, but by a gender-blurring North, full of strong-minded women and unstable gender roles. However, working against its own proslavery, pro-South agenda, the narrative depicts Frank's virility as beginning only when he dresses Caesar in his own foppish clothes: the white Southern male's masculinity arises only from his emasculating the black male. Whiteness, therefore, exists only as a social construct and wields power only insofar as a culture insures its perpetuation of gender, racial, and class polarizations. The text completes Frank's restoration to manhood when he falls in love with the novel's most feminized and sexualized character, the virginal Mary, who turns out to be a Southern planter's daughter stolen at birth by Caesar. Again contradicting its pro-South themes, the novel's subtext suggests that only the weak, blonde, ultrafeminine Southern woman can provide a background against which the Southern white male appears manly. Contrary to its intent, *The Ebony Idol* discloses an effete Southern patriarchy that defines and maintains itself only in opposition to what it can constrict and overpower.

As does Rush's *North and South*, Flanders's *Ebony Idol* attempts to advance its proslavery argument through mother-daughter relationships—and in doing so, contradicts its earlier advocacy for white women's rights. Though the Cary home, once an "Eden of domestic felicity," falls when the mother-Eve figure defies her husband's authority, the narrator applauds her rebellion—so long as it remains within the bounds of the white community's best interest and the welfare of her daughter. When the stereotypically licentious Caesar pulls the Carys' daughter Lucy onto his lap to kiss her, the wrathful Mrs. Cary demands that he leave, despite her husband's having staked his reputation on Caesar's metamorphosis into a model freedman. Rather than showcasing a woman's power, however, Mrs. Cary's assertiveness only protects the white virgin and the racial supremacy she represents. Eden is restored, but for whites only. Caesar's next hosts, the Hobbs, an aspiring abolitionist politician and his politically active wife, retain beautiful blonde Mary as both servant and foster daughter. Notably not a biological mother, Mrs. Hobbs verbally abuses Mary: "No epithet was too low, no accusation too absurd, no taunt too gross to escape her" (186). In the Hobbs household, the antislavery mother figure sacrifices her daughter on the altar of the father's professional ambitions by encouraging Caesar's assaults on Mary. The abolition that the narrative frames as the North's new religion has converted an acquiescent slave into a predator and a maternal protector into an aider and abettor of sexual assault. Demonstrating the result of women's political involvement, the scheming Mrs. Hobbs and the sexually frustrated Miss Dickey can be neither good mothers nor self-controlled, virtuous women. The proslavery, biologically "genuine" maternal figure Mrs. Cary, on the other hand, models the "good" mother because she defends whiteness and lets domesticity preclude all other concerns.

Perfectly illustrating Toni Morrison's analysis in *Playing in the Dark* (esp. 52–53) of white New World fears of nature and anxieties about freedom, Flanders paints Minden as a Puritanesque village vulnerable to the savagery lurking at the edges of its precariously maintained civilization. In this village, the religion of the Puritans is superseded by a fixation on freedom, with Miss Dickey as high priestess, while the inhabitants neglect "Christ," Widow Wellman. A symbol of the Enlightenment mind and its principles, Minden disintegrates into chaos when confronted by the disquieting presence of blackness, which becomes the space on which Flanders inscribes white anxieties.[47] These anxieties, though, coil back and complicate the text's intended depiction of an escaped slave's degeneration into savagery. When Minden's townsfolk finally decide that their abolitionist leaders have misled them, they tar and feather Mr. and Mrs. Hobbs, making them black victims of their own white barbarism, an act far more cruel than any suffering the text has imposed on a fugitive slave. In contrast to Flanders's intended narrative about white virtue, the savagery lurking at Minden's edges, this subtext shows, is the white townsfolks' own potential for brutality; rather than the apostasy of making an "idol" of a fugitive slave, Minden's heresy is the worship of whiteness.

Like *The Ebony Idol*, Mrs. V. G. Cowdin's *Ellen; or, The Fanatic's Daughter*, also initially seems to laud strong mothers, portraying its coprotagonist

Mary Danville as the Holy Mother and later as a Christ figure battling an inhumane, antislavery North—though such gender transgressions prove dangerous. Having made an improvident match with weak-willed Northerner Horace Layton, Mary must support her family while her husband devotes himself exclusively to abolitionist proselytizing, guided by the charlatan Parson Blake, who embezzles colonization society funds. Although Horace's firsthand impressions of the South had persuaded him that "slavery . . . [is] a system of judicious control over a race of human beings who, as yet, were incapable of self-government, or of thriving as a community upon the strength of their own intellect, unaided by superior natures and intelligence" (10), he persists in abolitionist zeal. The epitome of the passively submissive wife, Mary, the innocent, hyperpure mother of twins, fails to counteract her family's imminent destruction while Horace focuses exclusively on writing abolitionist articles. Even when their son fails to return home during a blizzard, only one parent braves the storm:

> [Mary] struggled onward, and stumbling against some object lying in the road, she threw forward her hand to prevent falling. A soft lock of hair met her touch. Ah, the mother well knew that silken tress, waving upon the snow, as if to mark the spot where a young heart had ceased to beat. With frantic haste she scraped the snow away and the moon shone brightly on the face of . . . Charlie. (52)

Though portrayed as the narrative's Christlike heroine in her perpetual lamb-to-the-slaughter sacrifices, Mary fails as a redeemer: the boy, frozen where he collapsed, is beyond saving. Even then, however, Horace has to see Blake sexually harass Mary before perceiving his villainy, and in the ensuing struggle, both men die. In Cowdin's answer to the male-authored, male-focused anti–Uncle Tom novels, her three central white males die early in the narrative and within a few pages of one another. The unflagging mother and daughter, meanwhile, struggle on, continually hounded by white men's political, economic, and sexual devices.

Unlike the domestic world, the narrative teaches, Northern industrialism is no respecter of gender or innocence, causing women and children to labor like machines and live in grinding poverty. Because her husband was weak, as most white Northern men portrayed by proslavery women are, Mary must move beyond a properly feminine role in trying to support herself and her daughter, replicating *The North and South*'s depiction of urban feminized men and masculinized women. The daughter, Ellen, however, as the surviving female half of fraternal twins, represents pure femininity, her sexual attractiveness and vulnerability heightened throughout the narrative.

As she struggles for survival in New York City, Mary moves from being depicted as the Holy Mother to a Christ figure, but this mother-savior proves both a naïve mother and a flawed savior, representing only unbounded self-sacrifice with no attention to justice, wisdom, or protection for the vulnerable. With misgivings, Mary allows her daughter to work for Madame Frivolli, who insists the young woman wear gaudy discarded finery and make herself attractive to male visitors. Apparently too pure for worldly wisdom, the fantastically naïve female Christ fails to recognize "Madame's" workplace as a brothel. In scenes both xenophobic and antifeminist, Cowdin sketches Mrs. Frivolli as a dark, "very masculine-looking woman" who represents Northern urban threats to femininity (98). Like Claudia, the brash, cast-off first wife of Mr. Moreland in Caroline Lee Hentz's anti–Uncle Tom novel *The Planter's Northern Bride*, an Italian woman is racialized; in her darkness, assertiveness, temper, sexual passions, and willingness to compete with men, she is close to black female stereotypes—indeed, she stands in for blackness. While the rich half-Italian male of *The North and South* could appear exotic and alluring, these narratives show that the ideal "Christian" woman, according to a theology of whiteness, is submissive, ultrafeminine, Protestant, fair (preferably blonde), behaviorally if not technically virginal, and selfless to the point of nonexistence. All these are incompatible with the full force of wild, Italian, papist blood. The surface text exposes the "black" Italian as a crass commodifier of white female sexuality; the subtext, however, points toward slavery's inverting the scenario, the white South's marketing of black female sexuality—but with this crucial distinction: unlike prostitution in nineteenth-century New York, slave auctions operated with the full sanction of the law and white Southern society's approval.

Urged by her dying mother, Ellen's desperate entreaties to Northern charitable societies provide Cowdin with her opportunity to denigrate women social reformers in rhetoric similar to that of Rush and Flanders, and to link women reformers' social justice concerns with sickness. Cowdin's spectacled "Woman's Aid Society" gathers "not to aid the suffering, but to gloat with fiendish exultation over the poor fallen ones, and to extort histories of depravity" (149). The John the Baptist to her mother's Christ, Ellen denounces them: "Go to the fountain of all light, for you now wander in utter darkness" (149).[48] Women reformers can be dismissed as spiritually diseased, and the reforms they champion, as sources of infection. Like Madame Frivolli and the "infection" her brothel represents, the text teaches, female sexual promiscuity produces the same effect as female social justice activity: desecrated womanhood.

Crucified by urban injustice, this novel's mother-savior is also framed by the text for having trespassed gender lines: her Christlike death at the hands of a self-righteous North reveals the gender, racial, and economic girders that uphold the narrative. Although chattel slavery itself never appears in the text, its polarizing, paranoid attempts to rigidify class, race, and gender definitions constantly confirm the signifiers that slavery invests with meaning, such as master and slave, white and black, industriousness and laziness.[49] According to the surface narrative, Mary dies in a filthy New York tenement whose free black owner, Hugh Jackson, and his listless, leering daughters demonstrate Africans' moral and social collapse apart from Southern slavery by selling the female Christ's body to Columbia medical students for dissection.[50] Echoing Mary Magdalene's distress over the apparent theft of Christ's body, Cowdin's Ellen weeps for her mother's stolen corpse and pleads, " 'Where have they taken my mother?' " (157).[51] The subtext suggests, however, that having enacted a male role, Mary is destroyed by her own assertiveness, while Ellen in her unadulterated femininity survives not in spite of but *because of* her gender-appropriate weakness. In an even more grotesque racial transmogrification than *The Ebony Idol's* Caesar, the text positions Hugh Jackson to illustrate how the North's urban "jungle" returns blacks to their natural savagery, since the manner in which he "captures" a human body and uses it to support his own physical needs suggests cannibalism. Evoking the plantation South's image of itself as a noble feudal society, the Southerner Cowdin juxtaposes the civilizing, "Christianizing" influence and clear boundaries of agrarian wealthy whiteness against the chaos and blurred racial, class, and gender lines of pagan urban industrialism.

The savior, Malcolm Sterling, who appears at this juncture, however, unravels the surface text's interwoven lessons on gender, race, and class. A Southern slaveholding male, Malcolm Sterling represents all that Mary Layton, an impoverished, politically powerless woman, could never achieve: his surname, Sterling, certifying his economic status, his character, and his whiteness, he is intrepid, bold, and efficient in countermanding Northern corruption. Earning Ellen's reverence, he rescues her mother's body and arranges a proper burial. In stark contrast to Stowe's mother-saviors who rescue others from slavery's degradations, Cowdin's mother-savior herself is degraded in death, only to be salvaged, lifeless, by a slaveholding male.

Despite the text's initial valorization of white women as opposed to white and black Northern men, Cowdin's proslavery tale must finally bow to Southern white men of privilege, who control what matters: money and its accompanying social and political power. The text finally reduces its own message to this: punishing one woman for holding strong political opinions and rewarding another for proper submission. Consequently, Malcolm Sterling ceases courting the daughter of abolitionist Mrs. Green, who is primarily interested in the planter's money, as her name suggests, and instead offers the pure-feminine Ellen the material security of marrying him. Though the narrative frankly suggests that he wins Ellen as much by the material security he represents as by any inherent qualities, it applauds her decision. Having learned from a mother who unwisely married a lowly schoolteacher for love and not money, the daughter more cautiously selects a husband who retains a godlike grip on his world by controlling a plantation's fiscal and human resources. Malcolm Sterling offers safety for a young woman whose self-giving mother-Christ could offer none. The subtext, however, suggests that the Southern male redeemer usurps the mother-savior's position by purchasing an economically vulnerable young woman's worshipful affection. Further, as a Columbia medical student himself, this Southern white male represents the financial incentive behind the Northern black male's sale of a dead body. Had Mary Layton not been the mother of the sexually desirable Ellen, she would have been dissected by Malcolm Sterling and others like any other corpse. As the power behind the commodified dismemberment and consumption of human beings (dissection), the white slaveholding male becomes the ultimate devourer of people—certainly a kind of cannibal—and by association, the white slaveholding Southern society becomes the real source of savagery.

In spite of the anxious attempts of *The North and South, The Ebony Idol,* and *Ellen* to show abolition as a threat to what they define as orthodox Christianity, these novels' theology of whiteness positions the wealthy white Southern male as God's earthly representative. In contrast to the women of *Uncle Tom's Cabin,* these novels' female characters undergo self-sacrificial suffering that leads to no one's redemption or rescue or repentance. For the anti–Uncle Tom woman writer, in the end only Southern slaveholding males can effectively liberate the oppressed white female, and happily-ever-after occurs only in the patriarchal, ordered bliss of the plantation South, a world away from the annihilating inhumanity of the urban North. Generally, Elizabeth Ammons and Jane Tompkins argue correctly that in place of man-made, male-led judicial courts, legislatures, and commercial markets, domestic fiction supplies alternative spaces of power: dinner tables, kitchens, rocking chairs.[52] In proslavery domestic tales, however, the reins of power remain in—or revert to—male hands, from Northern factories, tenements, and medical schools to Southern plantations. Whereas in *Uncle Tom's Cabin* a mother's love can strengthen civil resistance, and even deathbeds represent spiritual and social transformation, in these anti–Uncle Tom narratives mothers fail even to protect their domestic circle, and deathbeds symbolize only an end to daily victimization. Even in death, in fact, female victims of male violence and greed cannot rest in peace. Whiteness and wealth in the end cannibalize these narratives' own proslavery themes, leaving only the skeletal remains of racial, gender, and class definitions formed and held together by slavery.

In *Uncle Tom's Cabin,* mother-savior figures effect actual change, both physical and spiritual. Eliza liberates herself and her son; the Quaker women assist fugitives to freedom;[53] Mrs. Bird rebels against convention, federal law, and her senator husband's authority in order to protect fleeing slaves; Eva transforms individuals' spiritual health and sense of justice; and Augustine St. Clare's mother's influence, together with Tom's prayers, enables St. Clare to enter heaven exclaiming, "Mother!"[54] Contrary to Minrose Gwin's contention that Tom's "downward plunge in fortune to eventual death shows . . . that passivity gets him nowhere" (26), this maternal, self-sacrificing male slave actually achieves for others the greatest liberation of all: Gwin misses the point entirely. In purely pragmatic terms Tom has succeeded; his sacrifice results not only in Cassy and Emmeline's escape, but also in George Shelby's releasing his family's slaves.[55] Further, though, according to Stowe's Christian schema, Tom's emulation of Christ through "aggressive nonviolence" achieves, as Sundquist observes, the "extraordinary power [Stowe] intended the Christian ideal to offer" (*New Essays* 33). Stowe's narrative leaves Tom, the feminized black Christ, as the novel's ultimate redeemer: Tom wins.[56]

Downward mobility also occurs in *The North and South, The Ebony Idol,* and *Ellen,* but with no real female—or feminized—victors. Mother-daughter teams combat the commercial, political, and sexual worlds of men. Inevitably, however, female agency fails, as daughters die of consumption or languish in brothels while mothers auction off maternal claims, "rescue" the oppressed through their own victimizing manipulations, and surrender their own lives to no effect. Even female characters such as Mrs. Dunlap who achieve what they want do so through the power of a husband's slaveholding profits. In these novels, male-controlled markets and social systems win every time. Like other authors of domestic fiction, these proslavery women writers question wifely subservience, challenge male dominion, and appear to promote female independence, yet inevitably they capitulate to white antebellum Southern society's hierarchy.[57] While *The North and South*, *The Ebony Idol*, and *Ellen* attempt to present mother-saviors as persevering redeemers, comforters, protectors, and spiritual instructors, the books' a priori commitments to chattel slavery necessitate that their narrative arguments be built upon the foundation of wealthy white Southern males' economic self-interest. Behind the protection of slavery's three-sided fortress of class, race, and gender constructs, these texts reveal even their most noble women characters—and the writers themselves—to be only pawns in a vast patriarchal game in which the pursuit and maintenance of white society's wealth is made to appear humane and even—most crucial to their argument—holy. The theology of whiteness they profess finally defeats and devours them.

CHAPTER 3

Justified by Mother's Milk

Mammy and Mistress Figures in Proslavery
Fiction's Plantation South

ointing to white slaveholding males' sexual license with female slaves, abolitionist Wendell Phillips labeled the antebellum South "one giant brothel" (108). To counter such charges, proslavery advocates constructed the mammy figure to represent the mutual affection that bridged black and white worlds: plantation life as one big, happy, biracial family. Ironically, the black mammy became the slaveholders' central symbol of white paternalistic care. Whereas Stowe attacks slavery by showing its separation of black mothers from their black children, anti–Uncle Tom women writers defend it by showing how slavery insures that black mothers will never be separated from the white children whom, the novels insist, the mammies love more than their own.[1] Yet even in these novels, the mammy's role inevitably suggests what Joanne M. Braxton calls "outraged motherhood": the reality of motherhood being virtually unavoidable for a female slave who was outraged by "the intimacy of her oppression." A black woman's suckling of a light-skinned child symbolizes both nurture and victimization.[2] However, accentuating affection while ignoring and thus perpetuating oppression, anti–Uncle Tom women writers evade all hints of black females as objects of white males' sexual desire, and instead stress familial bonds between black surrogate mothers and the white owners whom they have nursed and now serve. Emphasizing the sisterhood of plantation women also becomes crucial for defenders of slavery, since white planter-class women could be portrayed as the ameliorating influence on slavery, softening its harsher aspects and maintaining harmony.[3] Consequently, these novelists feature the faithful, strong mammy and the compassionate, delicate mistress to sketch Southern mothering in black and white, depicting slavery as not only an economic necessity but also an ideal familial configuration. Defending slavery through their own supposed contentment with their alleged roles and in their care and concern across racial lines, mammy and mistress appear to thrive on the security of "belonging" to the white male planter. On closer examination, however, this mythology completely collapses in proslavery women's narratives, which dismantle their own and each other's arguments, exposing how the plantation South brutalizes enslaved black women and debilitates wealthy white women.

As Lillian Smith in *Killers of the Dream* has observed, motherhood in slave society presented an intricate knot of tangled maternity: two mothers of different races, different educational levels, different legal status, and different value systems—making the Oedipus complex appear a facile adjustment by comparison (110–35). Terming this pairing "biracial multiple mothering" in their psychoanalytic study of motherhood in the antebellum South, Bartlett and Cambor trace the resulting "bizarre and paradoxical" way of life that included the shame-free rape of one race of women and the simultaneous control and adulation of the other (21). Existing as obverse images of one another, the fictive mammy and mistress are both pious and asexual, yet the former is corpulent, masculininzed, outspoken, and subservient, while the latter is tightly corseted, ultrafeminized, submissive, and privileged.[4]

Mary Eastman's *Aunt Phillis' Cabin* offers just such female figures, created to connect black and white worlds yet ultimately highlighting the enormous social and economic chasm between them. The first and most widely read of the proslavery responses to Stowe, *Aunt Phillis' Cabin* sold eighteen thousand copies in a few weeks, but even in combination with all other anti–Uncle Tom novels never approached Stowe's staggering sales figures. Although like Stowe, Eastman capitalizes on mother-savior ideology and addresses slavery through the relationships of an eponymous, self-sacrificing slave, Aunt Phillis is not the protagonist. Rather, Eastman centers her story primarily around white female characters and details Phillis's saintliness only to illustrate the graciousness of slaveholding whites. In defending slavery to Northern college friends, planter's son Arthur Weston lauds the mammy who nursed both him and his father as children:

We have a servant woman named Phillis, her price is far above rubies. Her industry, her honesty, her attachment to our family, exceeds every thing. I wish Abolitionists would imitate one of her virtues—humility. I know of no poetry more beautiful than the hymns she sang to me in my infancy; her whole life has been a recommendation of the religion of the Bible. I wish my chance of Heaven were half as good as hers. She is a slave here, but she is destined to be a saint hereafter. (137).

In typical proslavery fashion, Arthur Weston avoids the word "slave" in direct relation to white ownership, revealing discomfort with its connotations. Phillis "*is* a slave," presumably the fault of external political forces and the accident of birth, but the Westons "*have* a servant woman," a power-evasive construction that relieves the white slaveholders of guilt, while also identifying Phillis as a possession and prestige symbol of the antebellum South's social elite (italics mine).[5]

Arthur praises Phillis specifically in areas that slaveholders stereotype as slaves' weaknesses: rather than laziness and lying, Phillis demonstrates "industry" and "honesty." Operating according to a theology of whiteness, which I have defined as the manipulation of religious language and ideology to augment wealthy whites' economic hegemony in order to denigrate non-whites and justify their subjugation, Phillis's spiritual virtues all center on her proper relation to her economic and racial superiors. She is admirable *because* she is fond of the planter family, *because* she has earned their trust, *because* she sang to the children. Rather than an argument for her humanity and therefore freedom, the slave mother's strengths here affirm slavery's "Christianizing" influence. In admitting " 'she is a slave here, *but*' " (italics mine), Arthur acknowledges Phillis's oppressed state and thus disqualifies himself from using the common proslavery argument that slaves are happiest in their current conditions and wish for nothing else. Yet he does resort to another common slaveholders' trope, reward in a heavenly "hereafter." To reconfirm the plantation's "Christian" atmosphere, Arthur Weston attests: " 'I know of no poetry more beautiful than the hymns she sang' "; but simultaneously this statement underscores the stereotype of blacks as mere mimics, incapable of creating their own sophisticated forms of poetry, music, and the other fine arts.[6] In appearing to praise the Westons' "servant," Arthur positions white slaveholders as generous admirers of their slaves while reinscribing blackness as inherently inferior, laudatory only through "improving" contact with whiteness.

Placing her " 'price far above rubies,' " Arthur Weston's soliloquy unintentionally evokes the fiscal realities of slavery: Phillis did indeed have a market "price," for which she could have been traded or auctioned at the whim of her master. Further, in alluding to Proverbs 31 here, the subtext evokes the disturbing contrast of Weston's mammy with a biblical maternal figure, a woman who buys and sells her own land with her own income, excels in mercantile activity, and clothes her family in fine linen—a far cry from the opportunities Phillis's life in bondage has offered.

Interestingly, contrary to proslavery fiction's depiction of Christianity as not only spiritually and morally uplifting but also socially pacifying and domesticating for slaves, historical documentation testifies to another reality. As one of a plethora of examples, Henry "Box" Brown, renowned on the abolitionist circuit as a fugitive slave who packaged and mailed himself across the Mason-Dixon Line to Philadelphia, believed that in attempting escape, he was acting "in accordance with the will of God" (Rose 272). Denmark Vesey, who organized a nearly successful slave uprising of enormous scale in Charleston, South Carolina, in 1822, had studied Christian scriptures assiduously, particularly those that related to God's setting captives free. Rather than producing a mollifying effect, "the religion of the masters," as reinterpreted by the slaves themselves, seems more often to have strengthened their resolve for liberation, human dignity, and equality.[7] As Eugene Genovese has observed in his monumental *Roll, Jordan, Roll,* "no matter how obedient—how Uncle Tomish—Christianity made a slave, it also drove deep into his soul an awareness of the moral limits of submission, for it placed a master above his own master and thereby dissolved the moral and ideological ground on which the very principle of absolute human lordship must rest" (165).[8] Eastman, however, clings to the proslavery script that features the Christian God as pacifier.

Stressing Phillis's familial intimacy with her white owners, Eastman portrays her as having always favored her white charges over her own children. Yet rather than demonstrating warm interracial regard, these depictions suggest slavery's violation of maternal affection.[9] As a boy, for example, the master's son Arthur commanded the coveted position of being held in Phillis's arms while "her own child, almost the same age, [lay] in the cradle near them" (253). With the master's niece, "never did mother hold to her heart child dearer to her, than Phillis, when she pressed Alice to her bosom" (248), while Phillis's own children were never allowed to touch the white children's toys painstakingly stored and later enshrined in the slave woman's two-room cabin. In games of make-believe with the master's progeny, Phillis consigned her own children to the roles of waiter and coachmen and instructed them to behave like white "quality." Neglecting her own children and ignoring her own needs, including meals and sleep, Phillis conducts another lesson in plantation priorities when she refuses to leave the white Alice Weston's sickbed. Through scenes such as these, the text applauds a slave mother's teaching white supremacy to black and white youngsters. "No master," Eastman concludes, "could be brutish enough to sell the [slave] who had nursed him and his children, who loved him like a son, even for urgent debt, had he another article of property in the wide world" (270). Yet as Bartlett and Cambor observe, black women represented for white male slave owners a shifting, liminal space; they could both embody memories of early childhood sustenance and serve as objects of adult sexual desire (21).[10] Antislavery Northerners were not the only ones to indict white male slaveholders on sexual grounds. Outside observers such as British commentator James Buckingham described them as "especially . . . indelicate in their thoughts and tastes; and [they] exhibit a disgusting mixture of prudery and licentiousness combined, which may be regarded as one of the effects of the system of slavery, and the early familiarity with vicious intercourse to which it invariably leads" (Clinton, *The Plantation Mistress* 208). As one white planter-class woman observed: " 'It occurs to me that if virtue be the test to distinguish man from beast the claim of many Southern white men might be questionable' " (qtd. in Scott 83). Further, despite Eastman's attestations of whites' affection for their slaves, her own words reconfirm every slave's legal status as an "article of property." Another anti–Uncle Tom novel, Maria McIntosh's *The Lofty and the Lowly*, portrays a kind-hearted planter, Colonel Montrose, being briefed on plantation matters after returning from a trip: " 'Sister Harriet's got a baby,' " the slave Cato reports, " 'and sister Judy—she lost a child, and ain't been well enough to work since,' " to which Colonel Montrose queries, " 'How much cotton have you got in, Cato?' " (1:197). The planter does not distinguish one property update from another: slave births, slave deaths, illnesses, the cotton crop. White material gain and black maternal grief, given equal weight by the text, merge as two parts of the overarching plantation business affairs. In the same novel, a prodigal Montrose son causes the family to pay his debts by selling their slaves, despite one of the white women's pleas to protect slave family and friendship ties—but business was business. And in *Aunt Phillis' Cabin,* even Eastman's insistence that "*most* of our Southern slaves are happy, and kindly cared for," reveals fissures in her confidence, particularly since she adds: "for *those who are not,* there is hope for the better" (277, italics mine). Although Stowe also depicts *most* slaves as kindly treated (on the Shelby plantation and even in the St. Clare household), the exceptions, such as Prue or Cassy or Legree's field hands, expose the "peculiar institution" for its inherently barbaric possibilities, showing the fallacy of any humanely operated human bondage. Interestingly, both *Uncle Tom's Cabin* and its fictive rebuttals, though aiming at opposite goals, make clear the same message, and often through similar means: there is no such thing as a "good" slaveholder.

In Mary Howard Schoolcraft's *The Black Gauntlet,* the cross-racial maternal bonds of the slave Phillis—about whom the narrator gushes, "No mother on earth could have been more loving than this sympathizing, adhesive slave" (346)—function as the novel's primary justification for slavery. The subtext, however, asserts a portrait of masochistic rather than mutual attachment. Like Eastman's Phillis, Schoolcraft's Phillis has "nursed this [white] child with her own infant, from her breast; and the acutest observer would have failed to ascertain which of the two babies this affectionate slave loved the best" (205). Intending to laud the mammy's role, Schoolcraft insists that

> the wide world does not contain a more affectionate, unselfish foster-mother, than the black family servant; indeed, the author has often seen more violent grief over the death of their white foster-child than she ever witnessed over the corpse of their own; and [white] children are regarded as more healthy and vigorous in their constitutions ever afterwards, who have been nursed by the good, kind Christian negro, on the patriarchal plantation. The affection thus germinated between the nurse and the child never becomes obliterated while life lasts; and in all the South, not a man could be found who would neglect or ill-use his foster-mother when she is advanced in years. (206)

Aligned with a theology of whiteness, the "good, kind Christian negro" would naturally feel more affection for the white children in her charge than for her own offspring, whiteness itself becoming part of what is to be worshipped, adored, and cherished. Further, in "germinated," Schoolcraft shows her hand and its pragmatic, fiscally driven motivations: the proslavery valorization of the black nurse–white child bond boils down simply to agricultural economics.

With the invention of the cotton gin and refinements to the cultivation of rice, the plantation South's "cotton is king, rice is gold" standard absolutely relied upon slave labor—or so planter-class Southerners believed. Lower-income, nonslaveholding white Southerners such as yeoman farmers and artisans were far less certain about slavery. Some white laborers resented the institution because it limited the leverage on employers they could apply: slaves could always fill labor gaps during a strike. In *The Impending Crisis of the South*, Hinton Rowan Helper, an abolitionist and virulently racist white North Carolinian, argued that slavery was economically unsound in its impact on whites.

To guard against possible divisions over slavery between upper- and lower-class whites, planter-class Southern leaders reinforced racial borders and suppressed economic disparities among whites by elevating the social concept of whiteness.[11] Although by 1860 fully three-fourths of the South's white population neither owned slaves nor had any economic interest in slavery, politically omnipotent planters managed to rally the voting population under a racial banner, creating at least the illusion of white unity.[12] Eager to convince not only skeptical Northerners but also uneasy Southerners that slavery was a "positive good," slaveholders advertised the beloved mammy.

Schoolcraft exemplifies this strategy. Like Eastman evading the term "slave," she touts the mammy's intimacy with whites. Almost but not quite part of the white "family," the black "foster-mother" is the "family servant." As a recommendation of her faithfulness to whites, Schoolcraft upholds her "violent grief" over the "death" of a white "child," while the black child becomes merely a "corpse," apparently evoking little emotional response. As the passage quoted earlier indicates, slavery's survival as an institution depended upon persuading whites of weak black-family ties. After the United States' 1807 prohibition of slave importation even as the Lower South's cotton and rice plantation labor needs grew, the domestic slave trade and slave "breeding" became planters' only sources of replenishing their labor forces.[13] As Catherine Clinton has asserted, antebellum slavery was not only "a system of production," but also "fostered a distinctive system of reproduction in the plantation South" (" 'Southern Dishonor' " 53). In addition to white male owners' rape of black women, which multiplied their own "property," slaveholders candidly discussed slave "breeding's" central role in profits, and some planters documented promoting promiscuity among slaves and voiding slave marriages—not legally recognized anyway—when one of the parties appeared to be sterile.[14] Some planters found it profitable to reward slave women for bearing healthy offspring. Senator James Hammond of South Carolina, for example, gave slave mothers a muslin or calico frock when their infants reached thirteen months, and another planter gave Saturdays off from work to slave women with six or more children alive at one time (Marable 409).

The mammy image was a crucial tool for recrafting slavery's public image. In the domestic slave trade, one million blacks were sold between 1820 and 1860, and in those last two decades, 575,000 of those were relocated from the Upper to the Lower South.[15] The vast majority of these would not have traveled as a family unit, since children over fourteen were considered prime field hands, and black women sold separately from their children brought higher profits. A few slave traders specialized in children eight to twelve years old. As historian John Hope Franklin observes: "Here and there one can find sufficient respect for basic human rights or ample sentimentality to prevent the separation of families, but it was not always good business to keep families together" (179). For whites to have credited enslaved blacks with human affections for each other would have undermined the entire system. Instead, planter-class whites argued for female slaves' "short-lived" maternal solicitude toward their own young yet the mammies' undying attachment to "their" white children.[16] Selling slave children away from their mothers, the argument reasoned, was less cruel than selling a faithful female slave away from her white owners.

Never naming but clearly responding to abolitionist charges of male planters' sexual misconduct, Schoolcraft insists that "not a [white] man could be found who would neglect or ill-use his [black] foster-mother when she is *advanced* in years" (206, italics mine), yet antislavery arguments never targeted slave owners' treatment of elderly slaves. In fact, a favorite *proslavery* tactic detailed Northern industrial centers' apathy toward sick and elderly workers, as opposed to the shelter, food, and clothing that slavery supposedly provided for the non–able bodied. By defending territory that had not been attacked, Schoolcraft inadvertently exposes one of slavery's most vulnerable points: male slaveholders' economic and sexual incentives to "ill-use" female slaves who were *not* "advanced in years." Schoolcraft's defending white

Southern males' treatment of older female slaves is beside the point—and the anxieties in her text reveal just that.

As *The Black Gauntlet* unintentionally shows, the South's "mammy," co-erced into nursing a child of her white oppressors, lengthens her own chains by providing strength and sustenance for one who will thrive and grow to perpetuate her exploitation. "As to the [black] infants being sold away from their mothers," Schoolcraft interjects into her meandering quasi-narrative, "it is not believed by the author that such a monstrosity ever has occurred in South Carolina as a mistress there universally takes more care of her little negro property, than a black mother ever does of her children" (45). Yet Schoolcraft destabilizes her own argument, implying both that slave women are negligent indifferent mothers and that separating them from their children would be a "monstrosity." The dichotomy she constructs between blacks as "property" versus blacks as "children" reflects the fundamental tension at the heart of the U.S. experiment in democracy: property versus humanity.[17] Further, the subtext suggests that under slavery, black mothers *could not* care for their children as they might have wished. Nutrition, shelter, clothing, prenatal care, work breaks for breast-feeding, and time spent with children were all determined by slave masters, and by definition were insufficient. As Richard H. Steckel has shown, contrary to Eugene Genovese's characterization of a slave's childhood as protected years, most slave children experienced malnutrition, particularly protein deficiencies, because planters could achieve higher investment returns by excluding meat from children's diets while feeding productive field-workers better. Unlike white planters' infants entrusted to black wet nurses, slave infants often suffered from attenuated breast-feeding because of their mothers' fieldwork schedules (Steckel 43–60). Slave owners who noted the high rate of infant mortality among slaves frequently blamed black women for poor mothering. Steckel, however, points to the correlation between increased rates of sudden infant death syndrome (SIDS) and fetal deprivation caused by erratic fluctuations in work, diet, and disease, all typical of slave field-workers' lives.

Repeatedly, Schoolcraft privileges white material possession of property over black maternal affection. Scorning "sickly sentimentality," she protests: "All this sensitiveness about children being torn from their parents in Africa by the slave trade, has no religion" (208, 210). Indeed, a theology of white-ness, based first and foremost on privileged whites' economic self-interest, committed the white "faithful" to practicing slave family dismemberment for the sake of profit maximization. Though Schoolcraft concedes slavery's systematic divisions of husbands and wives, she retorts that no white sympathy should be expended, since Africans are "all polygamists": "The sentimental abolitionist weeps over the separation of husbands and wives when they are sold; but if a woman or man has a half dozen husbands or wives, which one of the six is to be selected as the orthodox lover?" (43). Black mothers and children, she claims, are not divided in slavery, and the plight of black fathers fails to concern Schoolcraft because they are not white and are therefore presumably insensible to paternal affection.[18] Then, as if suddenly cornered by facts, Schoolcraft backs away from her own earlier claims, and her argument completes its self-destruction. Implicitly acknowledging slave children separated from mothers, Schoolcraft counters: "Can we [white mothers] keep our children about us always? Do none but black children go to the ends of the Union and become settled there?" (46). Then she attacks New England's divorce rate as evidence of the North's lack of respect for family values.

Schoolcraft admits that though she grew up in South Carolina, she lives as an adult with her scholar husband, does not own slaves, and "never again expect[s] to be a slaveholder" (v). Yet she maintains:

> If I were an absolute Queen of these United States, my first missionary enterprise would be to send to Africa, to bring its heathen as slaves to this Christian land, and keep them in bondage until compulsory labor had tamed their beastliness, and civilization and Christianity had prepared them to return as missionaries of progress to their benighted black brethren. (vii)

With the words "enterprise," "labor," and "progress," she reveals the white South's commercial motivation for race-based slavery: not so much religious converts as cheap workers for a labor-intensive agricultural society. Schoolcraft cloaks her white greed in "Christianity['s]" "tam[ing] . . . beastliness" with violent coercion and "civiliz[ing]" the "benighted" Africans through barbarous force.[19] Locating whiteness as the culturally normative and theologically orthodox space, Schoolcraft tags blackness as inherently deviant, always the monstrous Other to be feared, restrained, and punished.[20]

More than any other woman anti–Uncle Tom writer, Schoolcraft positions God as the primary enthusiast for chattel slavery and the white South as merely "obey[ing] God in all things" (47): "What right have we of the nineteenth century to profess to be more sensitive about God's creatures than their infinitely loving Creator is? God ordered His chosen people to take their slaves from the heathen nations around them, and He knew all the consequences of this command" (46). Having blamed divine authority for blacks' enslavement, Schoolcraft extends the guilt to blacks themselves for being "stubbornly obtuse to all *enterprising*," a word she has already connected with the economic motivation of ruling whites, whose material security depends on portraying blacks as innately lazy and unentrepreneurial (italics mine). "All history proves that idleness and vice is the only liberty the African aspires to" (49–50), she insists, illustrating Henry Louis Gates Jr.'s caution about race as a dangerous trope, driven by profit and "lending the sanction of God, biology, or the natural order to even presumably unbiased descriptions of cultural tendencies and differences" (*"Race," Writing, and Difference* 5).[21] Ladening her fiction with footnotes, Schoolcraft marshals the Bible, philosophy, anthropology, Greek mythology, history, and personal anecdotes to defend her racial invectives, strung together on a thin—and ever more thinning—narrative thread.

As two other woman-authored proslavery novels, *Recollections of a Southern Matron and a New England Bride* and *Liberia; or, Mr Peyton's Experiment* demonstrate, some slaveholders defended themselves by portraying slave women as untrustworthy, even dangerous, mothers prone to abuse and infanticide.[22] Yet neither novel seems to know what conclusions to draw from its own depictions. The plantation-mistress narrator of Caroline Gilman's *Recollections* positions herself in maternal relationship with "her people" and contrasts children of the urban North with what she insists is, at least relatively, an idyllic existence for the young chattel:

What a blessed thing to childhood is the fresh air and light of heaven. No manufactures, with their overtasked inmates to whom all but Sabbath sunshine is a stranger, arose on our plantation. What a blessed thing to *all* is it to enjoy that light, and bathe in that air, whatever may be their deprivations! Long before the manufacture's task in other regions is closed, our laborers were lolling on sunny banks, or trimming their gardens, or fondling their little ones, or busy in their houses, scarcely more liable to intrusion than the royal retirement of a Guelph or a Capet. (122–23)

Her theopolitical insertion of religiously charged language—"blessed," "heathen," and "Sabbath"—aligns divine favor with slavery, while Northern industrialism is coupled with imprisonment ("inmates") and "deprivations," with its overtones of both physical want and spiritual lack (i.e., depravity). Gilman intends to depict human bondage as a kind of heaven and urban freedom as hell. Yet fewer than fifty pages later, intertextual conflict defies Gilman's cheery depictions of life on a Southern plantation. The slave mother Bella, who is deaf and mute, serves the Elms plantation, where white boys regularly pretend to threaten the safety of Bella's one treasure, her infant.[23] Portrayed as brutelike, Bella responds with "a howl, wild, long, and fearful, burst[ing] from the dumb creature as she clasped the baby more closely to her bosom" (169). Bella lives only for her child's protection, feeling "no want with her babe in her arms; and language—oh! the language between these two creatures—the twining of arms, the gaze of eyes, the pressure of lips; and, when an attempt was made to take her child from her, how that strange howl thrilled the soul!" (237). Unintentionally, Gilman's portrait of a slave mother and child mimics *antislavery* depictions of profound mutual affection among black people. To undermine any such conclusion, Gilman describes Bella's own mother attacking her and her baby with a stick of wood. The infant dies of injuries incurred while in the arms of its most ardent protector. No longer caring to live, Bella herself soon dies.

The subtext, however, emits its own howl of protest. The white boys' tormenting Bella and her child suggests not merely a mischievous prank but genuine cruelty. Indeed in the historical record, white slaveholding men recall their coming of age as a process that instilled the emotional callousness toward blacks required for their adult roles as plantation masters.[24] And the derangement of Bella's mother, rather than casting a slave woman as a "bad" mother, points toward the structural abuse of slavery itself. As Nell Irvin Painter demonstrates, documented child abuse within slave families is traceable to the abuse of slave parents by whites under a socioeconomic system she terms "soul murder." Furthermore, although no physical abuse occurs toward white females, by the end of Gilman's novel the planter's bride–protagonist appears bored, isolated, and unfulfilled—hardly the depiction of ideal Southern domesticity that Gilman intended.[25]

Also working contrary to its author's purpose, Sarah Josepha Hale's *Liberia* illustrates Painter's point. The central black mother figure, Keziah, was "ill-treated from earliest infancy first by an unfeeling mother whose punishments were all so many ingenious tortures, and who had twice been prevented by her master from killing her own child, having hung her up once with her head down, and at another time being caught dashing her up and down against a pile of bricks" (27). Later, the narrator describes Keziah's next master as sadistic and capricious, and attributes her distrust of white men to his merciless beatings. The brutality of the second white master, not punishable under antebellum Southern slave law, suggests a system that breeds victimization. The text's concession of the white master's violence indicts the entire system under which he abuses without penalty and casts Keziah's raging mother as more victim than victimizer. Her attempt to take her own female child's life becomes an act of maternal protection against a life worse than death, the subtext suggests, and the white master's saving the infant Keziah's life becomes private-property protection rather than human compassion.[26]

If the mammy functions significantly in the arguments of Eastman's, Schoolcraft's, Gilman's, and Hale's novels, the same white-privileging figure makes an extraordinarily early entrance—in the preface—in Caroline Lee Hentz's *Planter's Northern Bride*.[27] Though a Northerner herself, Hentz testifies that she is thoroughly familiar with the condition of slaves, and that, when asking one if she never longed to be free, the woman replied:

> No, mistress, that I didn't. I was too well off for that. I wouldn't have left my master and mistress for all the freedom in the world. I'd left my own father and mother first. I loved 'em better than I done them. I loved their children too. Every one of 'em has been babies in my arms—and I loved 'em a heap better than I done my own. (8)

More than two hundred pages later, Hentz is still tracing the same image:

> The faithful servant, who has devoted the vigor of her youth and the energies of her womanhood to her master's interest, and to his children's service, and dandling his children's children on her aged knees, looks upon them with worshipping tenderness, and dreams that the babes of Paradise are cradled in her dusky arms. (233–34)

Hentz vividly employs a theology of whiteness. The "*faith*ful servant" (not slave) has "devoted" herself to the "service" of the white male planter–god, at whose scions she gazes with "worshipping" tenderness (italics mine). Linking the planter's children with "the babes of Paradise," Hentz renders heaven white and implicitly excludes the "dusky" Other from it. Perhaps the reason for this exclusion appears in this paragraph, covertly. In highlighting the female slave's serving the "master's interest" with "the vigor of her youth" and "the energies of her womanhood," the subtext suggests more than his child-care needs. The veiled sexual reference here, consciously or unconsciously, signals Hentz's underlying assumption that enslaved black women could not go to heaven because the sexual license of white masters renders them impure. Neatly, the white patriarchal system produces and then condemns sexual experience that it can then turn around and use to justify excluding black women from salvation: it is a logic that Hentz embraces wholeheartedly.

From its inception, the United States formed its laws on slavery to serve the "interests" of white male planters. The pre-Revolutionary Southern colonies offered considerable permeability in racial, class, and gender lines, partly due to early Southern evangelicalism's emphasis on the equality of believers.[28] As the economic stakes grew, however, racial lines solidified. In the seventeenth century, most of Great Britain's American colonies rejected British laws on slavery that declared a slave's status followed that of his or her father.[29] African slaveholders typically followed Islamic law, which stated that any slave fathered by the slave's owner would become free at the owner/father's death. Because these laws did not maximize profit, and presumably because the Islamic law might encourage patricide, colonists patterned their slave laws after those of ancient Rome: *partus sequitur ventrem*, following in the status of the mother. Female slaves' reproductivity, therefore, became directly related to capital increases. In images similar to Hentz's quoted earlier, male slaveholders defended their compassion for slaves by depicting their having been "suckled at black breasts." Yet as Catherine Clinton observes, the image often suggested sexual rather than sentimental messages and reduced the black woman to animal-like exploitation: "Mammies were to be milked, warm bodies to serve white needs" (*The Plantation Mistress* 202). Whether victims of mammary rape, such as Sethe in Toni Morrison's *Beloved*, or black wet nurses forced to bare their breasts for hungry white infants, the mammy image suggests sexual exploitation even more powerfully than its intended message, cross-racial affection.

Though not technically an anti–Uncle Tom novel because the author never directly refers to Stowe or her book, Elizabeth Wormeley Latimer's

Our Cousin Veronica; or, Scenes and Adventures over the Blue Ridge displays many of that genre's characteristics, lauding its mammy's unwavering loyalty in prioritizing a white child over her own children—which the text itself problematizes. Despite its initial abolitionist British setting and often conflicted presentation of slavery, which has led some scholars to misclassify it politically, its subtlely proslavery message determines the plot and characterizations, challenges abolitionists' motives, and ultimately promotes slavery as at least preferable to Northern poverty.[30] Beginning on a winter's night in England, the six-year-old Veronica's American father has just died, leaving her new in the country with only one immediate "family" member, the slave mammy, whose presence horrifies Veronica's British abolitionist cousins. As Veronica cuddles in her mammy's arms, her cousin, who refuses slave-grown sugar in her tea, confesses in Ophelia-like fashion: " 'I was ready to wish all the African race all good, I was ready to desire immediate emancipation, but I was not prepared to shake hands with a negro' " (2:165).[31] Veronica's father was returning to England because he "disliked owning negroes" (1:42), yet his ideological stand has wrenched a slave mother from her children. Remaining with her young mistress despite their nonslaveholding location, Mammy epitomizes both stereotypical faithfulness and laziness: " 'Laws!' " she exclaims, " 'you can't get nothin' out o' niggers, 'scepts you's all de time lookin' after them' " (1:50). Yet in Mammy's confession that she has been married to more than one man still living, since her first husband was sold away from her, and in the English nurse's self-righteous response, " 'I thought you called yourself a Christian,' " the text not only skewers misguided moralism but also acknowledges the horrors of slavery itself (1:51). And although this mammy, like Eastman's and Schoolcraft's, has "loved her master's child—her little white nursling—better than her own flesh and blood," Latimer's Mammy dies regretful: " 'I done left all my chil'en. My chil'en over thar, honeys. . . . I done love dis [white] chile of mine too well—too well, honey' " (1:69). While woman-authored anti–Uncle Tom novels display such cross-racial maternal ties as positive proof of slavery's beneficence, *Our Cousin Veronica* disrupts Mammy's deathbed testimonial of devotion to whiteness with frank anxieties, suggesting something deeply unnatural and disturbing in slavery's coerced reconfigurations of family. The text suggests what Toni Morrison terms the "choked representation of an Africanist presence," rendered in "estranging" dialect (*Playing in the Dark* 17). While Latimer grants Mammy speech, her ungrammatical utterance reinforces class and racial boundaries, and privileges the "correct" speech and social power of the whites standing, symbolically, over her.

Mammy-deathbed scenes being a common trope among anti–Uncle Tom novels by women, the Phillis of *Aunt Phillis' Cabin* uses her final moments for an evangelistic sermon that extols the glories of slavery. Surrounded by her twelve biological offspring and "the family," her term for her white owners and never her own children, the dying Phillis represents slaveholding whites' victory over blacks' self-definition. Admitting in a private exchange with her master that in her younger years, " 'There was a time, sir, when I was restless about being a slave,' " Phillis testifies she has generally " 'never had a want, I nor the children' " (257): serving the planter family has apparently fulfilled her every wish. As she admonishes her fellow slaves in theopolitical rhetoric to focus on an egalitarian afterlife, not on earthly injustices, Phillis reminds her owner, Mr. Weston: " 'Master, we will all meet there. We will praise him together' " (262). Conveniently for whites, this focus on the afterlife makes slaves' rebellion or even discontent unnecessary in their earthly existence.

Yet rifts here in Eastman's narrative disclose the white South's difficulty in reconciling the severe social and material inequalities of slavery with their biblical literalism, which insisted on a monogenic understanding of human origins, as opposed to the polygenists' argument for the white race as a separate species. As compensation for earthly inequalities, proslavery Southerners often invoked the afterlife, but this too proved problematic, as Phillis's "We will praise him *together*" suggests (italics mine). Read against the grain, Phillis's words become a defiant challenge to white hegemony and to white fears of amalgamation.

When Phillis's children offer their dying mother medicine to ease her pain, she moves close to a figure of the crucified Christ, offered drugged wine just before his death. But there the text stops, disallowing any direct connection between savior and slave mother. Refusing the drug, Phillis points away from herself: " 'I don't want medicine. Jesus is what I want. He is all in all' " (262). With the last of her breath, she preaches: " 'Keep close, children to Jesus. Seems as if we wasn't safe when we can't see him. . . . Blessed Jesus! take me—take me home' " (263). Though intended as a confirmation of slavery's "Christianizing" influence on blacks, Phillis's homily, "Jesus! take me *home*" (italics mine), points toward the disparities among her earthly home, a two-room cabin (one-half of it reserved exclusively for white children's playthings), the planter family's mansion home, and biblical images of heavenly mansions reserved for the faithful. Because of the wealth created by slavery, upheld by a theology of whiteness, slaveholding Southerners as sketched by Eastman have already achieved at least a material paradise.

Further, the subtext underscores "seems as if we wasn't safe" as a commentary on slaves' perpetual danger from the anger, whims, lusts, and greed of white owners. Eastman's Phillis, paragon of the contented female slave, coexists in the narrative with another elderly slave mother, Lucy, introduced and dismissed in a single scene in which a central white character, Cousin Janet, learns that all seven of Lucy's children have been sold away from her by a former master. Eastman creates the interchange not as a concession to abolitionists' accusations of slave-family separations, but as a demonstration of compassion by a white female Christ figure who repeatedly appears in crises with the words "God is here." The scene also affords a planter-class woman the opportunity to swear that she has never before heard of any child being sold away from its mother and that she "look[s] upon the crime with as great a horror as you do" (44). In Janet's feigned ignorance of slave-family separations and her labeling that reality a "horror," the text unintentionally condemns the economic foundation of the institution Eastman attempts to defend. Elderly Aunt Lucy's tale of betrayal and heartbreak at the hands of a white master undercuts fellow bondswoman Aunt Phillis's deathbed testimony of cheerful contentment. Further, Cousin Janet's expressed dismay, followed by compassion, followed by her never addressing the issue again, replicates white planter-class women's refusal to see their own complicity in a system that they often abhorred yet helped perpetuate by enjoying its material benefits and by failing to oppose it publicly (see Chapter 4). As Catherine Clinton notes, planter-class women "endured rather than endorsed a society based on chattel labor" and, believing themselves trapped, mentally set aside the question of slavery's morality: the political, familial, and economic consequences were too great (*The Plantation Mistress* 197–98). In accepting the role of white Southern goddess, planter-class women took to themselves positions of privilege that carried clear social expectations, including their silence on slavery.[32]

In the conclusion of the same novel that contains Lucy's tale of seven children sold away, Eastman sabotages her entire project. First, she complains:

Abolitionists do not help their cause by misrepresentation. It will do well enough, in a book of romance, to describe infants torn from the arms of their shrieking mothers, and sold for five and ten dollars. It tells well, for the mass of readers are fond of horrors; but it is not true. It is on a par with the fact stated, that masters advertise their slaves, and offer rewards for them, dead or alive. How did the snows of New England ever give birth to such brilliant imaginations!

Family relations are generally respected; and when they are not, it is one of the evils attendant on an institution which God has permitted in all ages, for his inscrutable purposes, and which he may in his good time do away with. (271)

With the term "romances" and its connotations of fanciful feminine narratives as opposed to hard facts, Eastman employs misogyny in attempting to discount *Uncle Tom's Cabin,* and to cast "shrieking" mothers as mere products of female hysteria. Using the same word, "horrors," that Cousin Janet chose with Aunt Lucy, Eastman replicates her earlier pattern, first denying slave-family separations, then backing off to a tentative "generally," followed by an anxious "and when they are not." Having admitted some family separations, Eastman invokes the white planters' divine scapegoat. According to a theology of whiteness, privileged whites' material security *is* God's "inscrutable purpose," and Northern abolitionists are the infidels who question God's "good time." The slave mother's very blackness muffles her shrieks; the God of whiteness cannot hear her cries.

With the sentence "It tells well, for the mass of readers are fond of horrors," Eastman alludes to the gothic aspects of *Uncle Tom's Cabin* and its antislavery ilk, and she attempts to dismiss such tales as mere escapist fiction, as if doing so could also dismiss the historical reality of the auction block.[33] Such atrocities as slave-family separations, she suggests, are mere figments of fanciful imaginations that can be safely contained within the pages of a best-seller and brought out again only for readers' entertainment. But Eastman's presenting as fantasies political realities that readers would have recognized as simple facts of life in the slaveholding South—the very existence of the infamous Fugitive Slave Law of 1850 testified to masters' advertising for and doggedly tracking down escaped slaves—only intensifies the feel of determined self-delusion in *Aunt Phillis' Cabin.*

As a narrative that polices the mammy figure lest she reject her role, *Aunt*

Phillis' Cabin offers a "fallen" version of Phillis, the escaped slave Susan, who desperately regrets being lured away by abolitionists from the infirm white infant in her care. Longing for the security of slavery and the sacredness of her former maternal duties, Susan looks to her employer, the transplanted Southerner Mrs. Moore, as a potential redeemer. This compassionate woman, the narrative suggests, might make amends to Susan's former owners and resecure her position: the proslavery white female Christ will "save" by reenslaving. As Hazel Carby notes: "The black woman has learned from the behavior of her master and mistress that if accommodation results in a patronizing loosening of her bonds, liberation will be more painful" (" 'On the Threshold' " 302). To Susan's having been brutalized by Northern urban poverty, Mrs. Moore responds: " 'She deserves it for deserting her kind mistress at a time when she most needed her services. God did not raise her up friends because she had done wrong' " (66). When Susan's former owners reveal that the white infant had died soon after her escape, the narrative rests all blame on the negligent black nurse-mother, for whom the urge to cross racial and class lines, attempting to live in liberty like whites, brought death and destruction. The subtext, however, raises questions about the white mother's apparent ineptitude. Rather than thriving on the Southern "ideal," dual maternity, the white infant apparently lived only for its black surrogate mother. The welfare of white children depends not on white but black women; white womanhood and white motherhood appear helpless and irrelevant. Further vexing the surface message, the white male God whom Mrs. Moore attests has refused to "raise up friends" for Susan and has allowed her deprivations, by the same theological reasoning must also have designed—quite intentionally—the white infant's death. Eastman's logic, bound closely to a theology of whiteness that protects wealthy whites from judgment or from any suffering brought on by divine disfavor, trips over itself at this point.

As an authorial comment on Susan's dilemma, Eastman adds:

> I do not mean to say liberty is not, next to life, the greatest of God's earthly gifts, and that men and women ought not to be happier free than slaves. God forbid that I should so have read my Bible. But such cases as Susan's do occur, and far oftener than the raw-head and bloody-bones' stories with which Mrs. Harriet Beecher Stowe has seen fit to embellish that interesting romance, *Uncle Tom's Cabin*. (63)

Including blacks in a generalized human preference for freedom over slavery and citing biblical support for this view sets Eastman apart from most proslavery writers, who insist blacks prefer slavery, dread the insecurity of freedom, and accept the divine mandate that has ordered it so. Throughout the text, Eastman concedes that slavery involves "evil," yet she maintains that the plantation South should not be blamed for continuing a labor system necessary to its economic survival. In other words, the subtext argues that "evil" which materially benefits whites and only harms Others must be tolerated, even protected. At one point, Eastman blames blacks for their own enslavement, citing the alleged Hamitic curse of Genesis.[34] As if sensing herself on shaky ground, Eastman suddenly shifts tactics and attacks the North, which, she insists, would still practice slavery had its economic interests required it, and so can claim no moral superiority (12–24).

Further contradicting the surface text's message and the white would-be mother-savior's assessment of Susan's not "*deserv[ing]* help," another of Eastman's fictive female slaves, Peggy, accused by her master of being ungrateful, retorts: " 'If I has been well treated, it's no more den I *desarves*. I'se done nuff for you and yours, in my day; slaved myself for you and your father before you'" (48, italics mine). Peggy's rebuttal identifies not only slavery's basic injustice but, with " 'slaved myself for you and your father,' " evokes the ever-present sexual threat to female slaves. The ambivalence apparent in Eastman's rhetoric typifies Peter Parish's characterization of white antebellum Southern society, never monolithic in its views despite the power structure's presenting the illusion of a unified political front.[35]

The deaths of two mammy figures in Caroline Gilman's *Recollections* offer opposing messages. Nanny, who refers to the plantation's white youngsters as "my children," prays on her deathbed that she would have " 'walk[ed] in dis worl' so to see missis in heaven' " (26). The religious education that proslavery advocates herald as a key benefit of slavery consists of no more than indoctrination into a theology of whiteness and its consequent sacralization of the slaveholders' skin color and socioeconomic status. In contrast to Nanny's peaceful expiring, the faithful slave nurse Binah's death occurs not in her bed surrounded by a graciously indulgent planter's family, but swallowed in the flames of the planter's burning mansion. While the white biological mother of the toddler Patsey stands watching, safely on firm ground, the black nurse Binah, with Patsey in her arms, is trapped on the mansion's upper story. When a handsome stranger—a planter-class male—arrives to save the victims, he succeeds in rescuing only the white child, and the text renders blackness expendable. The nurse's speechless terror just before the text incinerates her contrasts poignantly with Patsey's piercing cries each night thereafter for "mauma," not the white biological mother but the black nurse who always tucked her in bed. Like the mammy figures of the other woman-authored anti–Uncle Tom novels, Binah dies testifying—in her case, by her actions—to the absolute priority of whiteness. The subtext here, however, like the fugitive-slave Susan's story in *Aunt Phillis' Cabin*, depicts white *motherhood* as irrelevant to a white child's emotional well-being and black *womanhood* as dispensable. Though valuable in her role as protector and nurturer of white children, the black nurse has no inherent value of her own to a white woman author. Binah's burning to death demonstrates at what cost slave women "mothered" their oppressors' young. Slaves' collaboration with their white oppressors, the subtext teaches, assists their own destruction. In destroying a female slave, symbolically the site of both white male sexual desire and white children's affection, Gilman reveals white women's anxieties regarding black women's power.

The mammy's deathbed scene in Hentz's *Planter's Northern Bride* showcases the slave Dilsey as she disseminates a theology of whiteness and consequently deifies the white male planter. The elderly Dilsey's children and grandchildren gather around her, "but . . . it was on the face of her master she gazed with such an expression of affection, gratitude, and humility combined that his answering glance was dimmed with tears" (350). She catechizes the slave community to " 'rejoice that ye eber learn of de Lord Jesus and de bless hereafter. If we'd all staid in de heathen land, where all de black folks come from, we'd neber known nothing 'bout heaben. . . . Tink of dat, if Satin eber tempt you to leave good massa and missus' " (351). Informing her master that in heaven, she'll " 'be beautiful, white angel den,' " Dilsey affirms a theological paradigm in which blackness is sin; whiteness is righteousness; the plantation is paradise; the "jungles" of Africa and of the urban North are the fearsome earthly hells from which whiteness "saves" blacks by enslaving them; slaves' manumission and escape are both damnation; and the hope of heaven is a punitive tool by which whites enforce compliance.

Leading Dilsey's funeral procession is the master whom, Hentz's narrator attests, Dilsey "loved in life, and blessed in death" (*Planter's Northern Bride*

353), and who uses her death for his own benefit. The slaveholder Moreland, whose name signals his acquisitiveness, turns Dilsey's funeral into a service of religious rededication to himself, the omnipotent, omniscient, wealthy white male planter. He reminds the mourning slaves:

> "She told you to be grateful that you were brought away from a land of darkness . . . to regions where the light of the gospel shines upon your souls. . . . Did you believe her words? . . . Would you think freedom a blessing, if I should scatter you all at this moment to the four winds and heaven, give up all care and guardianship of you and your children, suffer you to go where you please, leaving you to provide for the necessities of the morrow and all future wants?" (354–55)

He then presses them to " 'renew your promises of fidelity and obedience,' " while he vows to " 'watch over your best interests for time and eternity' " (356). Having thus hailed himself as immortal, Moreland stands before his devotees as the setting sun "gilded the pale and earnest countenance . . . with a kind of supernatural radiance" (356). The death of the devoted mammy figure provides Moreland the chance to have "his people" worship him. Though Dilsey dies testifying her allegiance to the planter-god, the text prohibits any association of her with Christ, or even a prophet. She has no authority of her own, no countercultural message, no existence outside that which whiteness grants her. Rather, Dilsey functions only in relation to the planter-god; she is merely a mouthpiece for broadcasting proslavery propaganda.

Soon thereafter, however, a slave insurrection brews, and Moreland is "surrounded by the spirits of darkness," including some maternal figures by whom "he had been dandled and caressed when a little boy" (*Planter's Northern Bride* 499, 502). Meant to underscore the slaves' depravity and ingratitude, the text disables its own message. A turbulent subtext shows mammy figures who have helped raise the planter to manhood now standing among those ready to rebel violently. Cross-racial nurturing has apparently failed to convert the slave women themselves to the glories of slavery. Reinscribing the white Southern woman as the "softening" influence on slavery, Moreland announces that he promised " 'in the ear of a dying mother' " his kindness to slaves (500), who otherwise would be subject now to his wrath. Armored with racial and class invulnerability, the planter rails at his slaves:

"I would rather, ten thousand times, cultivate these broad fields myself, than be served by faithless hands and false, hollow hearts . . . if labour was the portion God had assigned me in the world. . . . Which of you wants to leave your master and follow him [the abolitionist Reverend Brainard]. Tell me, for I will have no Judas in the field ready to betray his too kind and trusting master." (502, 505)

In this theology of whiteness, Moreland becomes an avenging Christ, establishing his plantation-kingdom not by suffering with the faithful but by crushing the infidels, not by dying for the oppressed but by becoming the oppressor by threatening death to dissenters: " 'There is but one master here. Submit to his authority, or tremble for the consequences!' " (506). The subtext, however, mocks Moreland's tirade. More than just Moreland's class snobbery against "labor" keeps him from cultivating his own fields: economically, he is helpless without his army of bound laborers.

In "tremble for the consequences," Moreland shatters proslavery's careful construction of the mammy and mistress figures as symbols of a peaceful, familial plantation South. Slaves are slaves *not* because, as Hentz had framed the mammy figure in her preface, they prefer white owners to their own families and life choices, but because, as her narrative now shows, they are violently coerced to "submit." As South Carolina's Senator James Hammond, owner of more than three hundred slaves, admitted: "We have to rely more and more on the power of fear. We are determined to continue masters, and to do so we have to draw the reign [*sic*] tighter and tighter day by day to be assured that we hold them in complete check" (Takaki, *A Different Mirror* 111). By 1860, four million slaves lived below the Mason-Dixon Line, 35 percent of the population (ibid.). In the Nat Turner rebellion of 1831, the Denmark Vesey plot of 1822, and a host of other uprisings, white Southerners had vivid examples of what organized slaves could achieve. Some slaveholders convinced themselves they controlled their slaves through kindness, but all relied ultimately on systematic governance by fear, as the rifts in Hentz's narrative reveal.

Moreland's having proved himself a tyrant with his slaves reinterprets the text's portrayal of his first wife, the beautiful, rebellious Italian, Claudia. The cast-off Claudia, whom the narrative has meticulously positioned on one side of the virgin-whore dichotomy, tells her story to Moreland's second wife, the insipid, cowering Eulalia, positioned on the other:

"I thought I married a lover! he turned into my master, my tyrant!—he wanted me to cringe to his will, like the slave in the kitchen, and I spurned his authority!—I defied his power! He expected me to obey him,—me, who never obeyed my own mother! He refused me the liberty of choosing my own friends. . . . He even had the audacity to command me to shut the door upon my mother's face!" (*Planter's Northern Bride* 366)

Since *The Planter's Northern Bride,* like all women-authored anti–Uncle Tom novels, evades any allusion to white males' sexual liaisons with black females, the Italian Claudia must stand in for blackness. Born into a Gypsy family, Claudia becomes a plantation mistress who has transgressed class and racial lines, and in defying male authority, she also violates gender lines. She has been punished, no longer having the right even to see her own child. Departing the Moreland plantation, Claudia looks back from her carriage "with a wild, lingering glance, such as was once turned upon the forfeited bowers of Paradise by earth's first tempted and exiled" (372). Having jettisoned obedience to maternal authority, the surface text insists, Claudia could never tolerate appropriate subservience to a husband and now, like the biblical Eve, stands cast out. Unlike Stowe's rehabilitation of Eve's "mother of all living" status in the character of Eva, Eve for Hentz remains tied to the patristic scapegoat for all evil. Hentz's subtext also points to the Adam figure, who not only remains in Eden but also has himself usurped the place of God. When Claudia, whose demeanor reflects the "look of a lioness fighting for her young" (371), attempts to take her daughter back from Moreland, Eulalia debates whether Claudia has "purchased her child by pains of maternity" (369). When Eulalia finally concludes, " 'The child is *mine*—committed to my guardianship by the father, who has abjured your maternal right!' " (370), she reveals that her role as mother-savior rests solely on patriarchal power.[36]

Hentz presents Claudia as a powerful, almost supernatural presence, dark and demonic. Moreland, in fact, "almost believe[s] he had been the victim of an evil spirit, who, assuming the form of a beautiful woman, had ensnared his heart, and was seeking the destruction of his soul" (*Planter's Northern Bride* 375). Thus Hentz equates power, darkness, and beauty in women with evil, which threatens white male authority through seduction.[37] Replicating the plantation South's social formula, in which all sexual accountability rests with the woman, Moreland lays the blame on Claudia for his succumbing: he was the innocent victim of the dark woman's attractions. In contrast to the pro-slavery women writers' dark male characters such as Caroline Rush's wealthy Italian bachelor, portrayed as exotic, desirable, and socially acceptable, Hentz's Italian female is exotic, desirable, and a social pariah. Like Gilman's destroying the white planter-class woman's sexual and maternal black rival in the plantation fire scene, Hentz discloses her own anxieties about dark women by hypersexualizing and then killing off the sultry Claudia.

Similar to Caroline Rush's parents for purchase, this creation of Caro-line Hentz's, Claudia's own Italian mother, had relinquished all claim to her daughter when a wealthy white Southern woman pitied the vagabond child. As in *The North and South,* in *The Planter's Northern Bride* a maternal white Southerner's gold "redeems" Claudia from life with her biological mother. Once again, the supposed mother-savior of the plantation South operates, in fact, only as part of a market exchange. Hentz positions Claudia's dark mother, another stand-in for blackness, to support the irresponsible, emotion-ally detached black mother image proslavery advocates promote. Unlike the "good" white mother of *The North and South,* however, Claudia's "bad" Italian mother searches for and finds her child years later. In a scene of xenophobic rage, Moreland finds "his home a scene of midnight revelry," with Claudia's Italian mother at the center. "Command[ing] her to depart," Moreland prom-ises "to provide liberally for her future wants," while extracting her promise that she will never return (375). Money, which patriarchal power commands, wrests even maternal love to its will. Though her narrative has consistently equated the male planter with both the source of money and the desire for "More" land and profit, Hentz attempts to cast the dark woman as greedy, a strategy that the subtext sabotages.

In Claudia's deathbed scene, Hentz attempts to convey a message simi-lar to the death scenes of the faithful mammies: just as the mammy figures showed the reward of a black woman's devotion to whiteness, this transgress-ing "black" woman has defied the planter-god's "power," "will," "authority," and "command"—and must face the consequences. The surface text positions her to die unrepentant and pitiable: "A wife, without the protection or name of her husband,—a mother, disowned by her child,—a mistress, the vassal of her slaves" (*Planter's Northern Bride* 474). But with the arrival of an angry Moreland and his lordly insistence that she repent, Claudia's final moments have inquisitional resonances, the subtext suggests. Because she has rebelled against the planter-god's rule, the text must kill her, for as Jacqueline Dowd

Hall observes, "a challenge to the absolute dominance of the patriarch endangered slavery itself."[38] Hentz creates a dark, economically powerless female heretic who, in refusing to prostrate herself to the wealthy white planter-god, defies any theology of whiteness, and therefore must die.

Literally replacing this bad "mammy," Claudia, in Hentz's vision is the good mother-savior, Eulalia. Apparently understanding that the complicity of Southern white women was necessary for slavery to remain viable, Hentz dilutes her Northern female protagonist to an appropriately weakened Southern planter's bride, so that Eulalia never questions her place in the gender, racial, or class hierarchy, or her husband's despotism. A stronger character, physically and otherwise, before the Southern planter Moreland finds her in her Northern village, Eulalia performs her own housekeeping chores (albeit wearing gloves) and is originally portrayed in the narrative as a Christ figure. Learning that her abolitionist father, Mr. Hastings, forbids her to marry Moreland because he owns slaves, Eulalia prays with Garden of Gethsemane rhetoric: "Not my will, but thine, O, God! be done" (*Planter's Northern Bride* 127).[39] When Eulalia's father at last grudgingly allows her to marry Moreland, Hastings dreams that his daughter will "bind up the bleeding wounds and smarting stripes of the poor slave. . . . She would teach their darkened minds the way of salvation, and draw them out of their bondage and chains, into the glorious liberty of the children of God" (150).[40] Sent from the righteous North to the benighted South, Eulalia will be a female messiah, Mr. Hastings hopes. When she arrives in the plantation South, however, Eulalia no longer performs as a female Christ but rather is promptly demoted to a *mother of* God. Upon first seeing her husband's daughter Effie, Eulalia's "face lifted up with the holy expression of the Virgin Mother" (206). Even after bearing a child herself, she "retain[s] the expression of child-like, virgin innocence" (422). When Eulalia falls asleep, exhausted from having to care for her infant without the assistance of a slave, Moreland discovers her beside the cradle looking like "the virgin mother . . . [beside] the infant Jesus" (441). The abolitionist Reverend Brainerd offers Eulalia the biblical Mary's homage: " 'Blessed art thou among women, and blessed be thy offspring!' " (402). Yet toward her planter-god husband, Eulalia has "too much reverence" even to use his first name. Moreland, in turn, speaks to and treats her as a "simple-hearted child" (343). All-powerful, Moreland commands great wealth, out of which he bestows pocket change on his ecstatic wife because he cannot be bothered to "dispose of such a trifle" (343).[41] The Christ figure has disappeared entirely, and even the Marian images disintegrate. Instead of a mother-savior, Eulalia becomes symbolic only of a mindless devotee of the omnipotent planter-god. Physically enervated, Eulalia no longer performs any household tasks—there are slaves for every menial chore. Moving South and devoting herself to the plantation's gender, racial, and class definitions, the subtext suggests, debilitates Eulalia. Notably, Hentz creates her most submissive heroine in her novel that most polemically defends slavery.[42]

In McIntosh's *The Lofty and the Lowly,* a white planter-class woman reverses Eulalia's move from North to South, from strength to weakness. Having grown up pampered on a Southern plantation, Alice Montrose is forced to relocate to the frigid weather, unfriendliness, and affordable-housing rigors of Cambridge, Massachusetts, a move that strains her health and her hopes for survival. Yet in learning to negotiate Northern urban life and to support herself and her mother financially through teaching and her own creative entrepreneurship, she grows braver and more assertive. When her brother returns from sea and takes charge of supporting the family, he informs Alice: " 'You must remember, my dear child, now that I am at home, you are no longer to make bargains and hire yourself out as if you were free; you belong to me now' " (2:186), and she complies with relief. But in linking a white woman's role with a slave's, the text acknowledges a correlation between white women's economic dependence and their subjugation. Further, the new Cambridge-based Alice responds to her brother's assumption of household leadership by adding: " 'I am not sorry to know that I can help myself' "—a discovery she could not have made in the luxury and hierarchical constric-tion of the Southern plantation.[43] Just as the plantation South disables white women, these novels unintentionally illustrate, the urban North empowers them.

In contrast, anti–Uncle Tom novels by women allow a *slave* woman in the plantation South to be strong—so long as she remains loyal to the plantation's agenda. The strength of the mammy figure, in fact, highlights the delicacy of the mistress. In Sarah Josepha Hale's *Liberia,* the female slave who nursed the planter Charles Peyton as a child leads the evacuation of slaves and whites as they flee a rumored slave insurrection. Ignoring the dire predictions of their fleeing neighbors, the white Peyton women refuse to leave the plantation, because Charles Peyton's sickness prevents his being moved. When the only able-bodied male, overseer Mr. Burke, disappears with the Peytons' fastest horse, the white women remain undaunted, despite Charles suggesting to his wife and sister: " 'I know very well that, if I were not lying helpless here, you would all be trembling, and crying, and clinging to me' " (22). The text at least grants Southern white women strength beyond that for which Southern white men give them credit. In the model of a good, submissive Southern married woman, Charles's wife comes closest to collapsing in fear. The widowed Margaret Fairfax, however, a mother unencumbered by marital subordination, performs with Christlike courage, "never known to shrink from any duty her heavenly Father held to her lips"(9).[44] However, though the narrator depicts the white widow as the female Christ, it is a black female slave who leads the white family's eventual retreat from Cedar Hill, thereby "saving" the Peytons' slaves from being liberated by rebels. Keziah, the slave most maternally attached to Charles Peyton, strides ahead of the procession. "Woe to the first man that should cross her path," notes the narrator. "No womanish fears, no feminine tenderness was in her heart, but the fierceness and pitilessness of a lioness fighting for her young" (37). Ascribing bestial qualities to Keziah, Hale sets the black rescuer apart from the white women, and particularly from the one married white woman, whose delicacy and dependence demand appropriately feminine quaverings and at least the semblance of relying on a white man's judgment. Labeled by one character "the best man in the lot" (58) and thus masculinized as the mammy stereotype required, Keziah repeatedly proves herself superior to all other males and females, black and white, in courage and determination. Yet she fails to threaten white patriarchy, because as a black woman she is not a "lady." Although the narrative credits Keziah with the procession's safety, it never allows her autonomous selfhood, an authentic voice, or anything approaching the adulation bestowed on the white women characters.[45] Having successfully "saved" the Peyton family and slaves, Keziah eagerly accepts the freedom proffered by her master, a scene unusual in proslavery literature, though politically deradicalized by her adding with maternal affection: " 'Mas'r Charles, next to God Almighty, I love you. . . . If you want me to stay with you, I stay' " (56). Unlike Hentz, Hale is careful to frame Keziah's devotion for the slave master as *"next to"* and not synonymous with "God Almighty." Nevertheless, Hale skillfully deploys the stalwart mammy figure to reinforce the racial, gender, and class walls that uphold slavery and its planter-god.

Although the strong, masculinized mammy figure does not threaten the white male planter because she has not crossed gender boundaries, since she was never a real "lady," her presence does necessitate a weak, feminized—

often invisible—black male.[46] In *Liberia,* the manly Keziah, bent on moving
to Africa, belittles the central black male, Polydore, who says:

> "If you go, I go too. You's an unprotected single womin, and I can't
> see you go alone."
> "Hush! shut up with yer single womin. I's worth two of you any day,"
> replied Keziah.
> "Dese arms is wort' somethin,' Keziah," said Polydore, stretching out
> limbs that might have rivaled Samson's.
> "De arms is good enough," replied Keziah, scornfully, yet not without
> a certain degree of admiration in her look, which strength, either of body
> or mind, always extorted from her, "but what's de good of strong arms
> when de heart is a coward's?" (136)

A woman's blatantly admiring a man's physical assets and her candid disre-
spect toward him are allowable here only because the characters are black.
Similarly, In *Aunt Phillis' Cabin,* Bacchus, husband of the saintly Phillis, is
superstitious and silly and drinks too much, as his name implies, but excuses
himself by insisting: " 'Niggers ain't like white people, no how; they can't 'sist
temptation' " (32). The text makes clear that Phillis heads the marriage, allowable since the couple is not white. And in *The Planter's Northern Bride,* the
slave mother Crissy can refer to her husband, Jim, as " 'most a fool' " (250).
Without exception, the black male characters of the anti–Uncle Tom novels
by women are useless as men, husbands, and fathers.

By contrast, although Stowe feminizes her central male slave, Tom is not
irresponsible, emotionally detached, or weak: rather he voluntarily restrains
his own considerable physical strength for what Stowe frames as a higher
good. Given slavery's economic mandate, proslavery novelists could not afford
to invest their male slaves with anything remotely like honorable intentions,
personal integrity, or familial affection—and certainly not with a thoroughly
Christlike character in both power *and* self-sacrifice; that would be reserved
for depictions of whites only, and wealthy ones at that.

The anti–Uncle Tom women writers paint glowing portraits of nurturing, responsible, wise female slaves, so long as they privilege whiteness.[47]
Initially cast as a "good" mammy figure, Crissy of Hentz's *Planter's Northern
Bride* has already refused her freedom: " 'Don't want to be free, Miss Ilda;
heap rather live with you and Mars. Richard. Don't know how to take care

of myself no how. . . . What'll I do with the children? Lord bless you, missus! don't say nothing more 'bout that' " (250). Crissy demands that she accompany her mistress on a journey north: " 'You go, I go. . . . Never mind Jim and the children. Leave 'em to Lord Almighty' " (222). The slave mother functions as protector, to be sure, but always as protector of the planter's family over her own. When abolitionists lure Crissy away with displays of baubles and promises of finery—for which, the narrator explains, slave women have a predilection—the narrative portrays the "wanderer from her proper sphere" as wretched in freedom (391). In the narrative's response to the first fugitive of *Uncle Tom's Cabin*, Crissy also flees across the Ohio, but unlike Eliza, who carries her son with her, Crissy imagines her own distraught children back at the plantation calling for her; she regrets escaping even before she reaches the opposite shore. The subtext here invalidates Hentz's intended message on several levels. Proslavery fiction's claims that slaves prefer plantation life become vexed when a slaveholder such as *The Planter's Northern Bride's* Moreland refuses to let the children of a slave mother such as Crissy join her in freedom, but instead holds them as ransom—or revenge. Further, though the text scorns Crissy's being lured by material possessions, baubles, her legal status as a possession exposes similar material motivations on the part of slaveholding Southerners. Ultimately, Hentz's portrayal of Crissy crossing the Ohio teaches the same lesson as Stowe's Eliza: slavery, motivated by profit and possession, threatens mother-child relationships.

Several anti–Uncle Tom women authors employ the emancipated mammy figure to signify Northern racism. For all her misgivings about the South's "peculiar institution," the author of *Our Cousin Veronica*, Latimer, has insisted upon two points by two hundred pages into the novel: first, that Yankees who settle in the South inevitably become the harshest slave masters, reminiscent of Stowe's Legree and the overseer of St. Clare's father; and second, that manumitted slaves remain far from genuine economic and social freedom. Terrified by Northern urban unrest, the former slave Saph fears for her children's safety and asks to return to the plantation:

> "But your children?" cried [her former owner] Max, "they will be slaves again if you go back to Virginia. . . ."
> "Do'n want 'em to be slaves, Mas' Max, but do'n want to bring 'em up here." (2:397)

To the astonishment of British, antislavery Max, the slave family voluntarily returns to slavery because, the narrator explains, slaves have been "accustomed to depend on whites, and all their virtues fitted them for dependence" (2:398). White-defined maternal solicitude triumphs over a human urge for liberty. Because Saph is a "good" black mother, she reenslaves her children. In Hale's *Liberia*, the freed slave Clara must, like Gazella Harley of Rush's *North and South*, support children and an alcoholic husband in the urban North by her only available occupation, needlework. And though Hale depicts her black mother as more susceptible to moral temptation than is Rush's white mother, Clara perseveres for the sake of family. For all its ambivalence toward slavery, *Liberia* consistently portrays the North as inhospitable to the dreams and incompatible with the skills of former slaves.

Though a Northerner herself, *Liberia*'s author, Sarah Josepha Hale, unequivocally rejects the free states as a potential place of prosperity and genuine liberty for persons of African descent, and weaves into her narrative numerous subplots of emancipated or fugitive slaves in the northern United States and Canada who are starving, unemployed, freezing, and shunned by the whites around them.[48] Raised in New Hampshire and then, after her husband's death, rearing five children in New York, where she edited *Godey's Ladies Book*, a popular women's magazine, Hale often touts white women's capabilities, as well as blacks' potential to excel. Yet in *Liberia* she descends to racialized, sexualized, and class stereotypes, claiming: "The Saxon has not the indolent and docile nature of the African, but with stray passions and insatiate desire, he has mighty energies to incite them to activity" (94). She dismisses poor whites as possessing "vacant minds and undeveloped reason" (95). Reflecting on the degradation of slaves and former slaves, she attributes most of their laziness, vagrancy, and ignorance to social causes: lack of education, a dearth of elevating role models, and the "crushing superiority of the white man."[49] From the beginning of her narrative, Hale avoids blaming the South for slavery as she traces the history of the slave trade and charts discrimination against blacks in the North. One of her slaveholding characters, Charles Peyton, assesses the problem: in the North, blacks " 'are not regarded . . . with the same kindness and toleration as with us.' " Then he uses racial stereotypes to explain Northern hostility: " 'We [Southerners] are so familiar with their habits of improvidence and indolence, that it does not strike us with the same feelings of surprise and contempt that it does the thrifty Northerners' " (47–48). Indeed, violent antiblack riots and virulent discrimination in

Northern cities during the nineteenth century signaled a lack of "kindness and toleration."[50] In contrast to the South's more clearly drawn and heavily patrolled racial lines, which rendered whiteness more impregnable, working-class Northern whites often existed within more destabilized racial and class definitions (see Higginbotham). Like Southern slaveholding whites' vigilante groups, workhouses, and instruments of restraint and punishment such as shackles, the riots and general hostility of many Northern whites toward a growing population of blacks also suggest tremendous socioeconomic inse-curity, though for a different complex of reasons and without the same legal, institutionalized oppression.

Though women anti–Uncle Tom novelists typically employ black female slaves as the erring but finally repentant figures in their policing narratives, these writers occasionally allow white Southern women to illustrate the hazards of crossing class, racial, or gender lines.[51] In Eastman's *Aunt Phillis' Cabin,* the white Alice Weston has transgressed class lines by falling in love with an illegitimate, penniless white man. Alice's mother, who followed her own passions as a young woman and ran off with a man who squandered her fortune, extracts Alice's promise not to marry the impecunious Walter. Against her own ethical instincts, Alice submits to her mother's instructions not to confess the liaison to Alice's fiancé, her cousin Arthur, the Weston heir. With his guarantee of lifetime comfort, Arthur is not to be lost. Though Alice be-comes dangerously ill as a result of her dishonesty, Mrs. Weston never wavers in her insistence that Alice keep quiet: too much is at stake. The juxtaposi-tion of the white and black mothers, however, creates textual turmoil. As the white mother/mistress enforces Alice's illness-producing silence, the black mother/mammy, Phillis, deprives herself of rest and nutrition in order to heal her white surrogate child. In contrast to the comforting, self-abnegating black mother, the white mother demands compliance and guides her daughter ac-cording to dispassionate financial calculations. Though Eastman hints at the dangers of dishonesty by linking it with disease and possible death, she allows Alice to recover and marry the wealthy slaveholder. The text portrays Alice's silence as purchased by considerations of material security, replicating the pat-tern of white slaveholding women. Through her silence, Alice has submitted to a world that determines human futures according to market worth. She is ultimately faithful to the white planter–god and is financially rewarded for her devotion.

Yet, deconstructing Eastman's surface text, with its positive portrayal of whiteness, reveals that Phillis's daughter Lydia begins feigning headaches to appear more "white," thus linking whiteness with sickliness, weakness, and deceit. In an inverted black mammy–white child relation, the white Cousin Janet hears and instructs the black youngster Lydia:

> "[God] don't love me like he do Miss Alice, 'kase she's so white," said Lydia.
>
> "He loves all who love him," said Miss Janet, "whether they are black or white. Be a good child, and he will surely love you. Be kind and obliging to everybody; be industrious and diligent in all you have to do; obey your mother and father and your master. Be truthful and honest. God hates a liar, and a deceitful person. He will not take care of you and love you, unless you speak the truth. Sometimes you try to deceive me. God will not be your friend if you deceive any one." (141)

Though intended to showcase Southern whites' edifying religious oversight of their slaves, Cousin Janet's sermon to Lydia simply reiterates a theology of whiteness, a race-biased, fear-based religiosity dedicated to white supremacy. Antithetical to classic Christian theology, Janet depicts a deity who loves and befriends *if* the human subject is good, industrious, obedient, truthful—precisely the stereotyped areas of slaves' weaknesses, and precisely the demands of the white male planter–god.[52] Yet the narrative has just portrayed the white Alice intentionally deceiving her future husband and deciding against being "industrious" herself but instead marrying material security. Because they have slaves, the subtext suggests, whites need not be diligent. And if deceit promises economic reward, whites need not be honest. Finally, the subtext highlights Janet's inserting "me" into her speaking for God: in a theology of whiteness, nonwhites' relation to the divine must always be mediated through whites. In substituting for the black mother, this white surrogate reinscribes the black child's subservient role in the patriarchal plantation, and her secondary status in the eyes of its God.[53]

Anti–Uncle Tom women writers' portrayals of the plantation mammy and mistress demonstrate the serious flaws in the analyses of such scholars as Minrose Gwin and David Levy, who contend that "those who attacked slavery in fiction portrayed the races in precisely the same terms as those who defended it" (Levy 265). Gwin attempts to show that both Eastman and Stowe base their fictive, cross-racial sisterhoods "upon stereotypical characters founded in racial myth" (11) and that in Eastman, just as in Stowe, female bonds diminish male power and promote maternal nurture above the demands of the marketplace.[54] Yet Eastman frankly concedes her uneasiness regarding slavery and bases her defense of it precisely on marketplace demands that "require" the South to maintain its "peculiar institution." Neither Gwin nor Levy can possibly have read even the majority of the anti–Uncle Tom novels. Without any evidence of familiarity with their contents, Gwin alludes to seventeen novels written in response to Stowe, five of them authored by women, when there are, in fact, twice that many by women. The distinction between the proslavery novels and Stowe's work is unmistakable. Although Aunt Chloe in *Uncle Tom's Cabin* expresses affection for the white Shelbys, nowhere in the book does Stowe portray slave mothers as loving their masters' white children *more* than their own. On the contrary, in Eliza's escape, Prue's insanity, Cassy's degradation, and the drowning suicide of the unnamed slave mother on the riverboat, Stowe bases her novel's persuasive power on the opposite assumption. In contrast to proslavery fiction—where, as Susan Tracy rightly observes, slaves have no conversations, activity, or relationships outside those that deal with whites (143)—Stowe's black characters strategize escapes, recount life stories, plan futures, invent machinery, argue, preach, and assist one another without whites present. To be sure, *Uncle Tom's Cabin* does repeat and endorse nineteenth-century white racist stereotypes of blacks, from the mammy figure (Aunt Chloe) to the fiery young light-skinned rebel (George) to the kindly old Christian slave (Tom). As Sundquist and Stepto rightly argue, Stowe's antislavery novel is full of racist representations and assumptions.[55] There is no doubt about that. Yet there are key analyzable differences between *Uncle Tom's Cabin* and anti–Uncle Tom novels when it comes to how such representations of blacks are deployed and what ends they serve, as I hope this chapter illustrates. In other words, scholars who argue without qualification that *Uncle Tom's Cabin* and its rebuttals are "cut from a common mold" (Gwin 20) are right only in this: though quite unintentionally, proslavery portrayals of the plantation's mammy and mistress ultimately expose within their own pages slavery's exploitation of black and white women, a goal Stowe certainly did share.

CHAPTER 4

The Background that Belies the Myth

The Historical Record that Helps Explain
the Preponderance of Nonslaveholding
Proslavery Women Authors

> Embedded in the proslavery argument are assumptions
> about the nature of women.
>
> —Susan Tracy, *In the Master's Eye*

Harriet Beecher Stowe envisions powerful, prophetic white and black women—mothers, community leaders, preachers—as holding hope for the nation's societal healing and moral redemption. In replicating her techniques and ideology, proslavery women writers also script white and occasionally black female characters as angels and Christ figures unwavering in their mission, role, and faith in the South's slave-based economy. Yet in comparing these novels with the journals and letters of antebellum Southern white women, I find no indication that these diarists and correspondents viewed themselves as in any way like the characters meant to represent them.[1] Rather, white women's voices in the historical record resound with fears of slave insurrection and husbands' infidelities; resentment over arduous physical labor, overwhelming administrative duties, and their own limited opportunities; and profound uncertainties regarding the ethics of slavery itself. Often, their personal writings position them accurately as both oppressor and oppressed, a stance in no way reflected in anti–Uncle Tom novels either by men, which ignore and patronize white female characters, or by women, which sacralize them.[2] Still farther from the fictional land of flowers and fancy-dress balls through which maternal angels flit reassuringly, antebellum Southern black women's testimonials depict a world fraught with terror, abuse, and systematic dehumanization. This chapter's focus upon the

demythologized, often grim depiction in the historical record left by antebellum women, both white and black, offers helpful interpretive perspectives on the ideology that upheld and finally imploded the women-authored
anti–Uncle Tom novels.

Given the South's general rejection of *Uncle Tom's Cabin,* one might
imagine that white Southern women of privilege, the vast preponderance of
whom at least publicly acquiesced in their culture's socioeconomic system,
lined up to refute Stowe, the enemy, the slanderer. However, though the antebellum South may have boasted a substantial population of female literati, as
Elizabeth Fox-Genovese has suggested, only a handful responded directly to
Stowe's book.[3] Diaries, memoirs, and letters of the time suggest explanations
for the silence, as they reveal that some of these Southern women found, as
did Mary Boykin Chestnut, that certain of the atrocities critiqued by *Uncle
Tom's Cabin,* such as sexual abuse of slave women, too closely reflected their
own condition. Though she read the book at least twice, Chestnut found *Uncle
Tom's Cabin* distasteful, unfair, and misguided: "How delightfully Pharisaic a
feeling it must be, to rise superior and fancy we are so degraded as to defend
and like to live with such degraded creatures around us. Such men as Legare
[Legree] and his women" (*Mary Chestnut's Civil War* 307). Part of an elite
circle of Southern planter-politicians that included Jefferson Davis and his
family, Chestnut recognized the insult—and the political threat—which *Uncle
Tom's Cabin* hurled at members of her social class and their way of life. Yet in
her diary she repeatedly confesses outrage over the rampant miscegenation
that accompanied slavery, and she admits that she can find as many faults with
slavery as can the most ardent abolitionist.[4]

Participating as beneficiaries of a slave-based society, white slaveholding
women thereby also participated in their own oppression. Evidence of their
complete ignorance or utter helplessness or, perhaps, indications of their
evolving opposition to slavery that grew along with their years of experience
might help explain their complicity in race-based human bondage—but this
is not the case. They were neither wholly ignorant nor utterly helpless—nor
were they at complete liberty to express their thoughts without personal cost.
Granted, white Southern women stood to lose their economic security, their
social standing, and even their right to their own children if they too-vehe-
mently opposed their husbands or fathers regarding slavery. Certainly, the
average antebellum American woman, North and South, was schooled not

to make her political thoughts public, and clearly, the social, economic, and familial dangers for white Southern women who openly opposed slavery were terrifyingly real. Nevertheless, throughout history other groups of women have confronted social injustice at the risk of tremendous personal cost. Yet with the exception of Fanny Kemble, a British actress who married a slave-holder, and the Grimké sisters of Charleston, neither of whom married or had children before leaving the South, no other planter-class women are known to have engaged in active and persistent opposition.[5] Archives and secondary sources reveal that white slaveholding women's moral qualms over slavery appear more vividly and frequently in their younger years, then gradually dull as they accustom themselves to moral and ethical atrocities and convince themselves they are, as Catherine Clinton encapsulates it, "onlookers at rather than instigators of inhumanity."[6] Over and over again, the ethical trajectory of these women's life spans is heartbreaking to observe.[7]

Plenty of white Southern antebellum women abhorred slavery for the marital infidelities and tensions it created. Some despised the "burden" of overseeing the health and welfare of "their people." Some confessed being haunted by premonitions of God's wrath because of slavery. Visitors to the South record how white planter-class Southern women would admit tear-fully, in confidential conversations, how they loathed slavery and worried that it violated New Testament teachings. In other words, plenty of white planter-class Southern women—maybe even most—were opposed to slavery, privately. Publicly, however, almost none were. Male Southern antebellum leaders wrote frequently about the crucial link between white women's sup-port for slavery and its continuation. But white Southern women chose not to publicize the thoughts and premonitions that would have shattered the link and collapsed the whole socioeconomic structure.

Planter-class women allowed well-founded fears of economic and social vulnerability as well as, in some cases, material self-interest to "purchase" their complicity in supporting slavery, even while their private writings often concede their profound ambivalence about the "peculiar institution." This helps explain why, I argue, Northern and nonslaveholding Southern women wrote the majority of proslavery rebuttals to Stowe, and why the anti–Uncle Tom novels often do not even attempt to reflect plantation reality. As a prime example, by the 1850s Southern legislators had criminalized literacy training for slaves throughout the Lower South, yet nearly all the women-authored anti–Uncle Tom novels set in the plantation South depict a loving mistress—in South Carolina or Georgia or various Deep South settings—teaching her slaves to read.

On one level, given these authors' theopolitical a priori commitments, they had no choice but to depict slaves' learning to read. Relying heavily upon the argument that Southern slavery was a Christianizing force that was "saving" heathen Africans from moral degradation in this life and spiritual damnation in the next, these writers bound themselves to the Protestant missionary tradition, which from the sixteenth century had emphasized individual believers' ability to read and interpret scripture for themselves. For Protestant missionaries, therefore, translation of the Bible into the vernacular of any given culture was a priority, along with literacy training. Thus these proslavery women novelists who insisted upon slavery's having a missionary effect were being theoretically consistent in conjuring at least a scene or two of a plantation mistress surrounded by eager slave students bending over their books—almost always Bibles. Yet in reality, slave literacy was forbidden and feared—and legislated against. Englishwoman Fanny Kemble skewered white Southerners' defensiveness on the subject:

> If they [slaves] are incapable of profiting by instruction, I do not see the necessity for laws inflicting heavy penalties on those who offer it to them. If they really are brutish, witless, dull, and devoid of capacity for progress, where lies the danger which is constantly insisted upon of offering them that of which they are incapable? We have no laws forbidding us to teach our dogs and horses as much as they can comprehend. (4)

Yet just as the proslavery novelists present munificent planters cheerfully offering a favored slave his or her freedom, even though the political reality of the late antebellum period made manumission illegal or at least tremendously difficult, these women writers maintain a vision—a fantasy—of mistress-led literacy instruction that actually would have run counter to Southern states' increasingly repressive restrictions on slaves.[8] Precisely because the majority of female anti–Uncle Tom novelists were not themselves slaveholders and, unlike Fanny Kemble, were not faced with daily flesh-and-blood evidence, they could participate in self-delusion and embrace a plantation myth that featured well-clad, well-fed, and if not well-read at least literate slaves.

Previous chapters of this book have highlighted that half the leading women's anti–Uncle Tom narratives—and some of the most virulently racist, such as Caroline Rush's—were by Northerners, some of whom had visited the South only briefly, if at all, or, like Caroline Lee Hentz, had lived only a portion of their lives in slaveholding states.[9] Other anti–Uncle Tom women writers spent their childhoods in the South, but as adults neither lived there nor claimed any slaves as property: Maria McIntosh, Mary Henderson Eastman, and Mary Howard Schoolcraft, for instance. Mary Eastman, in fact, exemplifies the proslavery Southerners' often complex loyalties: though she was raised in one of the prestigious first families of Virginia and authored the best-selling of all anti–Uncle Tom novels, *Aunt Phillis' Cabin,* Eastman's Union officer husband became a commandant for a federal prison camp and her eldest son died after contracting an illness while in the Union army.[10] By any calculation, the substantial majority of women who deployed fictive shots at Stowe did not own slaves, and this chapter's examination of antebellum Southern white women's historical narratives suggests why: the writers who were not slaveholders could most easily romanticize plantation life precisely because of their distance from the day-to-day realities of human bondage.

Concurring with the work of historians such as Elizabeth Fox-Genovese, Catherine Clinton, and Anne Firor Scott, my own archival and secondary-source research shows frustration, injustice, and subservience in the lives of antebellum Southern white women. Anti–Uncle Tom novels by women, however, feature female figures who, when residing in the plantation South, revel in luxury and enjoy a security in which the concerns described in the archival documents rarely surface. Because of white privileged women's high literacy rate relative to those of either poor whites or women of color, and because of socioeconomic circumstances that increased the likelihood that families and historical societies would preserve the personal writings of privileged families, the preponderance of archival material represents the planter class. Illuminating the sociohistorical context in which white, literate, slaveholding Southern women of the 1850s lived, these texts emphasize race and gender relations, education, societal expectations regarding motherhood, and the realities that belied the myth of the pampered lady of the manor. Starkly contrasting with the fictional portrayal of the plantation belle, these documents often portray the typical day of a slaveholding woman as one of drudgery, exhaustion, uneasiness over a husband's sexual relations with slave women, and insecurity over her own position should she oppose her husband regarding, for example, the treatment of slaves.

In contrast to the idealized planter mistresses portrayed in fiction, the average white Southern woman labored long, exhausting hours throughout her adult years. Since three-fourths of the South's white population did not own slaves, and fewer than 5 percent of those who did held twenty or more slaves, most white Southern women were not at leisure to perform exclusively administrative duties.[11] Rather, the typical plantation mistress rose at five or six in the morning and was present in the kitchen when the cook arrived. The remainder of her day might be divided between nursery and sickroom, and include hog butchering and fieldwork, as well as making a rough dress for a slave and a silk ball gown for herself.[12] Even those who, like Mary Boykin Chestnut, could afford to keep their hands soft and uncalloused often found themselves married young, anywhere from ages fourteen to seventeen. Their private writings complain of complete lack of privacy and of feeling overwhelmed by the supervision of slaves (who could number more than a thousand on the larger plantations), in addition to performing the roles of medical professional and teacher (Scott 28–29).

Of all the duties that dictated the white Southern woman's days, bearing and raising children appears in the archival records as the most labor intensive and the most likely to block intellectual or artistic development. In 1835, in the *Southern Literary Messenger*, Thomas R. Dew theorized that rather than innate mental inferiority, the structure of women's lives, especially child rearing, necessarily rendered them more ignorant (qtd. in Scott 31). Ella Gertrude Clanton Thomas, mistress of a Georgia plantation, typifies the constraints of maternity, calmly informing her journal: "I have a sick stomach and headache and find that I am again destined to be a mother" (June 16, 1855). Three years later, she recorded in the now only sporadically filled volume that "housekeeping and married life are not compatible with keeping journals" (November 14, 1858).[13] Sally McMillen has shown that the typical Southern woman of privilege bore many children, usually nursing a newborn each year; suffered from a variety of health problems and exhaustion; and grieved over the grave of at least one of those children (3). Compared to wealthy Northern white women, Southern women of privilege were more likely to live in isolation on far-flung plantations and farms where medical assistance was scarce, and they faced a greater danger of disease, partly due to milder winters that failed to kill disease-carrying organisms. Further, in a culture that valued large families, Southern women bore more children than did Northern women. And though many Southern doctors were trained in the North, by the 1840s and 1850s, when the Northern medical professionals were questioning the efficacy of heroic measures, Southern doctors persisted longer and more vigorously in bleeding and purging as regular practices (McMillen 29–81). Anti–Uncle Tom novels, by contrast, typically depict white Southern mothers reveling carefree in the joys of maternity, except in cases when a Northern scoundrel defrauds them of their husbands' or fathers' fortunes. Fictive Northern mothers beset by the inhumanities of industrialization, on the other hand, often suffer to secure the most meager sustenance for their young.

Anti–Uncle Tom fiction and Southern reality likewise clash when it comes to black and white women's being drawn together by the births and rearing of children. Proslavery novels idealize the bond formed as mistresses and mammies or other female slaves share maternal concerns (see Chapter 3). The diary of Sarah Witherspoon McIver, a slaveholder in Darlington, South Carolina, however, bears witness to a different story. McIver bore only two children but also reared the orphaned daughter of her eldest brother. While her journal reflects little of her feelings regarding motherhood, it teems with matter-of-fact mentions of the births and deaths of infant slaves, coupled joltingly with notations of plantings, menus, and books: "Pender's Baby died yesterday—We have not had rain yet—I had catfish for dinner Monday which was very nice" (April 25, 1855); "Weather mild again. I have a sty on my eye which troubles me very much—Tamer lost her child Friday night supposed to have smothered it accidentally" (October 7, 1856); "Tamer had another girl last Friday morning (at daylight) the 13th of January, I told her to call her Hannah as Mary [one of the McIver daughters] requested it" (January 16, 1854). McIver's journal reports the slaves Sely, Flora, Beck, Bella, Sary, Pender, Minder, Choir, and Chain typically bearing one child a year, with McIver herself recording the event in dispassionate, accountant fashion.[14]

Like those of McIver's slaves, most plantation mistresses' and slave women's lives often centered around an incessant round of pregnancy and childbirth. Unlike the childbirths of white women of privilege, however, a slave woman's experience of childbirth involved little concern with her "delicate condition." As Adeline Jackson recalled of her days in captivity: "Yes women in family way worked up to near the time, but guess Dr. Gibson knowed his business. Just before the time, they was took out and put in the carding and spinning rooms" (qtd. in Hurmence 37). Rest for black women could mean, at best, only temporary transfer to less physically taxing labor.

In general, depictions of relations between white and black women in the novels bear not the slightest resemblance to those of slaveholding women's private writings. Anti–Uncle Tom novels depict virtually no tensions between good Southern mistresses, as they are all portrayed, and their slaves. Slave women, such as the eponymous black protagonist of Mary Eastman's *Aunt Phillis' Cabin*, eagerly serve their white mistresses and masters, considering it a privilege, in fact, to be considered trustworthy. Side by side, black and white female characters tend sickbeds of white family members; side by side, black and white female characters nurture the young. While nothing approaching equality exists, perpetual harmony does. The narratives' Northern matrons, on the other hand, regularly abuse their servants, as Caroline Rush's *North and South* demonstrates. Slaveholding women's private writings, however, sketch their struggles to perform in roles both menial and administrative in which they recognized themselves, though hierarchically superior, as functionally inferior. As Fox-Genovese has shown in *Within the Plantation Household*, female slaves, having gleaned knowledge from older slaves and from personal practice, almost invariably knew more than their mistress supervisors about cooking, child rearing, farming, medical care, and sewing, all key aspects of plantation life. Not surprisingly, black and white women's consciousness of the disparities in knowledge and experience exacerbated tensions between the mistress and the workers she sought to command, as reflected in Lucilla McCorkle's reminiscences: "Our servants are a source of discomfort. Their [*sic*] is a lack of confidence—so necessary to the comfort of that relation."[15] As Irving Bartlett and C. Glenn Cambor point out, slavery itself created an uneasy two-mother system in which white women lost their sexual and maternal identity, becoming fragile and childlike, while black women filled the role of either mammy or dark-skinned seductress. Univocally ignoring the latter possibility, implying as it did the unspeakable existence of sexual violence and amalgamation, female-authored anti–Uncle Tom novels set in the South laud the level-headed, nurturing mammy (see Chapter 3).

As Anne Firor Scott's instructive text *The Southern Lady* argues, in contrast to this fictional representation of harmony, many white Southern women worried about slavery, including its implications for their own lives—though few coupled antislavery action with their concerns. Mary Chestnut, often hostile both to the institution of slavery and to its victims, reflects the insecurities of a white woman in the alleged position of plantation control, insisting:

> These women [planter's wives] are more troubled by their duty to the Negroes, have less chance to live their own lives in peace than if they were African missionaries. They have a swarm of blacks about them as children under their care. . . . And they hate slavery worse than Mrs. Stowe does. (*Mary Chestnut's Civil War* 245)

In her journal, Chestnut reacts with "horror and amazement" when she learns that her cousin Betsey Witherspoon has been murdered by "her own people, her Negroes"; yet if she claims amazement at the specific instance, Chestnut seems familiar both with the fear of insurrection and the reality, recalling in the midst of her meditations on her cousin's death "when Dr. Keith was murdered by his Negroes" (*A Diary from Dixie* 139). Repeatedly, the personal writings of white Southern women intimate anxiety—occasionally, real fear—regarding their relationships with their slaves, sentiments never acknowledged in proslavery fiction except at a distance, as in Sarah Josepha Hale's *Liberia*. Even here, however, rumors of a slave rebellion on neighboring plantations cause the protagonists' slaves, particularly a turbaned Keziah, only to rally valiantly in defense of the slaveholding Peyton family. Unlike the historical record of white Southern women's lives, their fictional counterparts encounter nothing but sycophantic loyalty and maternal concern from the black women they retain in bondage.

As Scott has argued, in shattering the literal chains of enslaved women, the Civil War also liberated white Southern women, who were always constricted by and conflicted over their role in a slave-based economy that demanded their submission and support. Though too often Scott positions white Southern women's limitations alongside black women's literal bondage, as if the suffering of the two might be entirely comparable, she does helpfully illuminate the former's dilemma. Indeed, the personal writings of slaveholding women rail against the patriarchal and racial hierarchy that framed the antebellum South's social code (Scott 50–51, 96). Mary Chestnut, herself renowned for her intellectual prowess among Southern political and social leaders, repeatedly compares slaves and white women. Marriage in general seems to have reminded her more of the local Charleston slave market than of the blissful pairings portrayed in sentimental proslavery novels of the time.

"You know how women sell themselves," Chestnut observes, "and are sold in marriage, from queens downward. . . . Poor women, poor slaves" (*Mary Chestnut's Civil War* 15). Caroline Hentz, author of the anti–Uncle Tom novel *The Planter's Northern Bride*, similarly recognizes the commodification of Southern women, as she notes in her journal a certain Mrs. Dickey, who "is not handsome, not even pretty,—nor witty, but her father has four or five hundred negroes and that makes her lovely in this southern land" (May 20, 1836). Though her fiction depicts slaves as the enthusiastic vassals of angelic mistresses who pay little heed to financial concerns, Hentz's journal testifies that black bodies in bondage translate into a white Southern woman's market value.

In addition to having her own worth assessed in ways not dissimilar to that of her slaves, the plantation mistress's authority operated as a mere extension of her husband's absolute dominion; her sphere of control, no matter how far-reaching, always fell under her husband's overarching power (Fox-Genovese, *Within the Plantation Household* 135). Mary Chestnut, for example, continually frustrated at her own lack of economic autonomy, depleted her personal inheritance to pay debts her husband incurred before their marriage. Consequently, she is forced to "beg" him for money, a practice that fuels her resentment: "All married women, all children and girls who live in their father's house are slaves" (*A Diary from Dixie* 46, 486). Similarly, Frances (Fanny) Anne Kemble, a highly cultured, antislavery British woman who, in marrying Pierce Butler, discovered her husband's family holdings included a plantation on Georgia's St. Simon's Island, describes her position of combined subordination and authority as unbearable. Cast as potential mediator between chattel and despot, Kemble records in her journal that, when she arrived on St. Simon's, one of the slave women dropped to her knees and uttered a prayer offering "tanks to de good Lord God Almighty that missus had come, what give de poor niggar sugar and flannel" (206). When she vehemently opposes such practices as returning female field hands to back-breaking work only three weeks after childbirth, Kemble increasingly alienates her husband:

> [Mr. Butler] is weary of hearing what he has never heard before, the voice of passionate expostulation and importunate pleading against wrongs that he will not even acknowledge, and for creatures whose common humanity with his own I half think he does not believe. (210)

When Pierce Butler not only refuses her requests but declares that "he will receive no more statements of grievances or petitions for redress through me," Kemble discovers her own impotence as a white woman in Southern culture:

> The imploring cry: "Oh missis!" that greets me whichever way I turn, makes me long to stop my ears now; for what can I say or do anymore for them? The poor little favors—the rice, the sugar, the flannel—that they beg for with such eagerness, and receive with such exuberant gratitude, I can, it is true, supply, and words and looks of pity, and counsel of patience, and such instruction in womanly habits of decency and cleanliness as may enable them to better, in some degree, their own hard lot; but to the entreaty: "Oh, missis, you speak to massa for us! Oh, missis, you beg massa for us! Oh, missis, you tell massa for we, he sure do as you say!" I cannot now answer as formerly, and I turn away choking and with eyes full of tears for the poor creatures, not even daring to promise any more the faithful transmission of their prayers. (222)

Like Mary Chestnut, Fanny Kemble recognizes the ever-lurking threat of slave revolt but, unlike her Southern-born counterpart, sympathizes with the justifications that could motivate a violent insurrection. "I . . . really think I should consider my own throat and those of my children well cut," she confesses, "if some night the people were to take it into their heads to clear off scores in that fashion" (216). Ultimately, Kemble, who never learns passivity in the face of her husband's attempts at absolute rule, "persisted in paying what I considered wages to every slave that has been my servant; and these my laborers must, of course, be free to work or no, as they like." However, she functions as employer at the risk, she admits, "of producing a most dangerous process of reflection and calculation in their brains" (217)—and of irrevocably alienating her husband. Not surprisingly, Kemble and Butler eventually did divorce. And as a prime example of why more white planter-class women didn't actively oppose slavery, Kemble lost custody of her children. In the antebellum South, the cost to a woman for standing by her convictions could be excruciatingly high.

White women of privilege who, unlike Kemble, passively accepted or even embraced the South's inflexible gender, racial, and class hierarchy colluded with their own oppressors. As Gerda Lerner argues in *The Creation of*

Patriarchy, slavery became possible as a socially viable institution because of the prior subordination of white women (76–100, esp. 79–100).[16] Those who refused to participate in Southern culture's structural degradation of all but wealthy white males found themselves cast off, excluded. Embodying that experience, the lecturer and writer Angelina Grimké, a former Charleston, South Carolina, belle, repeatedly connected the oppression of slaves with that of white women, and in her 1836 "Appeal to the Christian Women of the South" attempted to reverse the process, encouraging the emancipation of the former by liberating the latter. In the female biblical figures Miriam, Deborah, Jael, Huldah, Elizabeth, Anna, Mary Magdalene, Lydia, Shiphrah, Puah, and Esther, she named role models who, as generals, judges, prophetesses, pastors, and mothers of the faith, resisted political authority and the domination of men in acting for justice. But in speaking out, in refusing to accept a socially prescribed—and economically advantageous—place, and then in willingly enduring the censure and eventual rejection of family, friends, and the socially elite of planter society, Angelina Grimké and her older sister Sarah represent exceptions to the rule. Even they, though, eventually grew weary of the prophet's role in a city that saw them only as pariahs: first Sarah and then Angelina moved north. And even they found that their own subordination overpowered their ability to speak out for long. Despite their philosophical adherence to egalitarian gender roles in marriage and society, both Grimké sisters found themselves progressively less able to lecture and write while attending to cooking, cleaning, and child care, particularly after opening a school for which they served as not only teachers but also housekeepers. Although Angelina married Theodore Weld, an ardent abolitionist and advocate for women's rights, her husband's travel schedule, her weakened health following a debilitating miscarriage, and the demands of child rearing pulled Angelina and Sarah, who lived with the Welds, increasingly from the public scene.[17]

In addition to taxing physical labor, tense relations with slaves, and subjugation to the whims of white men, white Southern women in their letters and journals suggest the writers' own paltry educations as another primary area of frustration. Sometimes the documents detail these women's ire; sometimes they merely hint obliquely at dissatisfaction over the limitations of past and future intellectual development. Either way, their disappointment—at times even grief—becomes evident (Scott 47). Yet, in women's anti–Uncle Tom fiction, Southern belles typically speak eloquently and possess knowledge of literature, languages, and fine arts at least sufficient to attract suitors. While comparable narratives by men may occasionally laud the feeble-minded but lovely young thing, as does Robert Criswell's *Uncle Tom's Cabin Contrasted with Buckingham Hall*, the novels by women more often extol a relatively erudite, if ultimately dependent, heroine. Only rarely does a woman-authored anti–Uncle Tom novel as explicitly express dissatisfaction with the education of Southern women as does Mary H. Schoolcraft's *Black Gauntlet*.

In reality, though, since training for young planter-class women elevated ladylike conduct and husband-catching accomplishments far above scholarly achievement, antebellum Southern females frequently lacked even fundamental academic training.[18] Though raised in a family with the leisure and financial resources to educate its daughters, Sarah Grimké wrote to Harriet Hunt: "The powers of my mind have never been allowed expansion. In childhood they were repressed by the false idea that girls need not have the education I coveted."[19] In her *Letter on the Equality of the Sexes,* Sarah Grimké insisted that in teaching young women to develop only those attributes that make them attractive to men, society made toys of women (47–55). After a visit with a Confederate colonel, Sarah Morgan Dawson recorded a similar regret: "when I . . . looked in my own heart and saw my shocking ignorance and pitiful inferiority so painfully evident to my own eyes I actually cried. Why was I denied the education that would enable me to be the equal of such a man?" (249–50).

One young mother in eastern Georgia, Susan Cornwall Shewmake, an aspiring poet who dreamt of and eventually achieved publication, confessed to her journal: "I look back at the past ten years of my life with much regret. I feel that I have not devoted this time to intellectual culture as I should have. My mind has I fear shrunk instead of expanding. . . . I must and will devote more time to study. Oh, that I could lend some aid to lift the cloud which obscures our Southern intellectual sky" (May 1, 1857). Yet Shewmake attacks those of her own gender and race who would take intellectual development too far:

We hear of women who have forgotten their sex and in their immodest love of publicity, have mounted the rostrum and poured forth incendiary harangues teeming with falsehood and disgusting revelation of their own depravity; but no black woman had so far belied her sex or forgotten her proper sphere. In this we discover one cause of hopeful gratulation for the race. (January 31, 1861)

Shewmake subscribes to the culture's message that for any woman to exercise her intellect publicly masculinizes her. Underlying this premise lies the threat to female virtue of sexual defilement: women who transgress against the social code endanger their purity, open themselves up to "disgusting revelation of their own depravity." Black females, as Shewmake reflects white Southern society's perspective, may be categorized as women only insofar as they adhere to a properly subjugated, acquiescent role, and even then the writer immediately marginalizes black women with her deprecating "*one* cause of gratulation for the race" (italics mine). Though subordinate themselves to white males, white women such as Shewmake participate in racial positioning by defending their own social territory. Women who trespass the boundaries that define their behavior and speech neither gain the benefits of the men they allegedly imitate nor retain their claim as women. Rather, the social code casts them, androgynous beasts, irrevocably from a bipolar civilization whose gatekeepers, white men of privilege, insist upon meticulous maintenance of gender, class, and racial lines.

Best-selling Southern novelist Augusta Evans Wilson offers examples of similar contradictions in her thinking.[20] Despite being highly educated herself in languages, history, and philosophy, Wilson insisted: "Surely utter ignorance is infinitely preferable to erudite unwomanliness."[21] Yet in a letter to Congressman J.L.M. Curry, she scorns Southern women who, though "often pleasant and graceful," generally display "information [that] is painfully scanty," and she judges "their judgement defective, their reasoning faculties dwarfed, their aspirations weak and frivolous."[22] Wilson cannot, in fact, abide the embodiment of that which she so forcefully advocates.

Granted, white Southern women's diaries do indicate that some had the luxury of time and education to read widely: Dickens, de Stael, Cooper, Irving, Richardson, Plutarch, Tennyson, Scott, Boswell, Milton, Shakespeare—and, of course, the Bible, which they quote extensively, along with works in French, in their journals.[23] Yet literacy rates for the South in general fell far below those of the North, and women of ordinary economic means faced far greater limitations on their intellectual pursuits relative to the planter elite.[24] The average white Southern woman faced the likelihood of a meager education, and the lowest economic stratum typically encountered great barriers to learning. Stephanie McCurry's book *Masters of Small Worlds* asserts that, given that white Southern yeomen joined the elite male populace in maintaining the South's rigid hierarchical system but, unlike their caste superiors, generally owned no slaves, some lower-class women may have served their husbands as substitute chattel. Anti–Uncle Tom narratives by women who were themselves products of the educated classes entirely ignore such indigent white women, with the exception of the Northern factory workers spotlighted in tableaux of urban misery, as seen in the early chapters of *The Planter's Northern Bride.* In *The North and South,* which might initially seem another example, the starving Harleys derive from highly cultured aristocratic stock and have fallen into poverty only through a husband's poor financial management, a class distinction that presumably makes them worthy of the reader's concern.

For the typical slave woman, literacy—much less erudition—was a dream never realized. Bearing even greater burdens of physical labor than those of their white mistresses, slave woman were prohibited from learning by legislation forged amid the white South's fears of insurrection. White privileged men structured antebellum Southern society around slavery and the unequivocal demand that its women, black and white, remain inferior mentally and physically. Just as the subordination of slaves depended on force—as well as, whenever possible, the slaves' low self-worth—the submission of a white wife relied on force and her devaluing of her own wishes, inclinations, and worth. Many, like Ella Gertrude Clanton Thomas, whose matrimonial experience taught her that women were created "to suffer and be strong," personified self-denial, at least by their own estimations (January 1, 1858).

To combat the resentment many Southern white women felt, Southern culture encouraged the idealization of the planter-class "lady," a process that attempted to shift focus away from the burden of her duties and areas of mandatory submission by lionizing of her multifaceted talents. Propaganda, from magazine editorials to proslavery novels, assisted this public image campaign. The November 1849 edition of *Southern Ladies' Companion,* for example, even while conceding the demands of the mistress's role, contributed to the pedestal-raising process by deifying it:

> Much is always expected of her [a woman of the planter elite], in all
> spheres of life where she is found. And particularly as a matron, where

the functions of wife, mother and mistress are all blended. She is expected to perform duties so complicated and important in character, and so far-reaching in their ultimate consequence, as would require all the tact of the diplomatist, the wisdom of the sage, and the graces of the perfect Christian. In a word, she is expected to be a living encyclopedia of human endowments and perfections. (169)

Fictive responses to *Uncle Tom's Cabin* reflect this image of white Southern women as exhibiting all "the graces of the perfect Christian," deifying key female characters despite the fact that the historical record presents women unhappy with the "complicated" nature of their responsibilities in a culture that demanded both their virtuosity in all things and their charming helplessness.

As political pressure mounted for the South to defend its economy and way of life, the plantation-romance novels, as well as the culture which spawned them, became increasingly fanatical in idealizing white planter-class Southern women (Taylor 123–55). Feeling more and more beleaguered, the South chose a socially reactionary course, rejecting Northern industrialism in favor of a precapitalist feudal society in which the planter class could play the part of an aristocratic elite.[25] Idealization of the "Southern Lady," to use Anne Firor Scott's term, augmented the position of the chivalrous cavalier. By valuing her weakness, the patriarch gained strength, as reflected in the views of antebellum Southern writer George Fitzhugh:

> So long as [the Southern lady] is nervous, fickle, capricious, delicate, diffident and dependent, man will worship and adore her. Her weakness is her strength, and her true art is to cultivate and improve that weakness. Woman naturally shrinks from public gaze and from the struggle and competition of life. . . . In truth, woman, like children, has but one right and that is the right to protection. The right to protection involves the obligation to obey. A husband, lord and master, whom she should love, honor, and obey, nature designed for every woman. . . . If she be obedient she stands little danger of maltreatment. (214–15)

Fitzhugh encourages artifice, ignorance, and passivity as the proper bait to lure men. Indeed, as the punitive stick that follows the carrot of white male approbation, his final sentence threatens danger to deviants. Concurring with

Fitzhugh's paean on white Southern women's helplessness, Virginian John Hartwell Cocke derides the "impudent clique of unsexed females and rampant abolitionists which must put down the petticoats—at least as far as their claim to take platforms of public debate and enter into all the rough and tumble of the war of words" (qtd. in Eaton 11–12). Following the publication of *Uncle Tom's Cabin,* Stowe became the target of innumerable such attacks.

Not surprisingly, white female characters in proslavery fiction are models of dependence. The protagonist of Maria McIntosh's *The Lofty and the Lowly* briefly exults in having faced financial disaster and survived through her own cleverness and hard work (and, notably, the help of a faithful former slave), but she ultimately welcomes the patronizing protection of her brother and, later, of her husband. Abolitionist women brazen enough to speak their own minds and behave accordingly, on the other hand, become in anti–Uncle Tom fiction masculinized monsters. One luridly detailed virago in *The Lofty and the Lowly* marches on a Cambridge, Massachusetts, residence from which she intends to liberate a slave who, she is humiliatingly informed, has remained voluntarily—and without pay—in the service of two Southern women. The privilege of serving a Southern woman of refinement, the narrative implies, abundantly compensates the simple, good-hearted slave. McIntosh's scathing portrayal of the antislavery crusader counters Sarah and Angelina Grimké's appeal to the sisterhood of all women for the emancipation of slaves and women. As Patricia Morton has suggested, antebellum white women in the North and South remained deeply divided by regional constructions of gender and race that pitted women against women (*Discovering the Women* 16–17).

In *Georgia Scenes*, antebellum Southern writer Augustus Longstreet gushes over the manifold virtues of his nephew's wife, a paragon of the good matron from Dixie, "pious but not austere, cheerful, but not light, generous but not prodigal" (108). Yet even his praise discloses the magnitude of her workload, as well as a brutal hierarchical system:

> To have heard her converse you would have supposed she did nothing but read; to have looked through the departments of her household you would have supposed she never read. Everything which lay within her little province bore the impress of her hand or acknowledged her supervision. Order, neatness and cleanliness prevailed everywhere. . . . And yet she scolded less and whipped less than any mistress of a family I ever saw. (108–9)

In his referencing the *"little* province" (italics mine) over which this woman holds sway, Longstreet sounds a note of paternalistic condescension. Even in his adulation, Longstreet observes the mistress whips *less,* which identifies violence as a regular practice of slaveholding women—a facet of antebellum Southern life decidedly never suggested in anti–Uncle Tom novels by women. Yet historical artifacts provide proof that even the most refined, generally well-respected slaveholding families employed such instruments as gagging irons, muzzles that wrapped an iron band the entire circumference of a slave's head and could be locked to prohibit talking, eating, or drinking.[26] Although the male-authored *Uncle Robin in His Cabin in Virginia, and Tom without One in Boston* features an abolitionist who, forced to live on her son-in-law's plantation, sighs over blacks in bondage but daily beats her poor white servants, proslavery fiction by women rarely concedes even the capability of white women for violence. When it does, such violence is strictly limited to Northern women, as in Caroline Rush's *North and South.* In anti–Uncle Tom fiction by white women, whip-wielding Southern mistresses simply do not exist. Harriet Wilson's *Our Nig,* viewed by some scholars as an anti–Uncle Tom text, provides a complication to this pattern, but Wilson's novel is antislavery as well, authored by an African American woman who does not hesitate to depict Northern *and* Southern mothers and mistresses as racist, negligent, and abusive.[27]

Symbols of a social structure's perfection, planter-class women maintained a precarious position: to question their own functioning in their own limited sphere was to question the entire system. Increasingly, the white South identified itself with the image of the Southern lady, since the "Southern woman's place in the Southern mind proceeded primarily from the natural tendency of the great basic pattern of pride in superiority of race to center upon her as the perpetrator of the superiority in the legitimate line" (Cash 118). Similarly, in *Revolt against Chivalry,* Jacquelyn Dowd Hall describes white women's place in antebellum Southern society as "absolutely inaccessible sexual property, . . . the most potent symbol of white male supremacy" (155). The reproductive system of the "Southern Lady," inviolable to all but white men of privilege, comes to represent patriarchal and racial power—and to assure its perpetuation. Indeed, the more dependent a white woman, the more virile and the more powerful became the plantation master, a dynamic replicated in nearly all the anti–Uncle Tom narratives set in the South. In *The Planter's Northern Bride,* the power of male protagonist Moreland (whose very name suggests acquisitive dominion) swells in inverse proportion to that of his increasingly diminutive wife, until the planter eventually becomes an extension of the divine.

Anne Firor Scott observes that despite countless examples of planter-class Southern women's abilities, the idealization of their character denied authentic selfhood and insisted upon selfless suffering, submission, contentment with their role, sexual purity, and religious devotion (4). The image of the Southern belle, in fact, increasingly symbolized for Southern white culture its notion of a moral, religious, racial, and social utopia.[28] Notably, however, the actual belles seem unpersuaded by the rhetoric of themselves as so very pure, so without religious or moral defect, for the biblical verse most often quoted in Southern women's diaries is Jeremiah 17:9: "The heart is deceitful above all things and desperately wicked: who can know it?" (Scott 11). Repeatedly, the historical record evinces Southern white women's awareness of the chasm between the flawless, romanticized ideal and their own reality.

For a white privileged Southern woman to question her subordinate place was to challenge the intricate patriarchal philosophy that fueled the entire economic machine of slavery. That is, to dispute the right of males to govern females was also to dispute racial hegemony and thus question the justice of a slave's still-lower position. In his incisive sociohistorical analysis of racial bigotry and class exploitation in the United States, *The Rise and Fall of the White Republic,* Alexander Saxton assumes, as do I, that bigotry arises as a rationalization for economic oppression. Similarly, in *Invention of the White Race* Theodore Allen traces the ruling planter class's intentional inclusion—even recruitment—of propertyless whites in culturally sanctioned racism in order to justify slavery. Racism, Allen contends, allowed those in economically superior positions to exercise social control, and maintenance of that control necessitated a unified white front: the planter class could not afford for poor whites—or, I would add, white women—to perceive themselves as oppressed lest they disrupt the reigning socioeconomic hierarchy. To question any element of the antebellum South's functioning was to question what white Southerners define in essays, speeches, sermons, and the anti–Uncle Tom novels as a divinely ordered creation in which men rule women, whites rule blacks, and masters must treat kindly but need not free their slaves. Some anti–Uncle Tom novels by women, such as *The Black Gauntlet,* defend this interpretation of the divine order in the form of theological tirades that regularly interrupt, at times countermand, the narrative.

Responding defensively to mounting political threats to its "peculiar institution," the white South suppressed any ideas of change, "any threat to stability, including, of course, definitions of lady and gentleman" (Scott 21). Understanding the inextricability of these links helps explain why more planter-class women did not publicly protest their positions, despite deep-seated ambivalence regarding their own lives, those of their slaves, and the relationship of plantation masters to both.[29] Theirs was a position of enormous social privilege and, at the very least, relative economic advantage. If they often had no legal right to their own children, property, and money, they remained in every way immensely better off than slave women, whose bodies could be brutalized and whose children could be abused and sold—legally—at the whim of a white man. If planter-class women bore myriad duties, they remained materially more secure than poor whites. Every motive of self-interest would have argued for their being convinced of the social good of slavery—or if unconvinced, at least to keep quiet.

Despite slaveholding women's public reticence, their private writings reveal their recognition that their own domestic experiences did not match any fictive romantic ideal. Though their letters and journals typically circumvent any direct mention of sexual violence, the abundant references to slaves' disrupting familial harmony and numerous intimations of female slaves as sources of temptation suggest white women's tacit understanding that their elevation by Southern patriarchal society was attempted compensation for white men's relations with black women.[30] As Lillian Smith puts it:

> The more trails the white man made to back-yard cabins, the higher he raised his white wife on her pedestal, when he returned to the big house. The higher the pedestal, the less he engaged she whom he put there, for statues after all are only nice things to look at. More and more numerous became the little trails of escape from statuary and more and more intricately they began to weave in and out of Southern life. (121)

Indeed, as Wilbur J. Cash asserts, just beneath the facade of white pillars and magnolia-framed verandahs lay perpetual violence. "How far the sons of slaveholders are in the practice of manufacturing Negroes for their fathers, their brothers, and their own services, no one enquires," observed an officer in North Carolina bastardy-court proceedings.[31] Rebecca Latimer Felton, a Georgian, also raged against the "violations of the moral law that made mulattoes as common as blackberries"; Felton later reflected that whatever Southern blood spilled during the Civil War did so as fit penance.[32]

Slave women, direct victims of such violence, harbored no doubts as to their own oppression.[33] As Mary Burgher observes in *Sturdy Black Bridges,* the "antebellum South's worship of helpless femininity clouded and debased the vigorous womanhood conceived and lived by Black women during slavery" (110). Though both were under the domination of white men, black and white antebellum Southern women shared nothing like the same predicaments. While a white woman could not afford to show her feet without being thought immodest, a slave woman could be ordered to strip for a presale inspection. As one slave remembered it:

> We was chained and dey strips all our clothes off and de folks what gwine buys us comes round and feels us all over. Iffen any de niggers don't want to take dere clothes off, de man gets a long, black whip and cuts dem up hard. When Marse Jones seed me on de block, he say, "Dat's a whale of a woman." (Sterling, *We Are Your Sisters* 20)

In this woman's testimonial, images of chains, stripped bodies, whips, torn flesh, and groping hands leave no room for mythologized visions of slavery as a potentially benevolent social system—or for the self-pity of white women who likened their own difficulties to slavery. Coupling sexual desire with the kind of matter-of-fact physical assessment appropriate to purchasing livestock, the words of "Marse Jones" frame the role of the antebellum Southern white male of privilege for whom sexual and economic acquisition could be achieved in a single purchase.

Slave narratives such as Harriet Jacobs's *Incidents in the Life of a Slave Girl* testify to one woman's years of living in fear of sexual assault, verbal and physical:

> My master began to whisper foul words in my ear. Young as I was, I could not remain ignorant of their import. . . . I turned from him with disgust and hatred. But he was my master. I was compelled to live under the same roof with him. . . . He told me I was his property; that I must be subject to his will in all things. My soul revolted against the mean tyranny. But where could I turn for protection? No matter whether the slave girl be as black as ebony or as fair as her mistress. In either case,

there is no shadow of law to protect her from fiends who bear the shape of men. (27–28)

As she herself notes, Jacobs was more fortunate than her plantation counterparts: she evaded, then, after seven years of hiding in cramped, miserable quarters, escaped the harassment of her master and managed eventually to secure the safety of her children.[34]

Louisa Picquet, a slave in Georgia who was taken by her master to Mobile, Alabama, lived through a similar cat-and-mouse struggle for her own sexual freedom. Initially, she avoided his ambushes, though

> in the mornin' he came to the ironin'-room, downstairs, where I was, and whip me with the cowhide, naked, so I'spect I'll take some of the marks with me to the grave.
>
> When he was whippin' me so awfully, I made up my mind 'twas of no use, and I'd go [run away], and not be whipped any more. (Sterling, *We Are Your Sisters* 22)

Though being sold the following day saved her further abuse, Picquet, like Jacobs, ultimately resorted to defending herself from one white man's stalkings by choosing to be the mistress of another white man. In an additional case of sexual terror, Louisa, maid to James Odom's wife, revealed to the recording litigator at the Odoms' divorce that

> Odom used to come into witness' bed-room and try to have intercourse with her, offered her one time two dollars to feel her titties; on one occasion to avoid Odom, she went up stairs and carried the children to sleep with her and locked the door; she nailed up the windows of her house to keep Odom out; he made these offers to her when Mrs. Odom was from home. Odom got into witness' window one night, and tried to throw her on to the bed; she told him if he did she'd halloo. She blew up the light to keep him off of her, and he would blow it out. (26)

Having tersely chronicled Mr. Odom's predatory behavior, the first chilling sentence ends in the recording litigator's unadorned declaration that "he made these offers to her when Mrs. Odom was from home," as if respondents would question not that a master might sexually assault a slave but simply how he managed to conceal such behavior from his wife. Only a courtroom's inter-pretation of sexual pursuit and terror, the testimony's very lack of emotional detail heightens its horror, making such an account seem commonplace and ending with no resolution as to Louisa's ultimate safety, as if repeated assaults of a black woman were relevant only as evidence in a white woman's divorce suit.

Other slave women, of course, were less able than Louisa to outwit or resist attack. One reminisced that

> Grandma say that she were near thirteen year old, behind the house tee-teein' when young marster came up behind her. She didn't see him but he put his hand up under her dress and said, "Lay down, Tildy. . . ." And so this thing happened, and her stomach began to get big.
>
> One day, Grandma and old mistress, they was putting up clean clothes. Old mistress had a pair of socks in her hand. She said, "Tildy, who been messin' wit' you down there?" Grandma say, "Young marster." Old mistress run to her and crammed these socks in her mouth and say, "Don't you ever tell nobody. If you do, I'll skin you alive." (Sterling, *We Are Your Sisters* 25)

The white woman wastes no time in covering for the white man's atrocity. Cramming socks in the mouth of the victimized slave, the white woman not only perpetuates violence herself but also threatens further force should the girl repeat her story. Though innocent of the original violation, "old mistress" sides against the oppressed, becoming herself another oppressor. Yet, in stark contrast to the verbal abuse, psychological terror, and rape to which slave narratives testify, nowhere in anti–Uncle Tom fiction by women does white men's sexual assault of black women occur. Rather, black men threaten white women, as in Mrs. G. M. Flanders's *Ebony Idol*, Mrs V. G. Cowdin's *Ellen, the Fanatic's Daughter,* and Caroline Lee Hentz's *Planter's Northern Bride.* Northern white men, on the other hand, harass helpless white women in urban wastelands that seethe with abolitionist activity, as in Rush's *North and South.*

Historically, gang rapes, like any white rape of a black woman, were not considered a crime in the Southern legal system. As one former slave woman remembered:

My sister was given away when she was a girl. She told me and ma that they'd make her go out and lay on a table and two or three white men would have sex with her before they'd let her up. She was just a small girl. She died when she was still in her young days, still a girl. (Sterling, *We Are Your Sisters* 25)

Slave women unprotected by small communities like Jacobs's and Picquet's resisted a white man's assault at their own peril:

I don't like to talk 'bout dem times, 'cause my mother did suffer misery. You know dar was an overseer who use to tie mother up in the barn wid a rope aroun' her arms up over her head, while she stood on a block. Soon as dey got her tied, dis block was moved an' her feet dangle, you know, couldn't tech de flo.' Dis ole man, now would start beatin' her nekked 'til the blood run down her back to her heels.

I asked mother "what she done fer 'em to beat and do her so?" She said, "Nothin 'tother dan 'fuse to be wife to dis man." (26)

Denying such relations, anti–Uncle Tom novels' depictions of antebellum Southern life advertise paternalistically caring white men who protect, rather than violate, black women, who are sketched into a backdrop of untrammeled gardens and tranquility.

Never does anti–Uncle Tom fiction acknowledge the existence of white Southern males as sexual predators or black females as their victims, even though the historical record is clear. Just as anti–Uncle Tom fiction portrays white women as enthusiastic supporters of slavery and paragons of virtue, it endows male slaveholders with nobility and high moral character. In the only exception to this, planters' sons sometimes briefly play the prodigal, as in McIntosh's *The Lofty and the Lowly*—yet even here, the Southerner is duped into gambling debts by a rapacious Northern merchant's son. Assigning to the planter's son only the faulty judgment of youth, the narrator of *The Lofty and the Lowly* never hints of sexual exploition, and certainly not of the assault of black women. Historical documentation, however, shows that white Southern society acknowledged the sexual appetites of white Southern males. In "Memoir on Slavery," published in the February 1838 *Southern Literary Journal*, South Carolinian Chancellor Harper expressed one popular justification of rape, noting that slavery freed Southern culture from the problem of prostitution by giving white men access to slave women. Further, he pointed out, such access increased the slave population, and thus white male property (1).

Few white Southern women responded directly to such an argument, but their journals and postwar memoirs indicate their horror of slavery's sexual atrocities. "I saw slavery in its bearing on my sex," Elizabeth Lyle Saxon wrote in her postwar reminiscences. "I saw that it teemed with injustice and shame to all womankind and I hated it" (14). In the late 1840s, Mary Pringle of Charleston, though a prominent planter's wife, wrote to her sons that "[slavery] is of itself revolting enough to every Christian and humane bosom, and does not certainly require the aid of misrepresentation to render it more distressing" (qtd. in Coté 181). Virginian Cornelia McDonald declared herself baffled that "the men I most honored and admired, my husband among the rest, could constantly justify it [slavery], and not only that but say that it was a blessing to the slave" (11–12). Similarly, Kate Stone expressed, if not explicit abhorrence of sexual injustices, a generalized revulsion of the institution that made such crimes perfectly legal:

> I was born and raised in the South. . . . Yet . . . my first recollection is one of pity for the Negroes and desire to help them. . . . [I] always felt the moral guilt of it, felt how impossible it must be for an owner of slaves to win his way into Heaven. (6–8)

Stone's frank confession voices the themes of social powerlessness in the face of injustice and the question of the South's "moral guilt," both of which frequently peer through even the most carefully masked meditations and reminiscences of Southern white women. Even Stone's "pity for the Negroes" and "desire to help them," however, apparently never progressed to outrage, or from outrage to action.

Occasionally, anti–Uncle Tom fiction by women depicts plantation mistresses as wishing that God, as defined by white antebellum Southern culture's theology of whiteness, had not condoned slavery. Here and there, an anti–Uncle Tom author points sadly to slavery in the Old Testament and insists that divine omniscience, which seemingly failed to forbid slavery in that era, must have reasons for its existence two millennia later.[35] Even these alleged regrets, however, remain narrowly focused, never attempting, for example, to defend polygamy on similar grounds of its existence in the Old Testament. Additionally, proslavery novelists always follow any concession of slavery's flaws with immediate finger-pointing at Europe, which first practiced slavery and imported it to an innocent South, now inextricably bound to the institution.

Historically, some white women did agonize aloud over the ethics of slavery. In a letter to James Russell Lowell, Charles Eliot Norton, a visitor to Charleston, South Carolina, contrasts the sexes in their evaluation of the "peculiar institution":

> It is a very strange thing to hear men of character and cultivation . . . expressing their belief in open fallacies and monstrous principles. . . . It seems to me sometimes as if only the women here read the New Testament, and as if the men regarded Christianity rather as a gentlemanly accomplishment than as anything more serious. It is very different with the women . . . but they are bewildered often, and their efforts are limited by weakness, inexperience and opposition. Their eyes fill with tears when you talk with them about it. (Norton and Howe 1:126–27)

However, like their fictional counterparts, some of these same women adroitly placed the blame for the South's "peculiar institution" on England or Spain, who brought slavery to their colonies, or on moneyed Northerners, who garnered fortunes in the slave trade before reinvesting in industrial production and condemning slavery in the South. Certainly, of those planter-class women whom postwar recollections depict as scandalized by slavery, few chose to articulate those views openly at the time—possibly because, as Norton suggests, they were both "bewildered" and paralyzed by their own social, political, and economic weakness relative to the antebellum South's real power brokers: wealthy white males. "It was a saying," former slaveholder Susan Dabney Smedes remembered, "that the mistress of a plantation was the most complete slave on it" (19). Yet Smedes's sympathies never expand to examine the dehumanizing physical, emotional, and material vulnerability of her own literal slaves. Like Smedes, some white Southern women evince more frustration at their own position, or at the position of all white Southern women, than any real feeling for the oppression of slaves. Fanny Moore Webb Bumpas, for example, of Pittsboro, North Carolina, complains in her journal:

> We contemplate of late removing to a free state. There we hope to be relieved of many unpleasant things but particularly of the evils of slavery,

for slaves are a continual source of trouble. They need constant driving, they are a source of more trouble to house keepers than all other things, vexing them, and causing much sin. (August 15, 1844)

Bumpas prays repeatedly for courage to speak her mind, to be less worldly, to "have opportunity of doing good," yet she seems to have managed none of that in relation to her own household.[36] Of her relations with slaves she worries: "We are compelled to keep them in ignorance, and much responsibility rests on us"; yet her plea "May the Lord direct us in this undertaking" never marches beyond private piety (ibid.) and her observation of slaves' "causing much sin" sidesteps specifics and any admission of slaveholders' guilt.

Like Bumpas, V. V. Clayton longed for emancipation, but probably not out of altruism: "I often said to my husband that the freedom of the Negroes was a freedom to me" (155). Like Bumpas, too, Mrs. Isaac Hilliard had other than humanitarian reasons for hoping to move out of the slaveholding South, meditating that "Negroes are nothing but a tax and annoyance to their owners" (June 16, 1850). Anti–Uncle Tom novelist Caroline Lee Hentz also figures among those whose personal writings reflect both profound bigotry and desperation to be freed from slavery's effects: "Oh! that we were far removed from the red men of the wilderness as well as the children of Africa" (Diary, May 24, 1836). Mary Chestnut, no advocate for the rights of slaves, joins those who detested slavery because of the prevalence of miscegenation and the powerlessness of white women:

A magnate who runs a hideous black harem with its consequences under the same roof with his lovely white wife, and his beautifully accomplished daughters, . . . poses, as the model of all human virtues to these poor women whom God and the laws have given him. From the height of his awful majesty, he scolds and thunders at them, as if he never did wrong in his life. (*A Diary from Dixie* 21–22)

Perhaps for similar reasons, one woman confessed to her diary: "Southern women are all, I believe, abolitionists" (Thomas, January 2, 1859). "In the end," Anne Firor Scott observes, "antagonism and love led to the same conclusion: slavery was an evil most Southern women who expressed themselves on the peculiar institution opposed and were glad when it was ended" (48). Yet their prewar opposition appears only in private forms such as diaries and letters, not in public statements or behaviors that might have endangered their social positions or economic security. And, for many of them, even their antagonism to slavery often smacks of self-interest. In the anti–Uncle Tom novels by women, however, no opposition whatsoever to slavery, either principled or self-protective, exists among white Southern women.

Just as Harriet Beecher Stowe calculated, some Southerners attributed their ambivalence toward slavery to maternal influence, although typically they did not articulate this until after the Civil War. Constance Cary Harrison recalled: "In some mysterious way I had drunk in with my mother's milk . . . a detestation of the curse of slavery laid upon our beautiful southern land" (42). Greatly influenced by her own mother's abhorrence of slavery, Mary Berkeley Minor Blackford, a blue-blooded Virginian and mother of six, responded with outraged compassion for the plight of those in bondage:

> Think what it is to be a Slave!!! To be treated not as a man but as a personal chattel, a thing that may be *bought* and *sold,* to have *no right* to the fruits of your own labour, *no right* to your own wife and children, liable at any moment to be seperated [sic] at the arbitrary will of another from all that is dearest to you on earth, and whom it is your duty to love and cherish. Deprived by law of learning to read the Bible, compelled to know that the purity of your wife and daughters is exposed without protection of law to the assault of a brutal white man! Think of this, and all the nameless horrors that are concentrated in that one word *Slavery.* (47)

Conducting a Sunday School for slaves that broke Virginia law because it involved literacy training, Blackford countered: "I know they cannot get any white witnesses to witness against me . . . and the colored people would not be received as witnesses in the eyes of the law even if they were willing" (44–45).[37] Blackford's convictions drove her to spend her spare time, her money, and whatever funds she could solicit from friends in buying slaves, manumitting them, and sending them to Liberia in the hope that there they might find racial equality.[38] When two of her own freed slaves refused to emigrate to Africa, she hired them as servants. Blackford's experience, however, illustrates the limits of maternal influence: despite her own repeated civil disobedience to oppose slavery and despite her urging her five sons to leave Virginia and the effects of slave society, all five sons fought for the Confederate army.

Consistently, the diaries and letters and recollections of antebellum Southern women, black and white, conjure images nothing like the female characters of anti–Uncle Tom fiction. Nowhere in the novels, for example, does a good Southern mother instruct her sons to abstain from defending the honor and nobility of the white South. Nowhere does a white Southern woman beat a slave, and nowhere does she rage over a husband's infidelities with slave women. Nowhere does a slave woman attempt to defend herself from the sexual assault of her master, and nowhere does she bear a child fathered by any white man accepted by the planter elite.

In this one way, however, fiction and history agree: the vast majority of planter-class women chose to use whatever influence they did wield in the service of the status quo. And while archival records depict white women of privilege as keenly aware of—and sometimes suffering at the hands of—antebellum Southern culture's brutal injustices, they may also have been the least likely of whites to protest slavery, given both their subordination to the patriarchal system and their interest in preserving what social and economic security they could claim. Yet they also left the job of defending slavery literarily to those who knew its realities far less well than they. The complexity of historical Southern white women's position as peculiarly both oppressor and oppressed assists in disrupting the univocally proslavery white and black mother-savior figures with which anti–Uncle Tom women novelists answer Stowe.

CHAPTER 5

Mothering the Other,
Othering the Mother

An African American Woman Novelist
Battles Slavery and Uncle Tom

*H*arriet Wilson's *Our Nig* triangulates the Uncle Tom/anti–Uncle Tom dichotomy, combining characteristics of proslavery novels, particularly *The Ebony Idol* and *The North and South,* and of the antislavery *Uncle Tom's Cabin*—and pointedly differing with both.[1] The author, a free African American woman living in the North, explains in the first paragraphs of her preface that she is publishing this narrative in the hope of earning sufficient income to support herself and her child; like Stowe's, Wilson's reasons for becoming a novelist are economically and emotionally tied to maternal protection and support. Yet Wilson's tale decidedly does not feature the mother-saviors of *Uncle Tom's Cabin* or anything akin to the derivative mother-saviors of anti–Uncle Tom fiction by women. Rather, with the exception of the author's allusions in the final chapter to her own attempts as a single mother to "toil for herself and her child," all Wilson's primary maternal characters are at best negligent and at worst monstrous. And while Wilson sides with Stowe politically, she rejects Stowe's primary tool of persuasion, the maternal savior. Wilson's protagonist, Frado, is the daughter of a grossly negligent, unfeeling white mother, and Frado later works as a servant for another white mother figure, Mrs. Bellmont, who is highly abusive, both verbally and physically. Further confounding easy categorization, *Our Nig* is unequivocally antislavery—Wilson repeatedly assures the reader she hopes her tale will add no fuel to slaveholding fires—yet it contains a secondary narrative remarkably similar to that of the phony fugitive slave Caesar of the virulently proslavery *Ebony Idol.* In what Henry Louis Gates Jr. has called a fictional third-person autobiography, Wilson seems intent upon voicing her own political and personal story, and appears to be crafting an antislavery anti–Uncle Tom pro-test—although on closer inspection, even this complex positioning becomes still more layered and multivalent.[2] As I demonstrate in the ensuing pages, Wilson stakes out unique territory, offering not a rebuttal but a firm revision of Stowe, then moves beyond *Uncle Tom's Cabin* toward a far more radical indictment of the endemic racial, gender, and class prejudices that infected the whole of American society, not just the slaveholding South.

With the exception of the author's stated devotion to her own child, *Our Nig* spins out its tale with relentlessly negative images of mothers—yet the end if not the means is similar to Stowe's. Born to a "fallen" white woman, Mag Smith, who takes up with a black man merely because she is desperate and deems herself unfit now for better, the protagonist, Frado, is a "beautiful mulatto, with long, curly black hair, and handsome, roguish eyes, sparkling with an exuberance of spirit almost beyond restraint" (17). When Mag abandons her daughter, Frado weeps to the compassionate Aunt Abby: "I ha'n't got no mother, no home. I wish I was dead" (46). Yet despite Mag's callousness and the regular beatings of Mrs. Bellmont, whose maternity has in no way augmented her compassion or tenderness, Frado continues to long for her mother, and the text, even as it portrays two vivid cases of motherhood gone awry, highlights just how profoundly destructive maternal deficiencies are, both to individuals and to society in general. Ultimately, it is precisely because Frado has no mother that she has no real home, no protector, no comforter—and her world falls apart. Initially seeming to contradict Stowe, Wilson creates mothers who not only are *not* saviors but also are more likely destroyers—of race relations, of gender equity, of socioeconomic class ne-gotiations, and of personal, familial, and public peace. Yet simultaneously, by demonstrating the far-reaching deleterious effects of motherhood gone wrong, Wilson underlines one of Stowe's key persuasive points: the critical role of the mother for the compassionate and just functioning of society. As in much of Stowe and her fictive respondents, men in Wilson's narrative prove to be either spineless or heartless, as they endlessly defer to women who either tear down or build up their families and communities.[3]

The author herself, the text has already informed the reader, is telling her story both as an act of social, racial, and economic reform and as a desperate attempt to regain custody of her child, removed to a poorhouse when Wilson was too sick and impoverished to care for him.[4] She both fails and succeeds. Like a slave mother's, her child has been taken from her by whites—not by

the slaveholding Southerners but by the social caste and economic entitlement of bigoted, self-concerned Northerners. While a few benevolent whites
attempt to assist her autobiographical protagonist, Wilson's North is primarily populated by those who are either too unfeeling or too weak to oppose
the actively abusive white racists. The research of Henry Louis Gates Jr. has
shown that Wilson's young son died not long after she self-published her
novel in order to care for him: tragically, she was unable to save his life. Yet,
the record of her son's death became the very item that confirmed Wilson as
the author of this text, thus resurrecting her and her jeremiad.[5] Though by
one estimation she failed as a mother to regain and rescue her son, according
to the terms of motherhood's societal influence, on which Wilson and Stowe
agree, Wilson succeeded: through her text and its rediscovery, she holds up a
mirror to American and specifically Northern social injustices—and the image
that looks back at the reader is not pretty.

In her corrective to Stowe's female-run utopia in which women assist
one another across racial and class lines in the name of maternal compassion,
Wilson depicts a world in which gender is no predictor of either stereotypical
feminine compassion or masculine strength. Her male characters typically
find themselves incapable of positive change, either dying young or collapsing
emotionally in the face of stridency and abuse, while her female characters
exhibit extraordinary cruelty. Like *Incidents in the Life of a Slave Girl,* the
authenticated slave narrative of Harriet Jacobs, written two years before *Our
Nig* but not published until two years after, Wilson's tale lacks Stowe's opti-
mism that black and white women will strive for social and racial justice side
by side.[6] Just as Jacobs's slave narrative depicts a thoroughly unpredictable
cast of female characters—including white slaveholding women who assist
her escape from the lascivious Dr. Flint but also including Flint's vindictive,
violent wife—Wilson's tale includes both the demonic Mrs. Bellmont and the
angelic Aunt Abby, members of the same white family.

Racially, too, *Our Nig* complicates any facile attempt at classification,
as the author repeatedly seems to embrace negative racial stereotypes and
slurs, only to play with those images and finally to turn, wielding the former playthings as weapons against whites and as tools of empowerment for
blacks. Throughout her narrative, Wilson remains in control of her own racial
discourse, calling her readers into shared experience with her physical, emotional, social, and economic suffering, then abruptly raising the color line to
remind white readers that they cannot possibly understand what it is to be

a member of the persecuted, despised free black minority in New England. Though throughout her narrative she describes herself in the third person as the predictably lovely mulatto of the long, smooth, and gently curling hair, Wilson toys with that nineteenth-century literary trope and its connotations, and—unlike Stowe's unsettling inferences that the mulatto characters of *Uncle Tom's Cabin* are more rational or more intellectually inclined because of the infusion of Anglo-Saxon blood—she adamantly refuses to attribute her own intelligence, self-reliance, or industry to anything other than native ability, determination, resiliency, and an inherent sense of self-worth. Like Stowe's light-skinned George Harris, who takes up arms against whites to defend himself and his family, Wilson's light-skinned Frado defends herself at one point by threatening her mistress with violence—yet again, Wilson never remotely connects this act of self-assertion with her "mixed" blood.

On the contrary, Frado repeatedly calls attention not to skin color but to the arbitrary racial categorization a bigoted North has assigned Frado: not just in the novel's title but throughout the narrative, she refers to herself as "Nig," a shortened version of the racial epithet frequently used by Mrs. Bellmont and other Northern whites. "Nig," in fact, becomes in Wilson's strategic handling of it a term that designates pride, fortitude, and independence from social pigeonholing. With this strategy, Wilson repeatedly disables the stereotype, as she refuses to reify whiteness or to reinscribe racial lines.[7]

Wilson also refuses to recognize the Mason-Dixon Line as a boundary that cordons off racial prejudice as a peculiarly Southern malady. While the author insists she is concerned that her focus upon the inhumanity of whites toward blacks in the North might undermine abolitionist arguments, she maintains that the abuse she faced at the hands of the Bellmonts was as bad or worse than any visited upon a Southern slave. She does suggest in her preface that her Northern mistress was imbued with "Southern" principles, yet her narrative suggests in its array of bigoted Northerners and her mistress's complete lack of association with the South or slaveholders in general that the disease of racial prejudice and its accompanying gender and economic discriminations plague New England just as dangerously as North Carolina. Adding, again in her preface, that she has "purposely omitted what would most provoke shame in our good antislavery friends at home," Wilson offers a statement which in itself opens the text up to triumphant cries from proslavery camps, many of whom argued in support of the white South by attacking Northern bigotry, greed, and inhumanity (see Chapter 2). Indeed, Wilson portrays Northerners at their worst, and in remarkably similar modes to such anti–Uncle Tom novels as Rush's *North and South,* including the abusive white family for whom the victim works; the weak, ineffectual, white father figure; and the inarticulate, silly, black father figure. White female characters initially manifest considerable influence and strength, but that strength degenerates into abuse of the weak, all typical of anti–Uncle Tom fiction by women.

Even more striking are the parallels between *Our Nig* and the polemically proslavery novel *The Ebony Idol,* published by D. Appleton, a New York house, in the year after Harriet Wilson's self-publication of her narrative.[8] Like *The Ebony Idol, Our Nig* includes (though unlike the former, does not feature) a black con artist who plays off the sympathies of good-hearted but gullible abolitionists—and Wilson implies that this occurrence is not rare: "A few years ago . . . there appeared often in some of our New England villages, professed fugitives from slavery, who recounted their personal experience in homely phrase, and awakened the indignation of non-slaveholders against brother Pro [proslavery]" (126). Her use of "often" and "professed" is every bit as damning as the proslavery narratives—as is Wilson's ensuing description of the phony fugitive with whom Frado falls in love and whom she marries. Leaving her increasingly often and for extended periods of time with the alibi that he is "lecturing," the charlatan—who at last admits he "had never seen the South, and that his illiterate harangues were humbugs for hungry abolitionists" (128)—abandons the penniless, pregnant Frado. Like anti–Uncle Tom combatants, too, Wilson supplies devastating reports of free Northern blacks' treatment at the hands of Northern whites: "[Frado was] watched by kidnappers, maltreated by professed abolitionists, who didn't want slaves at the South, nor niggers in their own houses, North. Faugh! To lodge one; to eat with one; to admit one through the front door; to sit next one; awful!" (129).

Yet in many ways, Wilson's tale of Northern racial woe resonates with *Uncle Tom's Cabin.* The key difference is Frado's assertiveness, a signifier of black-white relationships devoid of the under-over implications some scholars detect in Stowe. Lori Merish, for example, has expressed concern that "sentimental narratives [including *Uncle Tom's Cabin*] present a deeply conservative, paranoid view of power: power is figured as dangerous and intrusive, its effects uncertain and perhaps uncontrollable (power can hurt); satisfaction and ethical value lie in the voluntary, unregulated, deeply felt exchanges of interpersonal life" (3; see also 153–54). I would argue that writers who attacked the antebellum political status quo had good reason to be "paranoid" about power, particularly in regard to the white-wielded power that so clearly could "hurt" blacks irreparably, and I would point out that Stowe is working from an ethical paradigm which theoretically privileges self-giving love over power: in this paradigm, world-changing power actually derives from such love, as demonstrated by the nonviolent political philosophies of Mahatma Gandhi and Martin Luther King Jr.[9] Yet with *Our Nig,* Wilson answers Merish's point interestingly, for contrasted with Uncle Tom, Wilson's Frado far more readily recognizes the necessity of claiming and maintaining power—over her own body, her own work ethic, her own child, her own education—and her commitment to nonviolence as an ethical mandate goes only so far. In this, Wilson exhibits solidarity with Frederick Douglass and Martin Delany, whose novels *The Heroic Slave* and *Blake,* respectively, stop short of discrediting Stowe's considerable political achievement with *Uncle Tom's Cabin,* yet offer significant reformulations: protagonists willing to use violence, if necessary, to end slavery.

Certainly Stowe, like Wilson, pointedly skewered Northern bigotry—the antislavery New Englander Ophelia has an initial revulsion to black skin, and the worst villain of *Uncle Tom's Cabin,* Legree, is a native of Vermont; yet Wilson rejects Stowe's book as the final template for racial reform. In Frado's poignant struggle to accept and embrace her own skin, Wilson's text clearly resembles Stowe's portrayals of Topsy, who like Frado is motherless. Topsy, however, plays the part of a relatively ignorant respondent:

> "Who was your mother?"
>
> "Never had none!" said the child, with another grin.
>
> "Never had any mother? What do you mean? Where were you born?"
>
> "Never was born!" persisted Topsy. . . .
>
> "Have you ever heard anything about God, Topsy?"
>
> The child looked bewildered, but grinned as usual.
>
> "Do you know who made you?"
>
> "Nobody, as I knows on," said the child with a short laugh. . . . "I spect I grow'd. Don't think nobody never made me." (*Uncle Tom's Cabin* 2:209–10)

With echoes of William Blake's poetry, Frado adopts Topsy's script but with important political shifts—and it becomes something entirely new.[10] The heroine of *Our Nig* takes a more aggressive role in engaging her closest ally, James Bellmont, the white son of her persecutor, in theological debate:

> "Oh, I wish I had my mother back; then I should not be kicked and whipped so. Who made me so?"
>
> "God," answered James.
>
> "Did God make you?"
>
> "Yes. . . ."
>
> "Who made your mother?"
>
> "God."
>
> "Did the same God that made her make me?"
>
> "Yes."
>
> "Well, then, I don't like him."
>
> "Why not?"
>
> "Because he made her white, and made me black. Why didn't he make us *both* white?" (51)

The intelligent, physically attractive Frado stands as a sharp racial rebuke to Stowe's deeply troubling goblinesque depiction of Topsy. Yet both Frado and Topsy are brought to faith by white Christ figures, James Bellmont and Eva St. Clare, respectively, both of whom perish within the pages of the novels as if too good for earthly existence. Topsy, too, wishes at one point to be white, and though Frado exhibits a keen intellect from her earliest years, as opposed to Topsy's representation of the infantilizing, dehumanizing results of slavery on blacks, both grow to be well-educated young women.[11] Again, Wilson takes the racial ideal several steps beyond Stowe: rather than being tutored by a white woman as is Topsy, Frado is *self*-motivated, and while encouraged by a white friend, she is essentially *self*-taught.

In her portrayals of the vicious Mrs. Bellmont and her daughter Mary, Wilson seems to contradict Stowe's idealization of the mother as embodying and acting for the divine, yet Wilson's primary concern is broader: to decode and deconstruct a theology of whiteness as prevalent in Northern as in Southern society. Frado is "abandoned to the tender mercies of Mary and her mother. As if to remove the last vestige of earthly joy, Mrs. Bellmont sold the companion and pet of Frado, the dog Fido" (*Our Nig* 61). With "tender mercies," a term from Psalms 40:11 for a gift of divine comfort, Wilson sarcastically positions the Bellmonts as female deities, but only of wealth and whiteness. The theological interaction in *Our Nig* between Mrs. Bellmont and Frado allows Wilson to negotiate delicate territory: problematizing Stowe's implications of Christianity as a religion of liberation, but one in which only whites or light-skinned blacks (Stowe's white George Shelby, who strikes Legree, or the light-skinned former slave George Harris) may be agents in attaining their own liberty. Wilson's Frado, on the other hand, though ultimately framing herself as an adherent of Christian teaching, never hesitates to think for herself or stand up for herself, physically and verbally, and her spiritual growth accompanies—apparently even catalyzes—her sense of worth and her refusal to bow to white oppression. Mrs. Bellmont performs a role that combines the brutality of a Legree and the religious perversions of a Marie St. Clare: " 'Religion was not meant for niggers,' " Mrs. Bellmont professes (68). She regularly attempts to beat out of her what Wilson frames as Frado's natural theological curiosity, which is encouraged by the kind-hearted Aunt Abby, a version of the racially enlightened Ophelia, and by James, a male Eva, both of whom instruct Frado in Christian doctrine. Unlike Topsy, though, in Wilson's corrective to *Uncle Tom's Cabin*, Frado's pursuit of faith becomes rebellion against her white employer rather than capitulation. Informed by Mrs. Bellmont that "prayer was for whites, not for blacks," and that "if she minded her mistress, and did what she commanded, it was all that was required of her," Frado persists in both praying and in opposing her employer's outrageous demands (94).

Clearly intended as Wilson's stand-in for Eva, James Bellmont succumbs to physical demise in inverse proportion to his growing spiritual stature, and his deathbed scene borrows heavily from Eva's—but Wilson is doing far more here than merely riding on Stowe's commercially successful plot and characterization. Repeatedly and over the course of many chapters, James utters farewell words strikingly reminiscent of Eva's death scene, which takes many of its phrases and images from Christ at the Last Supper, particularly as depicted in the Gospel of John.[12] Like Eva, too, James dies after issuing earnest, heartfelt sermons to his family and servant (slaves, in the case of Stowe), and like Eva's, James's final words indicate his ecstatic first visions of heaven. But the beautiful child with the bewitching curls and the precocious mind in this case is not the wealthy white Eva but the abused black servant-girl Frado, while the gentle, Christlike male who must die in order for the plot to reach its climax is not Uncle Tom but the wealthy white James. In performing a gender and racial switch, Wilson allows her central black figure to survive the oppression of cruel whites and to profit from the instruction of benevolent ones: she is ultimately owned and mastered by neither.

Rather, Frado rises above the physical and psychic destruction of white abuse and avoids pure assimilation of either Aunt Abby's or James's quietly reasoned piety. Like Topsy, Frado is irrepressible, but Frado's boundless energy, the text propounds, derives not from childlike mischievousness but from her "native wit," "common sense," and "pertness." Unlike the whites of *Uncle Tom's Cabin,* even the best of whom wish only to tame and domesticate Topsy into civilization, the benevolent white characters of *Our Nig* value Frado's spunk and recognize it as an attribute that "might become useful in originating a self-reliance which would be of service to her in after years" (69). And contrasted with the initial racial self-loathing of Topsy, Frado embraces negative racialized discourse only to use it as a cudgel against whites and proclaim her own independence.

Refusing to feign mourning at the death of Mary Bellmont, Frado's mistress's perfidious, perjuring daughter, Frado claims and plays with Mrs. Bellmont's own racial and theological binarisms, then uses them against her: "Sposen [Mary] goes to hell, she'll be as black as I am. Wouldn't mistress be mad to see her a nigger!" (Wilson, *Our Nig* 107). Like Stowe's Prue, who didn't want to go to heaven if white people were there, Frado makes clear that she will forego any paradisical afterlife that she would have to share with Mrs. Bellmont: "Frado pondered; her mistress was a professor of religion; was she going to heaven? Then she did not wish to go. . . . She resolved to give over all thought of the future world" (104). Frado finally claims her right to an afterlife, but not as defined by wealthy Northern whites.

From its title onward, Wilson's novel, whose full title reads *Our Nig; or, Sketches from the Life of a Free Black, in a Two-Story White House, North. Showing that Slavery's Shadows Fall Even There. By "Our Nig,"* fearlessly negotiates borderlessness.[13] She refuses to assign compassion as a gender-specific trait and instead features two monstrous mothers—yet she underscores the potentially healing, protective, and reforming role of motherhood. Portraying a protagonist who is the product of amalgamation, trumpeted by racist whites as the supreme evil of abolition or, in the North, of racial equality, Wilson confesses the social difficulty of the black-white union yet insists upon its fundamental harmony and mutual protection.[14] Further, she holds up her heroine, and thereby herself, as an example not of the sterile grotesque forecasted by antebellum pseudoscience's predictions of interracial unions but as a lovely, articulate, independent, determined young woman who has borne and is desperately attempting to protect a child. In *Playing in the Dark,* Toni Morrison examines "canonical" American literature in which blackness haunts the narrative or exists merely to enhance the quality of white characters. In *Our Nig,* however, blackness loses its hard and fast lines—and by definition, so does whiteness, sapped of its superiority.

Wilson positions herself as an American prophet unafraid to call things as she sees them—and what she sees is a society fraught with inequities and institutionalized injustice in which white privilege cloaks its violence behind piety and social position to protect its own power and appear benevolent. Exposing race itself as an arbitrary designation completely disjoined from any moral, physical, or spiritual superiority, Wilson exposes this theology of whiteness for what it is: a systematic dehumanization of nonwhites for the economic and social benefit of wealthy whites. In both the slaveholding South and the self-righteous North, *Our Nig* insists, the emperor of whiteness has no clothes.

CHAPTER 6

Still Playing with Fire

Perpetuation and Refutation of the Plantation Romance in
Twentieth- and Twenty-First-Century Novels by Women

*A*s Theodore Gross asserts: "America is a civilization whose literature cannot be fully understood apart from the culture that has helped to shape it" (v). Conversely, American literature has shaped the culture that produced it. During the 150 years since the composition of the first fictive rebuttals to *Uncle Tom's Cabin*, Southern plantation mythmaking has continued to influence American fiction, even as the romanticizations have influenced the white South's image of itself as an Eden fallen since the arrival of the Yankee serpent.

In the years preceding the Civil War, as slaveholding states solidified their defenses of a beleaguered economic and social system, proslavery advocates from both within and outside the South constructed images of lovely, leisured, contented belles, of their worshipping cavaliers, and of the loyal black vassals whom nothing could induce to leave their beloved white owners. Proslavery advocates defended a "civilization" that never existed.[1] In the antebellum white South, the zeitgeist and the power structure insisted that benevolent paternalism administered chattel slavery and, inseparably, strict gender and class hierarchies. In reality, even the white South's most humane manifestations of slavery masked a crushingly oppressive patriarchy.

In *The Dispossessed Garden*, Lewis Simpson analyzes the relative lack of literary accomplishment among nineteenth-century Southerners, despite an elite planter class with sufficient leisure for artistic creation. Corroborating the lament of plantation-tradition writer William Gilmore Simms that "the South don't care a d--n for literature or art," Simpson posits that the antebellum white South, lacking the overarching sense of purpose and mission typified by New England Puritans and their descendants, groped for "philosophical amplitude and depth" through which to defend its own version of "truth"; in the end, the Southern plantation became "a symbol of the tyranny of slavery over the mind" (36, 40). In fact, primary among their literary concerns, antebellum Southern writers promoted slavery and the Southern "way of life."[2] In his study of nineteenth-century Southern literature, Ridgely suggests that the white South saw itself as an Arcadia in a moral wasteland, yet in the end, the South itself was exposed as a fiction (76). "When southern promoters blew the call for a native literature," Ridgely observes, "the trumpet gave no uncertain sound. They did not mean literature written *in* the South; they meant a literature *about*—and subservient to—basic southern interests" that precluded independent literary activity (74). Hinton Rowan Helper, mentioned earlier as, paradoxically, an antislavery crusader and virulent bigot, drew similar conclusions, noting throughout *The Impending Crisis of the South* that because liberty and literature flourish inextricably, the curtailment of one, as in a slave-based economy, inevitably limits the other.

As I have asserted, women anti–Uncle Tom writers who set their fiction in the plantation South both consciously and unwittingly conceded their qualms about slavery. Many of their concerns, however, focus not on slaves' sufferings, but on the damage done to white women. These novelists sketch planter-class women as gracious, refined, and articulate, though not scholars—bookishness they typically associate with single, unsexed, Northern women. Yet here and there, even the romanticizers bemoan planter-class women's intellectual shortcomings and connect them with the white South's slave-based power structure. Mary Howard Schoolcraft, for example, rages in *The Black Gauntlet*:

> The reason why so few [Southern] ladies direct their attention to authorship is not because they lack the genius to eliminate books, but because the gentlemen are so unadmiring of blue-stockings in South Carolina, that a spinster has only to get the odious reputation of pedantry, and the beaux shun her as they would the plague. (300)

Sarcastically linking literary accomplishment with excrement, learning with disease, Schoolcraft blames Southern gender expectations for white women's constraints. Ferociously defending female intellectual capabilities, she hails one white Southern woman for her "great conversational powers and . . . captivating wit, her withering sarcasm and her erratic independence of thought and action" (173). Condemning white antebellum culture's gender conventions in the midst of a narrative that defends that culture's overall social structure, Schoolcraft complains: "It is a singular fact, that a woman of genius is rarely, if ever, loved as a sister or a wife" (361). Further: "The greatest admirers of female beauty among men have decided that enterprise, learning, or any kind of serious or anxious thought destroys the fascinations of a dimpled, lovely face" (180). In the character of the second wife of a silly, unsympathetic planter, Schoolcraft creates a representative of the class of wealthy white Southern young women she deplores: "these tender-eyed, characterless, useless, pretty dolls. . . . Everybody waits on them, patronizing their good-for-nothingness because they are too weak to elicit envy or opposition" (190). Yet her subtext endorses their "good-for-nothingness" by connecting it with their position as oppressors in a system that signifies white indolence as a sign of privilege.

Northerner Sarah Josepha Hale more consciously links Southern planter-class females' lack of learning with slave-based culture, as articulated by a character from her 1831 novel *Northwood*.[3] Though the book's Georgia slave owner Charles Stuart focuses his critique primarily on slavery's perpetrators and not its African victims, he concedes the entire system to be " 'a burden and curse' ":

> "[Slavery] lowers the tone of morals; checks learning; [and] increases the ignorance and helplessness of women and idleness and dissipation of men; in short, it injures the white race more than it benefits the colored—so that there is an actual loss of moral power in humanity. Let me illustrate by the single example of *language*. The negro is imitative and capable of speaking the English language correctly; as a *slave*, he will never be taught to do so—but allowed to go on in his own idiomatic jargon. This he communicates to the children of his master, and thus our novel tongue is vulgarized and rendered disgusting to the scholar and people of refined taste. I have met southern ladies, elegant looking women, whose manner of speech and intonation were so 'niggerish,' that it required a knowledge of this peculiar dialect fully to understand them." (406)

Pointing to dialect as a way of distancing the Africanist presence and reifying whiteness, Hale casts enslaved blacks as the lucky recipients of whites' kindness.[4] Whites, meanwhile, corrupt and demean themselves—in fact, endanger the boundaries of whiteness—by contact with the Africanist Other. In the merging of speech patterns, blacks' "dialect" pollutes whites' "language." Language, according to the text, belongs to whiteness.

In her anti–Uncle Tom novel *The Lofty and the Lowly*, Maria McIntosh gives flesh to Hale's image of the "ignorance and helplessness of women and idleness and dissipation of men" caused by slavery. With the exception of Northern-born Alice, all planter-class women in *The Lofty and the Lowly* exhibit varying levels of haughtiness and idleness, plus insensitivity to suffering and helplessness in the absence of slaves. Raised on a South Carolina plantation and presumably writing from personal experience, McIntosh also pointedly depicts male planters as dissipated and profligate. Though Elizabeth Moss's examination of several domestic novelists incorrectly describes McIntosh as "transcend[ing] the bounds of culturally prescribed womanhood," Moss's study does highlight McIntosh's fears for what money and luxury could do to women, not least of all slaveholding Southerners. Because McIntosh insists that the infusion of Northern industry and religiously motivated compassion can redeem slavery from its abuses, her promotion of expanded rights for women becomes tangled in—and captive to—the slave-based South's intricately woven gender, racial, and class oppression.

Two generations after Appomatox, an impoverished, defeated white South had kept the myth of the paradisical plantation alive, but without the accompanying reservations and ambivalence regarding slavery that anti–Uncle Tom writers such as Hale and McIntosh confess. Unlike Kennedy's willingness in his 1832 edition of *Swallow Barn* both to fete and to make fun of the planter "aristocracy," postbellum novelists revise even the antebellum history recorded by Southern whites in order to elide any flaws in the alleged former Eden. The fifty years that followed the publication of *Uncle Tom's Cabin* allowed nostalgic white Southerners to gloss over and obscure daily realities of a slave-based South, so that postbellum plantation writers such as Thomas Nelson Page could add fresh and even more fantastical layers of romanticization to the fictional Dixie.[5] Adamant and confident, the surface message of Andasia Kimbrough Bruce's *Uncle Tom's Cabin of Today* never oscillates ethically regarding slavery, as did such predecessors as Mary Eastman's *Aunt Phillis' Cabin*. Safely distanced in time from its horrors and part of a national

wave of white supremacy that also swelled the ranks of the newly reborn Ku
Klux Klan, Bruce depicts the plantation South in glowing terms, and the Civil
War as a travesty of justice.[6] Describing Stowe's novel as the "master stroke
of a woman's pen—which brought sorrow to so many hearts and desolation to
so many homes," Bruce regrets that "out of the chaos of war and all its terrors
has sprung the freedman. Has the end justified the means?" (7). Her narrative
responds with a resounding *no*.

Unremittingly nostalgic about plantation life, *Uncle Tom's Cabin of Today*
depicts the antebellum South as "verily the 'land of flowers,. . . where masters
and mistresses sat in homes of luxury and ease" (7). In this mythical place,
"broad halls resounded with the feet of merry dancers, and the young and the
beautiful were gathered together at the festal board" (7–8). *Only* the young
and beautiful dwell in this Dixie. Just like the antebellum proslavery fiction
that Papashivly has termed "one great travel folder to entice the North on
a mass excursion trip below the Mason-Dixon Line," *Uncle Tom's Cabin of
Today* employs only superlatives for the beauty, grace, and unadulterated happiness of the former Arcadia. Opening with a wounded Confederate soldier,
William Berney, holding the hand of a "faithful 'black,' " the narrative emulates its proslavery predecessors and borrows a character name from Stowe:
"Tom [the loyal slave] pressed the hand which that day had fought to keep
chained in slavery" (8). Unlike her predecessors who frame the impending
conflict between North and South as an issue of states' rights or a region's
prerogative to define its "way of life," or via constitutional and biblical interpretations, Bruce unapologetically calls the Civil War a battle over whether
blacks would remain "chained in slavery."[7]

As do the antebellum anti–Uncle Tom novels, Bruce employs the trope of
the Northerner who, charmed by Southern flora, friendly manners, and pretty
women, converts to a leading enthusiast. Jaded, dissipated Northerner Ned
Atcheson has read *Uncle Tom's Cabin*, the narrator points out, and therefore
finds himself surprised by the utter contentment of the black "help" he en-
counters south of the Mason-Dixon. When the aged Uncle Tom saves Ned's
life, the faithful servant completes the Yankee's proselytization. Imitating
her forerunners, including Stowe's depiction of St. Clare and Simon Legree,
Bruce features a dead mother's influence upon a primary character. When
Ned confesses his love to the delicate, angelic—and insipid—Southern-belle
Helen, he cites his mother as his first mother-savior-teacher: " 'You—' he tells

Helen, 'the only woman beside my mother who ever showed me there is a Heaven' " (233).

Framed by the male protagonist as his evangelist, Helen initially seems to echo Stowe's Eva—until the subtext reveals her as more decoy than deity in female form. Ned testifies:

> "I came into your home almost an unbeliever in the very God that made me. I had no faith in man or woman, and when I saw you on your knees in prayer I tried to believe you were like the rest. Yes, I tell you . . . I'd gladly have shattered your faith—your pedestal of charity—and dragged you down to my level. But somehow you wouldn't let me. You were made of different stuff." (233)

Unlike Eva, however, this character's piety serves to direct attention away from the Africanist presence that haunts and disrupts each scene. Playing the role of the female redeemer, Helen saves a Northern male protagonist from his own lack of purpose in life; and repeatedly cast in feminine terms such as the "land of flowers," the plantation South itself becomes the ultimate female savior—for wealthy white males only.

In tying up its narrative loose ends, Bruce's novel reasserts its underlying social assumptions. Ned recovers, marries Helen, and arranges for a "young negro" from the bride's plantation to work up North in Dr. Atcheson's office, and everyone lives happily ever after. The narrative closes with the faceless "young negro" cheerily sweeping, dusting, and putting the white doctor's things in order, as he sings softly, " 'I wish I was in Dixie' " (244). "No longer in their [Ned and Helen's] home," the narrator concludes, "is there any North or South. The old days of prejudice are forgot in that one word Love. Uncle Tom's Cabin of to-day stands under the shadow of its protection" (244). As do the antebellum proslavery novels, Bruce defines prejudice in her postbellum polemic as misconceptions between white Southerners and white Yankees of privilege, not as racial bigotry. The white underclass merits little mention, while the only central black character, Tom, joins the other shuffling servants as part of the plantation backdrop. He steps into the foreground only to save two wealthy white males' lives. White women ultimately exist only to save and serve men. The female characters who populate *Uncle Tom's Cabin of Today* appear as spineless and uninteresting as those of the original anti–Uncle Tom novels by men. The white South's hierarchy, though it no longer supports slavery, continues to buttress gender, racial, and class divisions.

Three decades later, a Depression-era white South had not recovered financially from what it perceived as the "Yankee invasion." From this socio-economic anxiety and racial unrest sprang, in 1936, Margaret Mitchell's *Gone with the Wind*, which has arguably done more to perpetuate the plantation romantic myth than any other novel, before or after the Civil War. Southern belles sweep in lovely gowns through stately halls; household slaves remain faithfully beside a white family even after emancipation; handsome cavaliers ride spirited steeds; and pristine Georgian columns loom against a backdrop of cotton fields in full bloom. Yet despite popular conceptions created by the movie's portrayals, Mitchell presents an antebellum South not without its critique, at least regarding the white South's gender conventions. Despite her lavish depiction of the unmarried Southern belle and her perpetual whirl of parties, barbecues, and balls, Mitchell portrays plantation mistresses who more closely resemble historical planter-class women:

> Gerald's sharp blue eyes noticed how efficiently his neighbors' houses were run and with what ease their smooth-haired wives in rustling skirts managed their servants. He had no knowledge of the dawn-till-midnight activities of these women, chained to supervision of cooking, nursing, sewing and laundering. He only saw the outward results, and those results impressed him. (54)

In other words, the plantation mistress, once married, exists as a glorified manager of menial labor.

Though Mitchell's Scarlett more overtly combines protofeminist, strong-willed determination than does her plantation-romance predecessor, her means and ends reflect those of the belles a century earlier: with the unspoken offer of her body, Scarlett manipulates men into acting for her benefit. Unlike the authors of the earlier novels, however, Mitchell discloses the bargain antebellum white Southern women of privilege strike to maintain peace and material comfort for themselves:

> What Melanie did was no more than all Southern girls were taught to do—to make those about them feel at ease and pleased with themselves. It was this happy feminine conspiracy which made Southern society

so pleasant. Women knew that a land where men were contented, uncontradicted and safe in possession of unpunctured vanity was likely to be a very pleasant place for women to live. So, from the cradle to the grave, women strove to make men pleased with themselves, and the satisfied men repaid lavishly with gallantry and adoration. In fact, men willingly gave the ladies everything in the world except credit for having intelligence. (156)

Like her predecessors, Mitchell defines "women" as wealthy white women. Lurking behind her words, though, the subtext interrogates Mitchell's depiction of "satisfied" white men. Not only do white women of privilege contort themselves to please planter-class men, but also the Southern antebellum legal structure, which refused to restrict white males' unlimited sexual access to female slaves, conspires to keep Southern patriarchs "contented, uncontradicted and safe in possession of unpunctured vanity." Mitchell does candidly confess white women's market exchange of their autonomy and intelligence in return for "gallantry and adoration." Beneath the surface message, Mitchell's explication of white Southern gender relations suggests not gallantry but rather a system dependent upon planter-class men's chivalrous performances as a bribe to planter-class women, and those women's acceptance of the bribe that secured their acquiescence (Bartlett and Cambor 16).

Mitchell sketches religion's role in the antebellum South differently than did her proslavery antecedents. In contrast to the nineteenth-century texts, always anxious to establish their authors and protagonists as defenders of the faith—as defined by what I've called a theology of whiteness, whose founding principle is economic profit, whose primary religious practice consists of reinforcing racial, gender, and class boundaries, and whose God is indistinguishable from its wealthy white male enforcers—*Gone with the Wind* flaunts its irreligious female protagonist. Piety appears only in superspiritual, too-good maternal figures such as Mrs. O'Hara and Melanie Wilkes. And rather than use Judeo-Christian scripture to defend slavery, Mitchell sets issues of faith apart from all questions of race, gender, or class hierarchies. Instead, *Gone with the Wind* conflates religious faith with worship of the land, and biological mothers with the South as motherland: Scarlett "loved this land so much, without even knowing she loved, loved it as she loved her mother's face under the lamp at prayer time" (30). Scarlet finds the family prayers "a moment for adoration of Ellen, rather than the Virgin. Sacrilegious though it might be,

Scarlett always saw, through her closed eyes, the upturned face of Ellen and not the Blessed Virgin, as the ancient phrases were repeated" (73). In reminding his recalcitrant daughter of her heritage, Gerald admonishes Scarlett that "to anyone with a drop of Irish blood in them the land they live on is like their mother" (39). The Irish planter reinscribes this link between devotion to mother and devotion to land. But when Rhett Butler irreverently insists that "there is never but one reason for a war. And that is money" (229), the text inadvertently exposes the plantation South's true "religion," its theology of whiteness. There was but one reason for slavery as well, "and that [was] money." All theopolitical arguments had to be constructed to protect that one unspoken goal, the maintenance of material security and its accompanying white power.

Mitchell replicates plantation literary tradition stereotypes, such as the myth of the contented slave. But unlike nineteenth-century anti–Uncle Tom novels by women that depict white Southerners as happy, rich, and unreservedly proslavery and evade all mention of poor Southern whites, Mitchell highlights "white trash" to offset her planter-class whites' refinement, including their benevolence toward their slaves. Overseer Tom Slattery, for example,

> hated his neighbors with what little energy he possessed, sensing their contempt beneath their courtesy, and especially did he hate "rich folks' uppity niggers." The house negroes of the County considered themselves superior to white trash, and their unconcealed scorn stung him, while their more secure position in life stirred his envy. By contrast with his own miserable existence, they were well-fed, well-clothed and looked after in sickness and old age. They were proud of the good names of their owners and, for the most part, proud to belong to people who were quality, while he was despised by all. (52)

Clinging closely here to the slaveocracy's self-perception of paternalistic good nature, Mitchell also, like Kennedy in *Swallow Barn* a century earlier, presents a stereotypical mammy with godlike qualities: "Whom Mammy loved, she chastened," the narrator observes wryly (25).[8] Following anti–Uncle Tom tradition, Mitchell's mammy represents fierce black loyalty to whites, and whites' gracious condescension to blacks.

Unlike its predecessors, though, *Gone with the Wind* addresses slave-family separations casually. Positioned to display a soft heart beneath a gruff exterior, Gerald O'Hara, Scarlett's father, admits buying the slave girl Prissy along with the purchase he'd intended to make, her mother, Dilcey. When Scarlett chides her father for his lack of business savvy, saying, " 'The only reason you bought [Prissy] was because Dilcey asked you to buy her,' " Gerald defends himself by appealing to maternal attachment: " 'Well, what if I did? Was there any use buying Dilcey if she was going to mope about the child? Well, never again will I let a darky on this place marry off it. It's too expensive. Well, come on, Puss, let's go in to supper' " (34). With such insouciant allusions to the domestic slave trade, Mitchell passes off a black mother's near-loss of her child in a few short sentences. In contrast to her proslavery literary predecessors, she neither defends the practice nor hides its existence, but merely uses it to develop her characterization of a softhearted planter. In a gender-role reversal from the nineteenth-century anti–Uncle Tom novels by women, the white female protagonist here cavalierly speaks of slave-family divisions, and even teases a white male for his profligate tenderheartedness. A departure from the more softhearted, soft-spoken female protagonists of earlier plantation romances, this more liberated, outspoken, and unfeeling white woman serves to highlight the social, racial, and economic inferiority of her female rivals, black women. But the result remains the same: as in the narratives eight decades earlier, maternal love matters little when the mother is the enslaved and voiceless Other.

Far more blatantly than do the earlier texts, Mitchell's reveals the politics behind slavery and its profit-guided principles. Despite the narrative's depiction of the white male planter as loveable and generous, the subtext points to the words "let a darky on this place marry off it," stressing the tyrannical power privileged Southern whites held over black life and love and choice. Indeed, though political movements came from within the white South to outlaw slave-family separations, the ruling power structure ultimately found such a reform "too expensive," as I have explained. In truncating Scarlett and Gerald's conversation about the fate of a black family by having Gerald announce dinnertime, the text further lays bare its assumptions: white physical and material comfort always supersedes—and trivializes—any concern of blacks, including the most sacred family ties. Except for its more forceful female protagonist and its more candid observations about Southern planter-class motives, Mitchell's cult masterpiece shifts little from the earlier fictive worlds driven by wealth and defined by whiteness.

Published a half century after *Gone with the Wind,* Eugenia Price's 1983

New York Times best-selling novel *Savannah* nods here and there to more politically correct attitudes toward race, gender, and class but ultimately adheres to the pattern established by the plantation romances, its scenes often suffused, like its predecessors', with superficial lessons on devotion to a Judeo-Christian God, narrowly defined. In general, Price's more "modern" perspective amounts only to small doses of white characters feeling moral guilt, with no substantive change in behavior, and little in rhetoric. Reinscribing the trope of the converted Northerner, protagonist Mark Browning arrives in Savannah in 1812, having been raised by a staunch Philadelphia abolitionist. He begins his adult career in the South by assuring his new friend, Robert Mackay, a successful Savannah merchant: " 'Don't worry about my embarrassing you with my aunt's views, or mine, on the slavery issue' " (59). Such is the extent of his prophetic stand for his first several years in the city. Only years later, on his honeymoon in Philadelphia, does Mark Browning broach the subject of using hired immigrant servants rather than slaves for the new couple's domestic needs. His wife Caroline's response reflects her submissive, malleable nature, portrayed as attractive in a white Southern wife.

> "Wouldn't people think it awfully strange if we—Mark, I don't even know what I'm trying to ask you. I'm not upset. I'm just—mixed up."
>
> He turned her over and snuggled to her back, spoon fashion. "One of us with a clear mind is enough for tonight. I'm very clear about loving you with all my heart and I'm very clear about being sleepy. Good night, Mrs. Browning." (450)

Consistently, the narrative awards *Mr.* Browning the clear mind. *Mrs.* Browning, on the other hand, waits to form all her political and ethical opinions until she can know and replicate her husband's thoughts, as exemplified in this passage.

Price's allegedly more progressive whites fail miserably. Despite the Brownings' eventually hiring two poor whites and one free black as domestic staff, their cotton crop, growing on land inherited from Caroline Browning's grandfather, continues to be harvested by slave labor. Repeatedly, the narrative excuses white possession of black slaves, particularly if the individual expresses distaste for slavery and affection for his or her slaves, as in this conversation among Eliza Mackay, Caroline Browning, and Mark Browning:

"Am I being stubborn to insist upon hiring our help?" Mark asked openly. . . .

"You will always do what you believe in, Mark," Eliza said. . . . "My grandfather Smith hated owning other human beings."

"But he must have been good to his people," Caroline put in.

"Oh, he was. And he owned over a hundred at one time, counting his house servants. They'd always owned their help, their fathers and grandfathers owned theirs—it's the way we all live. . . . You were brought up to believe that slavery is wrong. . . . And I expect it is—very wrong. Only God has the right to be anyone's master." Eliza smiled a sad little smile. "I—would be totally helpless to try to change my way of living now. As you of all people know, Mark, I don't have any money for wages. Even tiny ones." (515)

The subtext amplifies the clash of "owning other human beings," "owned over a hundred at one time," and "owned theirs" with the impossible corollary of one human being being "good" to others. Eliza Mackay, always depicted as the paragon of Christian virtue, continues to find financial resources to purchase new ball gowns, operate a country estate, and feed, clothe, and shelter the "servants" she cannot afford to pay. Consistently, the narrative sustains what Ruth Frankenberg terms a "power-evasive" view of racism, locating injustice only in intentional individual acts, thus excusing not only the Eliza Mackays, who at least intend to behave differently if economic circumstances did not compel them to their current lifestyles, but also an entire culture, whose power structure can continue its lucrative functioning only if unmolested by those who would challenge racial or gender ordering (*White Women, Race Matters* 242).

Reflecting the trope of cross-racial mammy/mistress affection, a key scene in *Savannah* depicts Eliza confiding in her slave maid Hannah, as both women invoke "the Lord" to guide Eliza. Maternal Hannah briefly performs the role of mother-teacher for her mistress, but only under the authority of a white, male, slavery-tolerant God: " 'There you go, honey, jumpin' smack into the Lord's slippers again! He's the *only* one to know what you ought to do and say' " (385). Eliza Mackay responds to this spiritual instruction by glancing in the mirror, pinching color into her cheeks, and drying her eyes. The temporarily inverted hierarchy of teacher-student ends there, and Hannah reverts to the role of compliant, faithful household drudge. Being "good" to one's "people" in this novel, as in the proslavery novels of the mid–nineteenth century, has nothing to do with human freedom, dignity, or justice.

Like those of its literary predecessors, *Savannah*'s black characters never develop beyond cardboard cutouts. Like the beleaguered factory "hands" of Charles Dickens's *Hard Times,* field hands here remain distant, impersonal figures, mere "straw hats and colored bandanas bobb[ing] slowly up and down" (536). When the would-be radical Mark Browning inspects his wife's cotton fields, he offers no protest to his overseer's explanation of field labor:

> "They work as well as any nigras if they know I'm on a horse watching their every move." He grinned pleasantly. "The good Lord understood about nigras and cotton. If cotton grew any taller, they could hide in it. Knightsford nigras keep marching all day long, I'm happy to say. Our full-grown hands pick from a hundred fifty to two hundred pounds a day of seed cotton." (536)

Though Mark Browning frowns at the speech, he fails to counter its scurrilous racism or spurn the cotton profits. Instead, he commends the overseer on the year's lucrative crop. As in proslavery antebellum novels, economics guides the principles of wealthy whites.

Eugenia Price's politics of representation envisions all characters of lower economic standing as meaningless—or worse, as dangerous—in the narrative scheme.[9] The only significant white male character whom the narrative condemns, Osmund Kott, is illegitimate, irreligious, and poor. Like Mitchell's Tom Slattery, the economically and socially lower-class Kott merits only suspicion and derision. Following the precedent of antebellum proslavery novels, in *Savannah* only characters of significant financial means attract the narrative spotlight. All of them are slaveholders, or at least married to slaveholders. By contrast, the narrative dehumanizes Kott, his motives always suspect, his physical presence hiding, sneaking, dissembling; and he is perpetually feared. The narrator attempts to elicit a modicum of sympathy for the wealthy elite's despising Kott, until he shows himself irretrievably corrupt, cheating his employer by weighting the cotton bales—yet the surface text never challenges the ethical purity of those whose forcibly bound dependents raise the cotton.

Though Price sketches house slaves in the foreground along with whites, the slaves' faces never materialize as more than mere extensions of white egotism. As in the antebellum plantation romances, loyal slaves prove themselves fully committed to their owners' material and physical welfare. When slaveholding merchant Robert Mackay suffers heart failure, the feminized slave Hero is the only male character to weep:

> Hero, unashamedly, wiped tears with the back of his hand . . . "Yes, sir," Hero said, struggling to assure Mark with a not very convincing smile. "Could we take our time getting there, sir? It give me a chance to settle my heart. There ain't nobody anywhere—like Master Robert." Tears still wet his brown cheeks. "They come—just one in a box, sir, like him." (231)

Echoing Stowe's Uncle Tom, the feminized Hero plays the faithful mammy, linking blacks and whites, slaves and free, with his tearful affection, though Robert Mackay's closest friend, the white male character Mark, maintains his unemotional manliness. The protection of ever-vulnerable whiteness mandates that gender and class as well as racial lines not be crossed. Whereas Stowe could show white men weeping, here only the black male can be emasculated by the pro-white text.

Unlike its plantation-tradition predecessors, *Savannah* does depict black female characters conversing in the absence of whites—but only to discuss their relative rankings in relation to dominant whiteness:

> "Anybody trusted to be in full charge when the mistress is away most of the time is high up!" . . . Annie looked down her aquiline nose at Hannah and Emphie. "Some folks needs a mistress on top of 'em every minute!"
>
> "*Some* folks wouldn't know how to behave in town," Hannah declared. "Some folks 'bout have to be kep' in the country!" (472)

Though intended as a mildly amusing scene, the subtext rewrites its message as profoundly racist, blacks measuring their own worth solely according to whites' assessments: a foundational principle of constructing whiteness.

Savannah's white female characters, while allowed to wear silk and dine lavishly, develop only slightly more than do the female slaves—and ultimately cannot rival white women's narrative centrality in women-authored anti–Uncle Tom novels. A backlash to late twentieth-century feminism, Caroline Mackay never moves beyond a weak-kneed, dependent being who waits, like an already monied Cinderella, for her chosen prince to give her life purpose. " 'If anything happens to Mark out there tonight, Miss Eliza,' " she confides, " 'I won't have any reason to go on living' " (405). The role of white females has actually regressed in relation to some of the nineteenth-century texts, which distinguished themselves from their male-authored political allies by featuring strong female characters and maternal concerns. Whereas the women-authored anti–Uncle Tom novels made their cases for slavery through women's relationships, *Savannah* portrays female characters who confess to wiser, more clear-headed male characters that slavery is "very wrong" yet lack the will to act on their convictions and the courage to make the necessary financial sacrifices. In this, *Savannah's* characters reflect the miserably conflicted white women of the historical record. Nearly a century and a half since the fictive rebuttals to *Uncle Tom's Cabin,* Price perpetuates the myth of a Southern society in which beneficent wealthy white males rule; white women of privilege pine for their men; and maternal slaves devote themselves to the concerns of their owners. Mammies and mistresses unite to force the narrative to its happily-ever-after conclusion.

Toni Morrison tells no such story. Published in 1987, only four years after *Savannah,* Morrison's *Beloved* converts the plantation romance into a horror story and valorizes the tale of the owned, rather than the owner. In place of wealthy white slaveholder protagonists, Morrison features former slaves. Rather than worshipping the past and battling to retain its material and social privileges, *Beloved's* characters struggle to forget the past and heal mentally and physically from the scars of its atrocities. Morrison has said she based her protagonist on a historical case, well publicized at the time, of a former slave who killed her child rather than allow the child to be returned to slavery; the inspiration for Sethe and her infanticide prompted by the sight of Schoolteacher's white hat might well have sprung from the same or similar sources Stowe used in creating the slave mother on the riverboat and Cassy, both of whom commit infanticide. Like Stowe, Morrison locates the nexus of social change, compassion, and comfort in women's hands. Sometimes those centers of power revolve around traditionally feminine domains—kitchens and parlors, for instance—and sometimes the women create their own spaces of empowerment, as does Baby Suggs in the Clearing, a church without walls, restrictions, or impediments of any kind. Morrison offers Baby Suggs as a mother-savior figure, teacher, comforter, protector, and redeemer for the wounded community of former slaves she leads. All emotionally battered and most physically as well, the free blacks who live near 124 Bluestone Road look to Baby Suggs for healing, wholeness, and celebration, a source of strength beyond their still oppressed, still fairly bleak existence.

In *Beloved*, Morrison echoes Stowe's emphasis upon the healthy practice of religion as liberating, not only for individuals but also for institutional structures. Baby Suggs redefines "holy" as she redeems the past, transforms the future—and empowers women to lead the way. At the narrative's conclusion, as Sethe stands in the doorway with Beloved and confronts her assembled neighbors, their rapt faces, their singing, and their prayers remind her of Baby Suggs's services in the Clearing,

> "with all its heat and simmering leaves, where the voices of women searched for the right combination, the key, the code, the sound that broke the back of words. Building voice upon voice until they found it, and when they did it was a wave of sound wide enough to sound deep water and knock the pods off chestnut trees. It broke over Sethe and she trembled like the baptized in its wash." (261)

Holiness no longer belongs to wealthy white men and their money-driven definitions of religion, of family, of white and black, bestial and human, male and female, planter and lower class, "us" and "them."

In stark contrast to the absent poor whites of the nineteenth-century anti–Uncle Tom novels and the demeaned poor whites of twentieth-century plantation romances, Morrison elevates an unrefined homeless white female figure. Though she does not rival any of the central black female characters in narrative importance, Amy Denver, a "whitegirl" on her way to Boston, helps birth Sethe's youngest daughter and aids mother and child on their flight to freedom. Amy Denver represents another female savior figure, not only providing Sethe with physical salvation, but also suggesting hope for cross-racial relations in a world primarily dominated by abominable whites. " 'Looks like the devil,' " Amy Denver says of the tree whipped by School-teacher and his minions onto Sethe's back. " 'But you made it through. Come down here, Jesus, Lu made it through. That's because of me. I'm good at sick things' " (1:82). Blunt and crude, Amy Denver is Christlike in playing the role of healer, protector, comforter, and redeemer in the practical physical matters essential to the hunted Sethe.

Like Stowe's Cassy, Sethe represents the terrors of a system so brutal that mothers would murder their own children rather than surrender them to it.[10] As Nell Irvin Painter's definition of slavery's "soul murder" suggests, Sethe attempts to save her children by slaying them. Insisting on defining her own maternal rights, Sethe rejects white authority and white delineations of property; instead, she operates according to her own definitions of justice, family, and love. Ratcheting up the horrific detail from the riverboat slave mother's and Cassy's less vividly depicted infanticides in *Uncle Tom's Cabin,* Morrison strips slavery down to the utterly unbearable by envisioning a mother who commits a bloody, brutal act of love for her children. *Beloved's* Ella, too, a secondary character who both resonates with Sethe's predicament and abhors the bloody violence of Sethe's response, "had delivered, but would not nurse, a hairy white thing, fathered by 'the lowest yet.' It lived five days never making a sound" (3:258–59).

By and large, white men in *Beloved* oppress, abuse, and victimize. Refuting the revered beneficent slaveholders of the antebellum plantation romances, white Southern males here whip, rape, molest, chain, mutilate, incinerate, decapitate, and constantly terrorize slaves. *Beloved's* primary plantation mistress, Mrs. Garner of Sweet Home, reflects a weaker, more pathetic, version of Mrs. Shelby, though unlike Mrs. Shelby's and Chloe's sabotage of the slave trader Haley, Mrs. Garner weeps for Sethe but finally fails—physically and politically—to oppose a patriarchal system she never embraced. Emblematic of historical white planter-class women, Mrs. Garner sees slavery for what it is but does not speak against it. Powerfully symbolizing the consequences of injustice silently tolerated, Mrs. Garner no longer retains the gift of language. Her silence has become her life sentence.

Like Stowe's *Uncle Tom's Cabin,* Morrison's *Beloved* enlists the plantation myth to demolish it. Her story strips the romanticized antebellum South of its fantastical trappings, exposing the civilization for barbarism, the benevolence for self-interest, and the beauty of the homes and land as built upon the backs of the enslaved. Both Stowe and Morrison insist upon liberation and self-definition of the individual as well as the group: Sethe cannot be free until she can cease defining herself as a slave, as the victim of mammary rape, as a mother, and as a murderess and instead accept Paul D's insistence to her: " 'You your best thing. You are' " (3:273). Echoing Stowe's mother-savior ideology, Morrison takes the plantation myth, as perpetuated from the nineteenth century into the late twentieth, and retells the tale from the inside out. In anti–Uncle Tom antebellum novels and even the plantation literary tradition of the twentieth century, mother-saviors never exert real power, never preside over real change outside the possible pietistic conversion of a wealthy white man, who all along maintains his self-determination. In the earlier texts, surface narratives present white female slaveholding characters in seemingly enviable positions of privilege, even though they finally appear within the subtexts as bound themselves within a closed socioeconomy that denies them any real voice.

In *Beloved*, conduits for supernatural revelation, comfort, protection, and redemption exist in the form of abused, assaulted, impoverished, and socially outcast women. This time, the oppressed paint their own picture of a society built on their blood, their sweat, and their desecrated humanity. Sethe embraces her mother-savior role, and the results—like their economic cause, slavery—are horrific. Sethe is the female Christ who brings "not peace, but a sword" (Matt. 10:34). In stark contrast to the women anti–Uncle Tom writers who plead for harmonious North-South relations, Morrison, like Stowe, privileges justice over peace. Just as the women anti–Uncle Tom writers make their slavery arguments not through the debates and soliloquies of the male writers but through female characters' relationships, Morrison frames Sethe's violence against her most intimate relations as the ultimate refutation of slavery. In raising her saw to literally murder her own children, Sethe announces her absolute rejection of slavery's soul murder. And to that argument, there is no proslavery defense.

Published fifteen years later, in 2001, Lalita Tademy in *Cane River* and Alice Randall in *The Wind Done Gone*, both African American women, continue, like Morrison, to wage battle against the plantation myth; they also continue, like Morrison and Stowe and a host of female authors in between, to examine slavery's implications for women in particular. *Cane River*, a historical novel based on Tademy's own extensively researched family, begins in nineteenth-century Louisiana and follows the lives of four generations of women in the characters Elizabeth, Suzette, Philomène, and Emily. Each slave mother watches the onset of her daughter's puberty with anxiety and sorrow, but also with a tragic sense of inevitability and resignation as white men sexually use and then abandon them. Hearkening back to *Our Nig* as well as to many of the slave narratives and private writings of historic planter-class mistresses, there is little sisterhood of women that transcends racial lines— this is not Stowe's interracial sorority of compassion and maternity. Day to day, slaveholding and slave women work together harmoniously enough, but when financial crises arise, or when the mistress's husband begins pursuing a young black female "possession" on the plantation, slaves are sold without white women's remorse. Rather than covering cowardice or apathy in silence, as many white slaveholding women chose to do and as Morrison symbolically reflected in the silencing stroke of Mrs. Garner, Philomène claims silence as her stand against the unspeakable when her husband and mother are sold to pay for the white mistress's remarriage. Though both blacks and whites try to coax her back into speech, "there was nothing to say that anyone could bear to hear" (166). In the face of an economy that values black women as breeders and maids, even the kindest words offer no comfort, but rather "deliver a fist" (168).

In a key scene in *Cane River* that responds to a theology of whiteness witnessed throughout proslavery and plantation-romance texts, Philomène's grandmother Elizabeth attempts to calm her:

> "God will provide" [said Elizabeth].
> "I believe God will provide, too, *Mémere.* Just that sometimes He needs help to remember who to provide to."
> "I have always believed in your glimpsing [prophetic visions], child."
> "I am going to make it come true," Philomène said. (179) [11]

More akin to Harriet Wilson's Frado of *Our Nig* than to Stowe's Uncle Tom, Philomène reflects her skepticism of any slaveholders' God who requires reminding of just how to provide justice and basic provisions for the suffering, much less to assist a slave woman in fulfilling her visions. In this, Philomène will take aggressive action, not merely wait for favors from the divinity in whose church she was catechized alongside the white mistress who later sold Philomène's husband and daughter. Sexually, too, Philomène chooses to be nobody's passive victim, even in a world that legally offers her nothing more. Like the historical Harriet Jacobs, the fictional Philomène takes a white man as a lover for what little security she can grasp in a desperate situation.[12] Despite myriad interracial unions, most violent and involuntary, and despite an elite class of free, light-skinned, relatively well-to-do blacks, racial lines in *Cane River* remain penetrable but always present. Rather than seek to eradicate arbitrary racial categorizations, the mother-daughter generations of women in *Cane River* merely learn to negotiate racial crossings and work these treacherous navigations to their own advantage.

In Alice Randall's *Wind Done Gone,* a retelling of *Gone with the Wind,* the protagonist, Cynara, also takes economic and emotional refuge in a relationship with a white man—yet ultimately the plot disassembles the power and allure of whiteness, as Cynara's most significant relationships ultimately prove to be with other blacks. The white man who for years loves and financially supports her is none other than Rhett Butler. Having taught her in bed how to write, he has supplied Cynara with the very pen with which she is staking out her literary agency: Cynara uses her sexual power over him to gain her own voice, her own social power. The half sister of Scarlett—or Other, as Randall's narrator calls her, thus subverting the "othering" of white racisim—Cynara weaves a plantation narrative from the threads of her own and other slaves' experiences. Ashley Wilkes's plantation, Twelve Oaks, for instance, becomes in this racially revisionist novel Twelve Slaves Strong As Trees, since the house was constructed by slave labor—and Cynara cannot even recall the name whites used, consequently dismissing whites' labels as undeterminative, signifying nothing of import. In the end, in fact, whiteness itself vanishes like a vapor. By the final pages, it is not the white Rhett Butler's love that Cynara values, or that of her white father, whom she calls Planter (Mitchell's Mr. O'Hara). "I only did one great thing," the narrator announces. "I bore a little black baby and knew it was the best baby in the world," and it is precisely "a lifetime of hating Other [that] has made me fit for an eternity of loving her" (206, 114). Inverting antebellum whites' exploitation of black labor for their white economic and social gain, Randall casts the only benefit of whiteness in *Wind Done Gone* as its preparatory purposes for black fulfillment and contentment.

Systematically, Cynara chips away at whiteness plantation myths, particularly those of the captivating young belle, the saintly mistress, and the benevolent, lordly planter. The mistress, Mrs. O'Hara in *Gone with the Wind,* becomes "Lady" in *Wind Done Gone,* as if representative of the pedestaled Southern lady. Randall's Lady operates according to the romanticized script in her purity and religious devotion—to a farcical extreme: having been drunk each time she has conceived a child, and never having had sexual relations with her husband outside the conceptions, Lady becomes not the sacralized virginal-maternal figure of anti–Uncle Tom novels but a laughable Virgin Mary who, as the narrator indicts her, "like to pray, and . . . got her babies without ever knowing a man" (61, 28). Repeatedly, through such textual moves, Randall renders a theology of whiteness of the slaveholding class a mere joke, which all slaves recognize as such.

But at points, the damage done by a theology of whiteness is framed as far more serious, its personal and public effects far more destructive. Beginning to recognize the antebellum theopolitical social system for its capacity to enslave even outside the plantation venue, and for her own part in reinscribing its values, Cynara exposes the wealthy white Southern male as the slaveholders' true deity and recognizes her own obeisance to that point: "The Confederate and his quadroon. . . . I have let him be my God. He redeemed me and I have loved him for it. Where do I go, to go and sin no more?" (145). Significantly, the phrase to "go and sin no more," ascribed in John 8:1–11 to Jesus as he commands the release of the woman whom other men have caught in adultery, becomes in Randall a cry for release from the "sin" of capitulating to the potentially paralyzing worship of whiteness.

Wind Done Gone incisively reexamines perhaps one of the most vexed areas of the plantation romance, the profoundly problematic two-mother system. Just as anti–Uncle Tom women novelists position the mammy-mistress relationship as a key persuasive proslavery tool and therefore attempt to elevate and glorify the subservient maternity of the former and the unsullied refinement of the latter, Randall centers most of her narrative on Cynara's attempt to come to terms with the complicated dual mothering and lack of mothering during her own childhood. Cynara suffers throughout the book with believing that Other was the child whom Mammy truly loved, to the extent that Mammy consistently neglects her own daughter, Cynara, in favor of the white Other and even suggests that Cynara be sent to the Charleston auction block.[13] Yet Cynara eventually comes to terms with the atrocities of her personal past—and of the South's past. In addition to the most brutal oppressions of slavery regarding black women, Cynara recognizes how much damage the institution has done white women, not only in the infidelity of their husbands with slave women, but also, and perhaps more deleterious still, in taking from white mothers the privilege of nursing and caring for their offspring, and from white children the assurance that their primary caregiver, the mammy, genuinely loved them and had not merely obeyed plantation mores to nurture her white charges. Cynara observes keenly:

> I could see in Other's face the first moment it came to her the possibility that Mammy did for her not because she wanted to, but because she had to. Maybe Mammy loved her and maybe Mammy didn't. Slavery made it impossible for Other to know. "She who ain't free not to love, ain't free to love." (103)

As if in direct renunciation of the anti–Uncle Tom novels, Randall rewrites the deathbed-of-the-mammy scene to problematize any romanticized image of interracial harmony and of the one big black and white happy family. To her own mammy's deathbed, Cynara arrives too late, precisely because she has been emotionally disabled, conflicted by the cross-racial competing loyalties created by slavery.[14] First reconstructing, then deconstructing, the traditional mammy of plantation myth, Randall paints her black matriarch as fleshy, increasingly stout, and maternal—at least toward the white Other—but also as highly sexualized, volunteering her favors to Planter. Eventually, the text also reveals her as murderous, having quietly killed all the infant male offspring of Lady and Planter because, as another female slave defends her actions: " 'What would we a done with a sober white man on this place?' " (63). Randall criminalizes the enslaved female only to reverse the accusation: Mammy has only defended herself, her race, her gender, and her class, retroactively and proactively. The institution of slavery and its racial, gender, and class oppressions create an all-powerful position for wealthy white males, whose tyranny, the text suggests, invites violent opposition. Nonviolence, in fact, of the sort demonstrated by Stowe's Uncle Tom is less denigrated by *Wind Done Gone* than it is simply viewed as irrelevant, naïvely idealistic: "I read *Uncle Tom's Cabin*," Cynara observes early in her narrative. "I didn't see me in it. Un'cle Tom sounded just like Jesus to me, in costume. I don't want to go in disguise" (7). And it is this "disguise" that *Wind Done Gone* rejects as any step toward genuine social and racial reform. For Randall, change must come without pretense and passivity—or not at all.

All the texts considered in this chapter, as well as the nineteenth-century anti–Uncle Tom novels examined in earlier chapters, inform twenty-first-century moves toward racial reconciliation; *Beloved* in particular illustrates just how much is at stake. While few white Southerners today would defend slavery, many still defend the Confederate battle emblem embedded in state flags because it allegedly represents magnolias and mint juleps and the Southern "way of life" their great-grandfathers fought for: "Heritage, not Hate," the bumper stickers read. Charleston, South Carolina, is a case in point. The Carolinas' coastal jewel, Charleston is one of the most beautiful and historically well-preserved cities in the United States, and its race relations in some ways are exemplary. Since its seventeenth-century founding, Charleston has been an ethnically, racially, and religiously diverse seaport and cultural center. Yet while Gullah Tours wend their way past slave-insurrection instigator Denmark Vesey's birthplace, the former Charleston slave market, and the city workhouse where recalcitrant slaves were whipped, shackled, and collared, more lucrative tours dress their white guides in Confederate gray, post the "Stars and Bars" on the backs of horse-drawn buggies, and strike a wistful tone when speaking of the gracious lifestyle of planters' families.

More than 160 years later, no amount of polishing the plantation myth hides the disparities in income and opportunity for African Americans that remain the legacy of slavery. The novel *Our Nig* reminds us that this legacy extends to the presumably most enlightened regions of the United States—that American society, North and South, is shot through with the same race, gender, and class prejudices that held slavery intact for two hundred years and still permits aspects of its lethal, wealthy white male–privileging aftermath.

Many planter-class women despised the South's "peculiar institution" for a variety of reasons yet nevertheless performed a role of uneasy acquiescence. The often grim reality of the slave-based culture depicted by wealthy white women's journals and enslaved black women's narratives suggests it is no coincidence that most of the women anti–Uncle Tom writers did not own slaves. The women who lived amidst slave children's malnourishment, slave whippings, sexual assaults, legally invalid marriages, fractured parent-child relationships, coerced labor, and a thousand daily injustices often proved far from enthusiastic in slavery's defense. And even the women anti–Uncle Tom writers reveal their own anxieties and ambivalences about slavery in their texts and subtexts. Planter-class women, products of their own complicity, silently witnessed and enabled the systematic victimization of black women, men, and children. If they could possibly be cast as ignorant of slavery's brutal realities, it would be different. But their own private writings as well as the fictions written to laud them expose a system that held nothing sacred for a slave: not sexuality, not dignity, not motherhood. The children of the white antebellum Southern women—and men—of privilege and their children's children's children still have a price to pay for that conspiracy. Perhaps these things may be a beginning: acknowledging the daily privileges of this heritage; recognizing that polite, poignant expressions of white guilt unaccompanied by intentional social transformation never reverse injustice; and affirming that, as Fannie Lou Harner has taught us, the freedom of one race is always and everywhere "shackled in chains" to the freedom of another.[15]

NOTES

PREFACE

1. In this book, I examine the form—I would argue heresy—of Christianity preached by slaveholders as distinct from classical Christian understandings of human freedom, worth, and dignity.
2. Because of the racial epithet, I hesitated to tell this story. I finally chose to do so because it testifies to the ongoing impact of *Uncle Tom's Cabin,* and because, as Toni Morrison points out in *Playing in the Dark*, racism must be addressed with regard to its perpetrators as well as its targets.
3. Although slavery existed in the North until the late eighteenth century and many Northerners continued to profit from slavery later than that, race-based slavery became not only entrenched in the antebellum South's economy, but also a defining feature of the white South's much-touted "way of life." As some historians argue, the particular manifestation of slavery that evolved in the American South was unique among Western civilizations.

INTRODUCTION

1. Classical understandings of Christianity have never posited God as inherently male or female but rather beyond gender. The "Father" terminology in Christian scripture, for example, is intended to convey relationship and intimacy, not maleness per se, and the Hebrew (original language of the Jewish scriptures/ Old Testament) word for Holy Spirit is feminine, while the Greek (original language of the New Testament) word is neuter. Later chapters of this book examine feminine imagery for God in Hebrew and Christian scripture.
2. In the case against Samuel Green, the governor of Maryland pardoned the convicted man after two years, but only on the condition that he would leave the South. For a detailed discussion of the reception of *Uncle Tom's Cabin* in the South, see Thomas Gossett, Uncle Tom's Cabin *and American Culture.*
3. Though the coinage is mine, the concept that both pro- and antislavery proponents claimed scriptural and Constitutional authority has been explored by a number of prominent scholars. Eugene Genovese asserts that proslavery ad-

vocates saw themselves as—Genovese would say they *were*—the more careful biblical exegetes, and they insisted their hostility toward Northern abolitionists stemmed in part from what they perceived as Yankee liberalization of Trinitarian Christianity (personal conversations and public lecture, 3–5 November 1998, Wingate University, Wingate, N.C.). In his recently published book *The Theo-Political Imagination,* William Cavanaugh has coined the same term, although he seems to use it differently.

4.   On toleration as a stated goal of such writers, see, for example, the prefaces of Eastman's and Hentz's novels and Hale's *Liberia.*

5.   By my count, there are thirty-one anti–Uncle Tom novels. The count varies widely from scholar to scholar. For example, I exclude Mary E. Herndon's *Louise Elton; or, Things Seen and Heard,* which some include, because it seems to me not to fit into the anti–Uncle Tom category. I also exclude several anti–Uncle Tom poems, including "The Hireling and the Slave," and a children's story, *Little Eva: The Flower of the South,* because I focus on fiction targeted for adults. I include a novel by Caroline Gilman even though it was published before 1852 because it was republished as a direct rebuttal to Stowe, and it shares many characteristics with the other anti–Uncle Tom novels by women. For other lists of anti–Uncle Tom texts, see the *Uncle Tom's Cabin* Web site created by Stephen Railton at the University of Virginia, and Gossett, Uncle Tom's Cabin *and American Culture.* Gossett, for example, includes twenty-seven anti–Uncle Tom texts.

6.   Given the abundance of abolitionist material in the form of sermons, pamphlets, poems, and various nonfiction appeals, Stowe's use of the fictive form and its unprecedented social impact is intriguing in and of itself.

7.   Nearly half these authors were Northerners. For more information on authors' native regions, see Hayne and Gossett's list in the latter's Uncle Tom's Cabin *and American Culture* (430–31). Though they are not works of fiction and therefore not analyzed here, *Slavery in the Southern States* (1852) by "A Carolinian" and *Notes on Uncle Tom's Cabin being a Logical Answer to Its Allegations and Inferences against Slavery as an Institution* (1853) by E. J. Stearns merit inspection as intriguing examples of anti–Uncle Tom literature. Stearns, for example, in addition to squabbling with Stowe over translations of the Bible from Hebrew and Greek, takes issue with the Declaration of Independence and insists that "men" are in reality *not* born free. Although some scholars include Calvin Henderson Wiley among anti–Uncle Tom novelists, I do not.

8.   Latimer never specifically mentions Stowe or her novel. Interestingly, too, Latimer may not have intended to write a proslavery novel, though I would argue that is what she produced.

9.   Although *The Patent Key to Uncle Tom's Cabin; or, Mrs. Stowe in England* by "A Lady in New-York" is an extended poem and therefore not included in this book's purview, it contains blatant examples of theopolitical argumentation and a typically proslavery treatment of women's rights, and therefore invites further examination.

10. This number does not include Latimer, though I do examine characteristics of her work where relevant in Chapter 3. Categorizing her by region is even trickier than most: born to cosmopolitan parents, one American and one British, she was raised in London, Boston, and Baltimore. She spent her adult life in Maryland, a slaveholding state that did not join the Confederacy.

11. Focusing on the justice and compassion of God, God's particular concern for the economically disadvantaged, and the need to change social systems, not just engage in charity, liberation theology was formally conceived as such in Latin America, though adherents would point out that its basic concepts run throughout Jewish and Christian scripture.

12. Flanders, Gilman, Hale, Hentz, and Rush were native Northerners. Gilman and Hentz spent the majority of their adult years in the South. See Gossett, Uncle Tom's Cabin *and American Culture,* 430–31. South Carolinian Maria McIntosh moved away from the South in her early adulthood, as did Mary Howard Schoolcraft (in McIntosh's case because financial losses necessitated her living with her brother in New York; in Schoolcraft's case because of her marriage to an ethnologist who studied Native American culture).

13. Though these are not Catherine Clinton's words verbatim, this is her basic assertion. See particularly *The Plantation Mistress.*

14. See Gates's substantive introduction to *Our Nig,* which also provides important background on the author's life.

15. Carol Bleser also makes this point well in the introduction to the collection *In Joy and in Sorrow.*

16. In the North, Degler points to the Garrisonians as being genuinely concerned for the welfare of the slave; in the South, he singles out the Quakers.

CHAPTER 1

"To Woman . . . I Say Depart!"

1. To some extent, Stowe and her respondents also wrote within and against the slave-narrative tradition, as I will address more fully later. See Castronovo for a fascinating consideration of a "reverse" American literary genealogy, with slave narratives as the generative genre.

2. Carl Degler's *The Other South* is particularly incisive on the rise and subsequent suppression of the South's antislavery groups and individuals before 1830.

3. See Yellin (*Intricate Knot* 19–29) and Susan Tracy (47–63). Though the two scholars differ in their perspectives on just how critical George Tucker was of slavery in his writing and his own life, both Yellin and Tracy contribute significantly to interpreting Tucker's work. See also Ritchie Devon Watson Jr., who observes in Tucker the very "tensions and unresolved conflicts which eventually split the nation" (79), and Lucinda H. MacKethan's "Domesticity in Dixie."

4. See Yellin and Tracy for important insights and background on *Swallow Barn.*

5. I am indebted to Yellin's research for initially pointing me to the discrepancy between the two editions of *Swallow Barn*.

6. Although as MacKethan points out, even in the later edition Kennedy allows such characters as the slave mother Lucy, mad with grief over the loss of her child, to create "an unsettling conclusion to [his] pastoral idyll" (231).

7. See, for example, Sewell's *The Selling of Joseph* (1700), discussed by Gaines (30).

8. Complete lists of anti–Uncle Tom novels by men and women appear in the introduction.

9. Simms's later work in particular is unequivocally proslavery, and he wrote disparagingly of Stowe. After the 1852 publication of his novel *Woodcraft,* he announced that he did indeed intend it as a response to *Uncle Tom's Cabin.*

10. In all, Simms wrote more than eighty books and, viewing himself as a Southern man of letters, collected an impressive personal library. He expressed his frustration, however, with the antebellum South's dearth of literary culture, in an 1847 letter to his friend James Henry Hammond: "Here I am nothing and can be and do nothing. The South don't care a d--n for literature or art. Your best neighbor and kindred never think to buy books. They will borrow from you and beg, but the same man who will always have his wine, has no idea of a library. You will write for and defend their institutions in vain. They will not pay the expense of printing your essays" (December 24, 1847, 65). Oliphat, Mary C. Simms, Alfred Taylor Odell and T. C. Ducan Eaves, eds. *The Letters of William Gilmore Simms*. Columbia: Univ. of South Carolina Press, 1952-82 (6 vols.).

11. In *The Dispossessed Garden,* Simpson interestingly explores this redemption, though his proposal that Tom functions as priest in the eucharistic union of master and slave works less well (59).

12. See, for instance, *The Planter* (11) and *The Slaveholder Abroad* (463).

13. Ritchie Devon Watson Jr. interestingly analyzes the South's (by which he means primarily white Southerners') early and ongoing enthusiasm for historical romances, idealistic reconstructions "of what that past might have been or ought to have been" (ix). And ironically, though Simms inveighed against the South's cultural stagnation, he made his living by writing in a genre considered outdated among literary circles in other parts of the United States.

14. Watson and Michel Kreyling offer intriguing examinations of the cavalier figure as it appears in the fiction of male antebellum authors such as Tucker and Simms.

15. Lucinda H. MacKethan's "Domesticity in Dixie" is especially insightful regarding Widow Eveleigh, noting that she "masters the values of the marketplace" and "takes the field, using men's language and men's arguments to fight for the first of all patriarchal values—her rightful ownership of property" (235–36).

16. *Emancipator* was no doubt a play on Garrison's *Liberator.*

17. Wyatt-Brown analyzes the plantation South's code of honor as a kind of theology, "a set of prescriptions endowed with an almost sacred symbolism" (*Honor and Violence* 15).

18. In the anti–Uncle Tom novel *The Sable Cloud* by Nehemiah Adams, a Southern planter's wife cries, in a pattern similar to Annie Mildmay's: "I believe I am the only slave on the premises. I am sure that no one but myself is watching for a chance for escape. I would run away from these people if I could. But what shall I do with them? I am not willing to sell them, for when I have hinted at leaving, there is such entreaty for me to remain, and such demonstrations of affection and attachment, that I give it up. . . . It is the Negroes who are a curse, not their slavery" (65–66). Adams, a Boston clergyman, had earlier infuriated some of his parishioners with his nonfictional *A South-side View of Slavery; or Three Months at the South*.

19. For historical examples of white Southern women's complaints of their own "slavery" and the burden on them represented by their slaves, see Chapter 4.

20. Dueling also appears, with the narrator expressing some disapproval, in James Hungerford's anti–Uncle Tom novel *The Old Plantation*, in which female characters function only as kind mothers and objects of male conquests.

21. While Thorpe is the more obviously gloomy of the plantation-tradition writers, Wyatt-Brown insightfully examines elements of despair and despondency in Tucker and Simms.

22. Mary Howard Schoolcraft's *Black Gauntlet*, examined later, contains similar reasoning regarding Africans' alleged savagery, though with the significant theological difference that Schoolcraft frames the Middle Passage as having been, in retrospect, a missionary effort.

23. Often the abolitionist characters of anti–Uncle Tom fiction are not only racially bigoted but also adulterous and lecherous, as is Alfred Orton of Mathews's *Old Toney and His Master.* See also Flanders's *Ebony Idol* and Cowdin's *Ellen*, analyzed in Chapter 2. The anonymous author of *Yankee Slave-Dealer* similarly inveighs against Northern hypocrisy and abolitionist agitation. He concedes that the slavery depicted in *Uncle Tom's Cabin* is indeed horrific, but that Stowe has not "faithfully portrayed" her subject (328).

24. In *Frank Freeman's Barber Shop*, Baynard Hall employs the image of the mammy devoted to her white charges as a primary defense of slavery: "Meet a bear robbed of her whelps; but attempt not to tear away the white babes from the black woman's heart! She would rend you, as if she were a raving maniac! And true it is, that usually the foster children love their black mothers almost like their white (15). As in *The Cabin and the Parlor*, slaves are more like wild animals or faithful pets than like humans.

25. Similarly, in Joseph Baldwin's *Samuel Hele, Esq.*, a Yankee schoolmistress, upon arriving in a small Southern town, dares not only to earn her own living but also to form her own political opinions, which leads her to funnel information to Harriet Beecher Stowe and, the narrator insists, to "double-sex" and "unsex" herself simultaneously (292). I am indebted to Stephen Railton's excellent Web site on *Uncle Tom's Cabin*, which led me to this text.

26. Tracy's *In the Master's Eye* offers trenchant insights regarding how proslavery narratives attempt to disguise social atrocities with paternalism (e.g., 7).

27. For a chillingly cheerful account of a slave auction, see Ingraham's depiction of a Natchez sale quoted in Rose, *A Documentary History* 164–67.

28. Hale's *Liberia* and McIntosh's *The Lofty and the Lowly,* for example, are particularly well written. Hale was a Northerner and McIntosh a Southerner who as an adult settled in the North.

CHAPTER 2

Sanctified by Wealth and Whiteness

1. Scholars commonly use the terms "domestic" and "sentimental" fiction interchangeably.

2. Of the three authors most closely examined in this chapter, Rush and Flanders are Northerners and Cowdin is a Southerner. Of the three, Northerner Rush may well be the most virulently racist—though it is a difficult call, given the extraordinary bigotry of all three.

3. "One reason religion was valued," Welter propounds, "was that it did not take a woman away from her 'proper sphere,' her home," leaving the markets and legislatures, domains of competitive force and aggression and real societal power, to men ("The Cult of True Womanhood" 152–53). See also Welter's *Dimity Convictions* (esp. 87) and Alexander Cowie, who claims nineteenth-century domestic novels functioned as morality police.

4. One key factor that motivated Stowe in writing *Uncle Tom's Cabin* was the death of one of her seven children, Charley, which, she said, led her to contemplate slave women's being forcibly separated from their own children. "In those depths of sorrow which seemed to me immeasurable," she wrote to her husband, "it was my only prayer to God that such anguish might not be suffered in vain. . . . I felt that I could never be consoled for it, unless this crushing of my own heart might enable me to work out some great good to others" (C. E. Stowe 123). In a letter to the Earl of Shaftesbury, Stowe insisted: " 'I wrote what I did because as a woman, as a mother, I was oppressed and broken-hearted with the sorrows and injustice I saw' " (qtd. in Gossett, Uncle Tom's Cabin *and American Culture* 52).

5. For more recent perspectives on what Mary Kelley has termed "literary domesticity," see the essays in Samuels, *Culture of Sentiment*; Kaplan, "Manifest Domesticity"; and Brown, *Domestic Individualism.*

6. See, for example, Carmen Manuel Cuenca, who argues that Eulalia, the central female character of Hentz's *Planter's Northern Bride,* is the reconciler of racial and regional divisions, and that Hentz "tries to undermine a patriarchal system and restore the basis of democratic America with an idealization of women's role" (91). Elizabeth Moss wrongly contends that domestic fiction, including that of Hentz and McIntosh, two anti–Uncle Tom writers, provided "female readers

means and motivation to transcend the bounds of culturally prescribed woman-hood" (3).

7. Because slaveholders self-consciously attempted to model themselves and their precapitalist society after ancient Greece and the Roman republic, as seen in their naming slaves Cato, Cicero, and Caesar, Clinton suggests the term "penarchy," a deliberate bastardization that mixes Latin and Greek and also highlights the profoundly sexualized nature of Southern slavery ("Sex and Sectional Conflict" 44).

8. Wilson herself, daughter of a prestigious, socially prominent family, provides a particularly paradoxical figure, insisting as she did upon female inferiority even while displaying her own formidable intellect and literary talents.

9. See particularly Bynum, *Jesus as Mother,* but also Lerner, *Creation,* and Wacker.

10. Attending a graduate seminar with Elizabeth Ammons and later reading her essays on Stowe first led me to consider what Ammons calls "the odd equation of mothers/Eva/Tom, an equation which, if followed through to its logical con-clusion, argues the radical substitution of feminine and maternal for masculine values" ("Heroines" 163). From there, I began making connections with feminist theology's assertions and examining the rebuttals to Stowe for similar theological themes.

11. See *Living Female Writers of the South* 30. Between 1840 and the 1870s, Dupuy published two dozen serialized gothic novels. Her financial stability suffered heavily, though, from the failure of her publisher and the loss of her copyrights.

12. See, for example, *The Curse of Clifton,* in which one subplot highlights Hortense Armstrong's jealousy of her daughter's affection for the girl's father and for a mulatto slave.

13. Herself a fitting subject for sentimental novels, Cutler suffered, while still a child, the loss of her mother and later, the death of her lover. While Cutler was giving a literary reading, her dress caught fire and the member of the audience who leapt to her assistance visited her regularly as she convalesced from her burns. When fully recovered, she married him.

14. Relatively new to fiction writing, Rush had published her first novel only two years earlier, in 1850.

15. "Misdirection" is the stage magician's term for using seemingly well-motivated gestures to direct the audience's attention away from the crucial action.

16. Many antebellum Southerners, witnessing New England's most prominent Protes-tant pulpits being filled by a new breed of Harvard-trained Unitarian ministers, viewed themselves as the true defenders of orthodox Christianity.

17. See Harris, "Whiteness as Property," and the other essays in *Critical Race Theory: The Key Writings that Formed the Movement.*

18. Morrison in *Playing in the Dark* uses the term "fetishization" and explores the concept as a racial strategy of white culture to assert categorical absolutisms (see esp. 68).

19. See Gossett, *Race* 15, 48–50, for quote from White and discussions of White and the reactions of the scientific and religious communities in general to mono- versus polygenics. Institutional Christianity has traditionally repudiated the idea of separate origin of races. The Catholic Church so strongly opposed polygenics that its authorities burned two advocates of the theory, Vanini and Bruno, at the stake.

20. Morrison discusses the racialized "fear of merging" (*Playing in the Dark* 67).

21. Ironically, political interests drove the slaveholding South to argue that slaves should be counted as whole persons, implying their full humanity if not their equality, while the "free" North argued for a subhuman accounting, quantifying enslaved persons in fractions.

22. In "Incidents in the Life of a White Woman," Castronovo suggests that the flow of exchange in antebellum literature moves from slave narrative to the proslavery sentimentalists' manipulating the fugitive tale to highlight white women's alleged sufferings, so that the plantation narratives are the dependent genre, not the other way around as is often assumed.

23. Chestnut, *Diary* March 14, 1861. See also Clinton, *Plantation Mistress,* and Fox-Genovese, *Within the Plantation Household,* both of which explore self-pity among planter-class women.

24. Born in Boston but spending the majority of her adult life in Charleston, South Carolina, Gilman's loyalties were initially divided, though by the Civil War she consistently sympathized with the South. Like Stowe, Gilman had borne seven children and suffered the death of a child. Of Gilman's children, in fact, only four survived to adulthood.

25. In *Gothic America,* see particularly Goddu's incisive discussion of Stowe and Har- riet Jacobs, their literary and interpersonal relationship, and their very different uses of the gothic.

26. On the issue of voyeuristic pleasure, see, for example, Lori Merish's handling of *Uncle Tom's Cabin* in *Sentimental Materialism,* as well as her assessment of other scholars' weighing in on this topic, such as Saidiya Hartman (esp. 152–63). See Goddu for her extended argument that gothic American literature has not been merely escapist but deeply engaged with historical concerns.

27. The Harleys had originally been rich, accounting for their sophistication and for the text's deeming them worthy of compassion.

28. See, for example, Chestnut, *Diary*, March 14, 1861, and also the fourth chapter of this book.

29. On such foreignness and defending borders, see Amy Kaplan's "Manifest Domes- ticity."

30. For example, Thomas Jefferson's *Notes on Virginia* (1786) depicts black males as "more ardent after their female" than the more reasoned, reflective white male. See Gossett, *Race* (42).

31. For Kaplan's observations, see the introduction to Kaplan and Pease, *Cultures of United States Imperialism.*

32. In a similar pattern, Tryphena Blanche Holder Fox moved from Massachusetts in 1852 as a governess to a Mississippi planter's children. Responsible for financially supporting her mother and siblings in New England, Fox married her employer, on whom she was economically dependent. Fox apparently never spoke out against slavery. See the compilation of her letters, *A Northern Woman in the Plantation South*. Fox's experience demonstrates the inextricability of racial, economic, and gender concerns.

33. See Scott, Bleser, Clinton's *Plantation Mistress*, and Fox-Genovese's *Within the Plantation Household* for examinations of slavery's damage to slaveholding families. Liberation theology and womanist theology both address the oppressors' ultimately suffering from perpetuating oppression, one reason some liberation theologians advocate violence if necessary as a means of "loving" oppressors by disallowing their oppression. See the work of Latin American liberation theologian Gustavo Gutierez, black liberation theologian James Cone, and womanist theologian Delores S. Williams.

34. Feminist theologian Sallie McFague examines how exclusively patriarchal language for and imaging of God promote social constructions of race, class, and gender that favor affluent white men.

35. See Higginbotham for a discussion of the metonymic identification of African Americans with welfare, drugs, and urban violence. She also explores domestic novels' calling upon "womanhood" but failing to see white women's complicity in limiting whom womanhood's definition includes (94–95).

36. Stowe herself hints at Eva as allegorical being (1:126).

37. Eva proclaims: " 'The time is coming that I am going to leave you' " (2:240); " 'It's only a little while I shall be with you' " (2:245); " 'I am going to leave you. In a few more weeks, you will see me no more' " (2:251). " 'I've felt that I would be glad to die,' " Eva insists, " 'if my dying could stop all this misery. I *would die* for them, Tom, if I could' " (2:240). The Gospel of John, known as the Evangelist, presents Jesus as saying: "I am going there to prepare a place for you. . . . In a little while you will see me no more." (14:2, 16:16).

38. For a compelling journey through various theological assessments of Eve over the centuries, see Gerda Lerner's chapter "One Thousand Years of Feminist Bible Criticism" in *The Creation of American Feminist Consciousness*. On Stowe's mother-savior imagery, see Ammons, "Heroines" and "Stowe's Dream."

39. E.D.E.N. Southworth, for example, often features strong female characters finally victorious after having been abandoned or betrayed by an unreliable or deceitful man.

40. On twenty-first-century white feminism's myopia, see, for example, the work of feminist bell hooks and womanist theologian Delores S. Williams.

41. See, for example, Lora Romero's *Home Fronts* for Stowe as a critic of middle-class women's oppression.

42. On the implications of Stowe's white maternity as a foundation that implies white ownership, see, for example, Merish, *Sentimental Materialism* (esp. 154).

43. The story in Matthew references an Old Testament prophecy, Jer. 31:15.

44. See Higginbotham's analysis of *State of Missouri v. Celia,* in which a female slave was denied what Missouri statutes had defined as woman's right to resist unwanted sexual advances: essentially, she was deemed not a woman (97–98).

45. The Northerner Flanders replicates the social scare tactic of Southerner William Gilmore Simms, who in his review of *A Key to Uncle Tom's Cabin* suggested Stowe's "perpetual bedfellowship" with her black character George Harris for depicting him as handsome (223, 229). I am indebted to Gossett's Uncle Tom's Cabin *and American Culture* for leading me to this quote.

46. Some nineteenth-century abolitionists themselves feared amalgamation. Harriet Beecher Stowe's father, renowned Congregational minister Lyman Beecher, insisted that such social intermingling as Theodore Weld advocated in Cincinnati would encourage mongrelization, while evangelical reformer Lewis Tappan countered with his calm, apparently cheerful assumption that blending of the races was inevitable and that eventually neither truly black nor truly white skin would exist. See Wyatt-Brown, *Lewis Tappan* (esp. 177).

47. See *Playing in the Dark* for Morrison's take on such white anxieties, e.g., 51–53.

48. See John 1:4–9, which refers to Christ's relationship to John the Baptist and echoes Isaiah 9:2: "The people walking in darkness have seen a great light."

49. Higginbotham explores race as it "came to life primarily as the signifier of the master/slave relation" and attempts to decode the "metalanguage" of race, which M. M. Bakhtin calls "the power of the word to mean" (Higginbotham 96–97; Bakhtin, *The Dialogic Imagination* 352).

50. Again, Merish's insights apply: that just as Stowe signifies civilization in her characters' proper housekeeping, so, I would argue, Flanders pronounces tenement owner Hugh Jackson unfit for polite society and incapable of handling freedom by highlighting the squalor of his building and his own living quarters.

51. See John 20:11–18, in which Mary Magdalene mourns, "They have taken my Lord, and I do not know where they have laid him."

52. See Tompkins (*Sensational Designs* and *"UTC"*) and Ammons ("Heroines" and "Stowe's Dream").

53. The sisterhood of women working together for change that Stowe envisions in *Uncle Tom's Cabin* (the Quaker women, Cassy and Emmeline, Aunt Chloe and Mrs. Shelby) reflects the novel's creation: Stowe was able to write with five children and one on the way only by her sister Catherine Beecher's giving a year of her life to care for the Stowe household.

54. When Yellin discerns a "note of hysteria" in *Uncle Tom's Cabin* and argues that at stake is not just political or economic manumission but the "salvation of the immortal soul" (135), she exhibits antifeminism herself, for her detection of "hysteria" implyies a weak, irrational, stereotypically female response to trivialities.

55. For a trenchant discussion of the "idea of the black Christ," see Sundquist's *To Wake the Nations,* in which he examines resistance and salvation as linked in the

black experience. Resonances of black Christ imagery have appeared throughout literature in the past two millennia. Langston Hughes's "Christ in Alabama" presents an interesting example: "Christ is a Nigger,/ Beaten and black—/ *O, bare your back.*/ Mary is His Mother—/ *Mammy of the South,/ Silence your mouth.*/ God's His Father—/ *White Master above,/ Grant us your love.*/ Most holy bastard/ Of the bleeding mouth:/ *Nigger Christ/ On the cross of the South.* Images of the female or specifically maternal Christ appear throughout the Christian tradition, as seen in the medieval mystic Julian of Norwich.

56. On Tom as the feminized black Christ, see Ammons, "Heroines." In his essay "The Racial Factor in the Shaping of Religion in America," C. Eric Lincoln asserts that African slaves who embraced the Christianity of their masters were not embracing their master's racial hierarchies—quite the contrary, in fact: "The strategy of American Christianity failed in its effort to make black Christians a class of spiritual subordinates in concert. For, in accepting Christianity in America, the Africans were not necessarily accepting American Christianity. The God they addressed and the faith they knew transcended the American experience" (185).

57. George Fitzhugh was among antebellum male proslavery apologists who recognized how crucial the subordination of white Southern females was to the patriarchal authority that maintained slavery. Susan V. Donaldson and Anne Goodwyn Jones address Fitzhugh's views in "Haunted Bodies" (2).

CHAPTER 3

Justified by Mother's Milk

1. In this book's final chapter, I analyze the twenty-first-century response to *Gone with the Wind,* Alice Randall's *Wind Done Gone,* in which a mammy's devotion to a white child relative to her own daughter highlights, by contrast, the horrors of slavery.

2. See Susan Tracy on the black mammy as bridge between white and black worlds (117); Braxton on "outraged motherhood" (19); and Collins on the female slave's "motherwork," challenging social constructions of family and work as separate spheres, and "othermothering," caring for other children besides her own, which often augments her power in the plantation hierarchy (59).

3. In their groundbreaking studies on antebellum Southern women, Anne Firor Scott, Elizabeth Fox-Genovese, and Catherine Clinton each explores whether or not the plantation mistress was actually an ameliorating influence on slavery. I would contend that some white planter-class women did at least attempt to soften some of the harsher aspects of slavery, but that this very "softening" contributed to slavery's perpetuation, since slaveholders could delude themselves that most slaves were treated kindly.

4. Catherine Clinton explores the idea of the mammy and what she terms the "Lady" as obverse images of one another (see, e.g., *The Plantation Mistress* 200–206).

5. See Ruth Frankenberg's *White Women, Race Matters* on power-evasive construc-

tions and Patricia Morton's *Disfigured Images* on the mammy figure as a signifier of the Southern elite's "right to rule" (35).

6. Thomas Jefferson reflected this view in observing that "never yet could I find a black had uttered a thought above the level of plain narration; never saw even an elementary trait of painting or sculpture." "Religion has produced a Phyllis Wheatley," he wrote, "but it could not produce a poet. The compositions published under her name are below the dignity of criticism" (140).

7. The civil rights movement in the twentieth-century South provides another complex example of Christianity's being embraced by both white bigots and black and white reformers—the reformers often choosing to meet and rally their supporters in churches. For a remarkably multilayered analysis of how Christianity operated in the slaveholding South, both for the owners and the slaves themselves, and how "even this diluted and perverted Protestantism lent itself, in various subtle but discernible ways, to the creation of a protonational black consciousness," see Genovese, *Roll, Jordan, Roll* (esp. 159–284).

8. While Genovese is clearly employing the term "Uncle Tom" in the pejorative sense it has come to connote, I take issue with its use here as synonymous with absolute obedience, since Stowe's depiction of Tom actually illustrates Genovese's point: that though irritatingly tolerant of whites' machinations, Tom's religious beliefs also motivate his ultimate subversion of white authority.

9. Genovese has analyzed slave mother-child relationships in *Roll, Jordan, Roll* and has surmised that the few cases in which a slave mother might actually have appeared less than passionately devoted to her offspring could easily be attributed to any number of factors, including the possibility of her having been raped, her own perpetual physical exhaustion, and a "self protective hardening of parents' attitudes toward their children, reinforced under slavery by fear of sale" (496). All of these, of course, undermine the proslavery argument for slavery as a beneficent institution.

10. As examined in this book's final chapter, Randall's *Wind Done Gone* emphasizes this particular intersection of the maternal and the sexual, especially regarding male slaveholders and their relationships with their families' mammies.

11. See Higginbotham on the ability of race to subsume other sets of social relations (95). See Morrison's *Playing in the Dark* on reifying whiteness and Takaki's *A Different Mirror* on reinforcing racial borders.

12. And of the one-fourth of the white population who were slave owners themselves or part of a slaveholding family, 88 percent had five slaves or fewer, meaning that the majority of slaveholders were yeomen farmers, not gentry (Franklin, *From Slavery to Freedom* 186). See also Takaki's *A Different Mirror* for percentages of Southern slaveholders (113). Both Takaki and Haney-Lopez, in *White by Law*, examine slaveholders' strategies for creating unity among Southern whites. Takaki argues that land-owning white colonists in the mid–seventeenth century who were having increasing difficulty controlling white laborers made a clear decision, whether conscious or not, to favor slave laborers, politically powerless

and denied the right to bear arms, so that planters could maintain both racial and class hegemony (see, e.g., 51–67).

13. Samuel Eliot Morrison's 1927 *Oxford History of the United States* reflects this utilitarian view of black women: "Negro wenches on cotton plantations were such poor breeders that the labor supply had to be replenished by purchase" (Morton, *Disfigured Images* 30).

14. In "Groundings with My Sisters," Manning Marable discusses slaveholders' sexual license with female slaves, promotion of promiscuity, and slave "breeding" practices.

15. According to Herbert Gutman. See Marable 408.

16. Arthur W. Calhoun's *A Social History of the American Family from Colonial Times to the Present* (Cleveland: Arthur H. Clark, 1917–1919) reflects this view, claiming that slavery destroyed maternal solicitude among blacks (see Morton, *Disfigured Images* 30).

17. In *White by Law*, Ian Haney-Lopez explores this property-versus-humanity tension that was present from the democracy's beginning. See also Morrison, *Playing in the Dark* 56.

18. Interestingly, given Schoolcraft's vitriolic tirades against Africans' alleged savagery, her husband was a respected explorer and ethnologist whose first wife of almost twenty years was a part-Chippewa woman who embraced Native American culture and passed this respect for her heritage to her children, who after her death became Mary Howard Schoolcraft's stepchildren.

19. When David Walker's 1829 "Appeal to the Colored Citizens of the World" made similar accusations of white savagery, even radical abolitionists such as William Lloyd Garrison condemned the declaration as inflammatory. Walker, a free black born in North Carolina who moved to Boston as an adult, died under mysterious circumstances the following year. See Takaki, *A Different Mirror* 106–11.

20. Frankenberg's *White Women, Race Matters* analyzes case studies that illustrate maintenance of the racial order and location of privilege in whiteness (e.g., 242).

21. "The sense of difference defined in popular usage of the term 'race,'" Gates asserts, "has both described and inscribed difference of language, belief system, artistic tradition, and gene pool, as well as all sorts of supposedly natural attributes such as rhythm, athletic ability, cerebration, usury, fidelity, and so forth. The relation between 'racial character' and these sorts of characteristics has been inscribed through tropes of race" (*"Race," Writing, and Difference* 5).

22. Though originally published in 1838, prior to the publication of *Uncle Tom's Cabin* and therefore not technically an anti–Uncle Tom novel, *Recollections* was republished as an answering shot to Stowe and shares many key characteristics with Stowe's direct detractors, making it worthy of consideration here.

23. A secondary character in Lalita Tademy's *Cane River*, examined in this book's final chapter, is also a mute slave woman; her sufferings bear comparison to Bella's, and both these bear comparison to the *choice* of white slaveholding women to remain mute in the face of atrocity.

24. See the work of Nell Irvin Painter, particularly "Soul Murder and Slavery."

25. See MacKethan's analysis of *Recollections* in "Domesticity in Dixie" 231–34.

26. In her novel *Beloved* (discussed in this book's conclusion), Toni Morrison explores a black mother's decision to take her own children's lives rather than allow them to live under slavery.

27. Hentz's life history was remarkably similar to Stowe's. Both lived in the Cincinnati vicinity during the same period and belonged to the same literary society there. Both were married to academic men who made little money in their professions. Both suffered the death of at least one child, and both became the primary income producers for their families.

28. In *The Devil's Lane: Sex and Race in the Early South*, editors Catherine Clinton and Michele Gillespie examine how early America negotiated complex social relations.

29. Not until the eighteenth century did Maryland finally conform to *partus sequitur ventrem*.

30. Latimer herself is hard to classify regionally. Born in London, she was raised in England, Boston, Virginia, and France and spent her adult life writing and raising three children in Baltimore.

31. Stowe's Northern character Ophelia is also antislavery and afraid to touch non-whites.

32. Phyllis Marynick Palmer's "White Women/Black Women" explores the historical tensions between black and white women. Catherine Clinton has shown that white Southern men, frightened by Northern examples like Abby Kelly and Lucretia Mott, generally considered white Southern women too "soft" on the slave issue. Many white Southern women seem to have "hardened" in their views as they grew older. Clinton notes that while younger planter-class women tend to complain in their letters and diaries about slavery, the older, more experienced mistresses complain about the slaves themselves. See *The Plantation Mistress* 182–85.

33. For an insightful examination of the function of the gothic in American literature, see Teresa A. Goddu's *Gothic America*.

34. One of the nineteenth century's leading proponents of monogenics, the theory that all races originated as one, was a Charleston, South Carolina, slaveholder and Lutheran clergyman, John Bachman, who, apparently to help stabilize the logical precariousness of his position, also cited the theologically specious Hamitic curse to defend the enforced subservience of blacks. Ironically, Bachman's primary opponent, Philadelphia physician Samuel George Morton, and most of the scientific community of the 1850s argued for polygenics, separate species among the races—which would have been a far more useful view to promote the justice of one race's owning and treating another as a lower form of life. Most Southerners, however, considered polygenics inconsistent with both primary biblical accounts in Genesis 1 and 2 of the origins of humanity—which greatly complicated proslavery defenders' rhetorical task. See Gossett, *Race* 58–64.

35. In *Slavery: History and Historians,* Peter Parish evaluates the paradoxes and contradictions of antebellum Southern society. Parish's work is flawed, however, in neglecting some of the leading women Southern historians—Fox-Genovese and Clinton, for instance.

36. For an intriguing analysis of the ideal plantation "patriarch" as seen in characters of different genders, see Lucinda MacKethan's comparison of the male writer Simms and the female writer Hentz and the protagonists of their anti–Uncle Tom novels.

37. Hentz herself was apparently beautiful. Her perpetually jealous husband challenged several men to duels. The Hentzes' frequent moves—five Southern states in twenty years—may have been partly related to this.

38. "Guilt over miscegenation," Jacquelyn Hall notes, "and undercurrents of female discontent reinforced a pervasive uneasiness about the loyalty of white women to the peculiar institution" (20).

39. Recalling Christ's prayer before his arrest and crucifixion: "Father, if you are willing, take this cup from me; yet not my will, but yours be done" (Luke 22:42).

40. His dream reflects the Old Testament messianic prophecy in Isaiah, quoted by Christ in New Testament reference to himself: "The Lord has anointed me to preach good news to the poor. He has sent me to bind up the brokenhearted, to proclaim freedom for the captives and release from darkness for the prisoners" (Isa. 61:1 and Luke 4:18).

41. Yet in her own married life, Hentz first supplemented and then from 1854 on earned the primary family income with her writing.

42. For comparative analysis of Hentz's other novels, see Baym's *Woman's Fiction.*

43. Minrose Gwin has observed: "Just as black women were forced to be strong, white Southern women often were compelled to appear weak" (*Black and White Women* 4).

44. Matthew 26:39–42 depicts Christ praying, "Let this cup pass from me" and later, "If this cannot pass unless I drink it, your will be done."

45. Hazel Carby examines this depiction of black women in fiction (see, e.g., *Reconstructing Womanhood* 168).

46. Pointing to Richard Wright's *Black Boy* and Ralph Ellison's *Invisible Man,* Donaldson and Jones examine "how white understanding of blackness excludes African American males from any aspiration to visible manhood" (3).

47. Reflecting the perpetuation of the "good mammy" stereotype, Georgia's Black Mammy Memorial Association, established in 1910, began soliciting support for a vocational school modeled after Booker T. Washington's Tuskegee Institute. Students would be trained to perform menial tasks in the service of whites (Morton, *Disfigured Images* 35).

48. Another defender of colonization as the only viable alternative for free people of color to flourish, Louisiana planter John McDonough allowed his slaves to work themselves out of slavery but then required their removal to Liberia. At least one of his former slave emigrés exchanged affectionate letters with McDonough that

confirmed Liberia as a place of unequaled liberty for former slaves. See Arthur G. Nuhrah, "John McDonough: Man of Many Facets," *Louisiana Historical Quarterly* 33 (1950): 125–26.

49. Though Hale's reasons for supporting colonization of Liberia may have stemmed, like Stowe's, from genuine concern for the continued oppression of freed slaves who remained in the United States, many who supported that cause did so for less altruistic reasons. In her diary, Keziah Goodwyn Hopkins Brevard records: "I wish the Abolitionists & the negroes had a country to themselves & we who are desirous to practice *truth and love to God were to ourselves*" (January 22, 1861). Both Anne Firor Scott and Elizabeth Fox-Genovese deal with Brevard, a fascinating study in human complexity. See, for example, Fox-Genovese, *Within the Plantation Household* 365–66.

50. On Northern riots and discrimination, see, for example, Takaki, *A Different Mirror* 106–10.

51. See Morrison's *Playing in the Dark* for her perspectives on policing narratives.

52. The primary tenet of classic Christian theology maintains that God loves *first* and without regard to any behavior, appearance, or character trait, precisely the opposite of Janet's God, who "will not take care of you and love you, unless . . ."

53. Elizabeth Ammons explores the term "patriarchal plantation" and its being used synonymously with slavery. She also discusses Stowe's use "in provocative ways" of the terms "patriarch," "patriarchal," and "antipatriarchal" ("Heroines" 174n).

54. Elizabeth Ammons has shown this dynamic in Stowe in "Heroines" and "Stowe's Dream."

55. See Sundquist's introduction to *New Essays* and Stepto's chapter in *New Essays on Uncle Tom's Cabin*.

CHAPTER 4

The Background that Belies the Myth

1. In the Southern Historical Collection's archives at the University of North Carolina, Chapel Hill, where many of these writings are filed, I followed the pioneering paths of historians such as Catherine Clinton, Elizabeth Fox-Genovese, and Anne Firor Scott, and also wandered on my own.

2. Black female characters in anti–Uncle Tom novels by men do sometimes explicitly appear as oppressed (see Chapter 1). This is rare, however, in anti–Uncle Tom literature by men and almost nonexistent in that by women.

3. Personal conversations, November 3–5, 1998, at Wingate University, when Fox-Genovese was a visiting lecturer on campus.

4. See *A Diary from Dixie* and *Mary Chestnut's Civil War*, esp. 245–46 of the latter. Repeatedly, too, Chestnut comments upon her husband's and her in-laws' losing money on their plantations, and she often suggests that most Southerners, particularly women, would gladly do away with slavery immediately if they knew how. During the Civil War, she scoffed at the assumption that the South

was fighting for slavery: "Can that be, when not one-third of our volunteer army are slave-owners—and not one-third of that third who does not dislike slavery as much as Mrs. Stowe or Greeley. And few have found their hatred or love of it as remunerative an investment" (*A Diary from Dixie* August 18, 1861).

5. Kemble, her opposition to slavery, and her marital and maternal fate are discussed later in this chapter. Sarah Grimké never married; Angelina Grimké, after relocating to the North, married and had children with Theodore Weld, an ardent abolitionist. The Grimkés are also addressed later in this chapter.

6. See particularly Clinton, *The Plantation Mistress* 196, which includes the quote. Clinton's work, especially, persuaded me of this pattern from outrage or distress to apathy or complacency. I must admit my own initial resistance to this trajectory—perhaps because I wanted to "excuse" white Southern women by virtue of their having been also victims of a cruel system. Perhaps I wanted to view white Southern women as legally, economically, and socially trapped, as having no real choices. Certainly, as Kemble's loss of custody of her own children shows, the consequences of white women's opposition could be unspeakably severe. Yet, as the Grimkés' lives manifest, women of the planter elite were making choices in how they used, or didn't use, their voices—particularly relative to the real victims of slavery: the slaves.

7. I trace a similar ethical path, typically driven by personal economic concerns, in several male proslavery authors' lives (see Chapter 1).

8. South Carolina, for example, prohibited manumission in 1820 (see Johnson and Roark 100). Because of the ever-tightening restrictions on manumission, free blacks who lived in the South sometimes circumvented Southern law by purchasing friends or relatives as slaves, which Genovese believes accounts for the vast majority of black slaveholders, whose numbers by any count were never large. Regarding this phenomenon and manumission in general, see Genovese, *Roll, Jordan, Roll* 51, 399, 406–9.

9. Hentz, for example, spent her childhood and young adult years in the North and ended her days in Florida.

10. The first families of Virginia were commonly known as F.F.V.s. Mark Twain mockingly includes an F.F.V. among his cast of characters in *Pudd'nhead Wilson* (1894).

11. According to Tracy, 50 percent of white families in Alabama and Mississippi were slaveholders, and 25 percent in Virginia, North Carolina, Kentucky, Tennessee, and Texas.

12. Scott 28–32; for a long list of the plantation mistress's duties, see Grimball, December 29, 1860.

13. See Fox-Genovese, *Within the Plantation Household,* and Scott for substantially more on Thomas.

14. Notably, McIver never mentions the Civil War until July 20, 1861, at which point her references shift from "our negroes" to "negro laborers" (e.g., January 1, 1867), possibly indicating a developing awareness of the workers as at least employees and not merely extensions of herself and her property.

15. Fox-Genovese quotes McCorkle in *Within the Plantation Household* as one of numerous examples of mutual distrust (136); though it focuses primarily on the most upper-class women of the planter elite, the book explores this dynamic of shifting racial and gender hierarchies throughout.

16. Elizabeth Fox-Genovese and Eugene Genovese also discuss the relationship of the subordination of women to men, and the subordination of blacks to whites, both hierarchies preached as divinely ordained in the plantation South. See, for example, Fox-Genovese's "Family and Female Identity" and Genovese's "Our Family, White and Black."

17. See Gerda Lerner's *Grimké Sisters from South Carolina.*

18. See, for example, "A Folder of Student Compositions, 1840," Iverson L. Brooks Papers, Southern Historical Society, University of North Carolina at Chapel Hill. A few Southern men of prominence encouraged women's intellectual and literary pursuits, as did Reverend William Hooper, who urged, in his *Address on Female Education, Delivered before the Sedgewick Female Seminary, Feb. 27, 1845*: "Give us girls as can understand and delight in such a work as *Paradise Lost*, more than in . . . the trashy, insipid chat of town gossip, and I will soon show you a new race of men, ambitious to merit and to win the noble hearts of such a race of women" (qtd. in Scott 70). Even here, though, Hooper advocates the education of females only insofar as it benefits the development and interests of men.

19. Sarah Grimké to Harriet Hunt, December 31, 1852, Weld Papers, William L. Clements Library, University of Michigan.

20. Born near Columbus, Georgia, Wilson moved with her family to Texas, then to Alabama, where she made her adult home. In 1859, at age twenty-three, she published *Beulah*, the first sentimental novel to deal seriously with a woman's religious doubts. It sold twenty-one thousand copies in a little over a year (*Living Female Writers* 270).

21. Wilson, *St. Elmo* (New York: Dillingham, 1887–1897) 395, qtd. in Fidler 141.

22. Augusta Evans Wilson to J.L.M. Curry, July 15, 1863, J.L.M. Curry Papers, Manuscript Division, Library of Congress.

23. See Fox-Genovese, *Within the Plantation Household,* and Scott.

24. In *Revolution and the Word*, Cathy Davidson not only shows discrepancies among regional literacy rates, but also analyzes how and why those differences may have developed.

25. For one of the most thorough analyses of this process, see Genovese, *The World the Slaveholders Made.*

26. See, for example, Richard Coté's inventory of the prominent Pringle household in Charleston, South Carolina (184).

27. I argue in Chapter 5 that *Our Nig* is actually a revision of Stowe and a move beyond her racial template, rather than a rebuttal.

28. Among the many scholars who make this point, Papashvily argues it particularly well in regard to women's novels.

29. I began my research looking for white Southern women who were opposed to

slavery. Months of archival digging unearthed astoundingly—tragically—few examples.

30. One of Cash's theses in *The Mind of the South* concerns white male guilt over miscegenation and the attempt to compensate white women by glorifying them. See also Jones, *Tomorrow Is Another Day*.

31. Benjamin Hedrick, manuscript of speech, B. Hedrick to B. S. Hedrick, Benjamin S. Hedrick Papers, Manuscript Room, Duke University Library, Durham, N.C.

32. Felton's *Country Life in Georgia, in the Days of My Youth* is quoted in Scott (79).

33. In *Discovering the Women in Slavery*, Patricia Morton testifies to the extraordinary variety of enslaved worlds, which problematizes the "typical" experience of slave or slaveholding women.

34. An abundance of late twentieth- and early twenty-first-century scholarship has provided intriguing insights into Jacobs's life and work, as well as her professional and personal relationship to Harriet Beecher Stowe. See, for example, Yellin, Introduction; and, more recently, Goddu.

35. Christian abolitionists, on the other hand, pointed out that the biblical text never condones chattel slavery or race-based slavery as practiced in the American South. In addition, they highlighted the Exodus event, the Hebrew people's celebrated release from slavery, as a central metaphor of the Jewish and Christian faiths. Lyrics of slave spirituals also focus on Egypt, crossing over Jordan, pharaoh, and so on, as code language that signifies liberation from bondage. See, for example, West and Glaude Jr., *African American Religious Thought*.

36. Throughout her journal, and specifically February 17, 1842.

37. In the 1850s, the Virginia legislature spurned a petition that called for the repeal of the statute which prohibited teaching slaves to read, and the legislature refused to institute legal constraints on the separation of slave families (Degler 36).

38. Though often championed, at least initially, by those concerned for the welfare of former slaves, colonization efforts sometimes also worked against free blacks. Degler finds that by the end of 1831, in the wake of Nat Turner's rebellion, two hundred free blacks were compelled to emigrate to Liberia. Sarah Josepha Hale's novel *Liberia* reflects humanitarian concern for enslaved persons of color, though the impetus for the book's creation ranks it among anti–Uncle Tom narratives.

CHAPTER 5

Mothering the Other, Othering the Mother

1. Later in this chapter I discuss the implications of Wilson's full title: *Our Nig; or, Sketches from the Life of a Free Black, in a Two-Story White House, North. Showing that Slavery's Shadows Fall Even There. By "Our Nig."* I am indebted to Teresa Goddu for suggesting that I consider triangulating Stowe and the white anti–Uncle Tom writers with African American women's writing. I chose here to focus on Wilson's *Our Nig* because its fictive form offered more consistent

comparisons with the other novels I have examined. Harriet Jacobs's *Incidents in the Life of a Slave Girl*, however, also confounds any easy formulation of pro- or anti-Stowe and offers considerable possibilities for further examination in the context of the texts covered in this book. See Jean Fagan Yellin's introduction to *Incidents* for the background of Jacobs's dim view of Stowe.

2.   In his introduction to *Our Nig,* Henry Louis Gates Jr. provides helpful insight to Wilson's novel, and to what little has been discovered of Wilson herself. To my knowledge, it is largely thanks to Gates's efforts that Wilson is known to us at all in the twenty-first century.

3.   The one possible exception to this, the good-hearted James Bellmont, never opposes his mother's cruelty in any effective, long-lasting way, and while he leads Frado to a growing religious faith, he fails to save her from physical and emotional harm before he himself dies young, leaving his own wife and children to fend for themselves.

4.   Womanist theologian Delores S. Williams celebrates a "black history in which women took the lead, acting as catalysts for the community's revolutionary action and for social change" (64). Wilson would fit well into Williams's paradigm.

5.   See Gates's introduction to *Our Nig* for the discovery of Wilson as author. See also Sacvan Bercovitch's *American Jeremiad*; although Bercovitch's work almost exclusively concerns itself with the writings of white males, both Stowe and Wilson would fit nicely into his paradigm.

6.   Jean Fagan Yellin's preface and introduction to *Incidents* describes her long process of authenticating as Jacobs's the manuscript once thought to be a fictional creation of Lydia Maria Child.

7.   In *Playing in the Dark*, Morrison conducts several examinations of American literature in which racial stereotypes are reinscribed. Part of her book's message is a call for critical studies that disable these stereotypes.

8.   Appleton published several anti–Uncle Tom and generally proslavery novels.

9.   For several magnificent essays on the theology and culture behind the power of the black church and of King in particular, see West and Glaude Jr., *African American Religious Thought*.

10. See particularly Blake's "The Little Black Boy," "The Lamb," and "The Tyger." Wilson informs the reader in the final chapters that she embarked on a self-directed course of literary study, so she may well have been familiar with Blake's poetry, written a half century earlier.

11. On Topsy's wishing to be white, see, for example, *Uncle Tom's Cabin* 245.

12. See, for example, Wilson, *Our Nig* 69, 88, 93, 95–97, and Stowe, *Uncle Tom's Cabin*, chaps. 24, 25.

13. See Morrison's incisive discussions of borderlessness and traditional canonical American authors' fears of it (*Playing in the Dark* 51).

14. On the evils of racial equality for Northern racist whites, see, for example, Schoolcraft, *Black Gauntlet*, and Bolokitten, *A Sojourn in the City of Amalgamation, in the Year of Our Lord 18—*.

CHAPTER 6

Still Playing with Fire

1. Wilbur J. Cash became famous (and infamous) for his contention in *The Mind of the South* that the South depicted by the plantation romances and myths never existed. In attempting to explain the antebellum white South's perception of itself as a distinctive culture, recent scholars invoke the region's remaining fundamentally agrarian and thus necessarily relying primarily on familial relationships for social interaction, education, and production of goods, while the industrializing North increasingly allowed for individualism and the possibility of financial autonomy. See, for example, Fox-Genovese, *Within the Plantation Household*, and Morton, *Discovering the Women in Slavery*.

2. Louis Rubin Jr., among many others, draws this conclusion in his analysis of John Pendletom Kennedy, Nathaniel Beverley Tucker, William Alexander Caruthers, and John Esten Cooke.

3. As Watson notes, the education of nineteenth-century planter-class men, unlike the cavalier images of fiction, also was often lacking. Travelers' diaries reflect planter-class males' focus on "slaves, crops and shooting matches," and little concern for literature, or for learning in general. Certainly, however, their opportunities for education, whether taken or not, would have been far greater than those of their female counterparts (64).

4. Historian Anne Lewis Osler insightfully describes Hale's opposition to slavery in *Northwood* as "born of a desire to protect free labor" and Northern whites' self-interest (62). In fact, even her slaveholding characters who explicitly express their abhorrence of slavery never release their own slaves. Osler rightly suggests that with the publication of *Northwood*, Hale (and Catherine Sedgwick with her novel *Redwood*) "helped transform a congressional debate over slavery into a contest over revolutionary inheritance, a tactic that would eventually render sectional compromise impossible" (40).

5. In addition to Page, other postbellum apologists for the plantation South—including Joel Chandler Harris, author of the Uncle Remus stories and other novels, and Eugenia Jones Bacon, author of *Lyddy: A Tale of the Old South*—were widely read and were published and feted by New York houses. Bacon explicitly states that she is responding to Stowe, and in Harris's *Aunt Minervy Ann*, for example, black characters reflect the stereotypes of proslavery antebellum fiction: male slaves tend to be lazy, deceitful, and not terribly bright, while female slaves are bossy and overbearing, particularly toward black men, but always faithful toward whites. Exploring the interworkings of race, gender, and class, Lucinda H. MacKethan offers an incisive introduction to *Lyddy*.

6. Thomas Dixon's *The Klansman*, the basis of the white supremacist movie *Birth of a Nation*, was published in 1905. Some Deep Southerners still refer to the Civil War as "the War of Northern Aggression," or, particularly in Charleston, South Carolina, "the Late Unpleasantness." In the rural North Carolina hamlet where I

lived a few years ago, I once passed a bumper sticker that boasted a Confederate battle flag and the words "One Hundred Thirty Years of Foreign Rule: Time to Rebel."

7. Bruce's identification of the Civil War as a battle over slavery is intriguing, particularly given its contradiction of such commentators as Mary Chestnut, whose contemporary assessment of the Civil War was that not even one-third of the Confederate soldiers were themselves slaveholders, and not even a third of that third, the slaveholding soldiers, would actually frame slavery as a good idea. See her entry of August 18, 1861, in *A Diary from Dixie*.

8. Cf. Proverbs 3:11–12.

9. On politics of representation, see bell hooks, *Outlaw Culture* 7.

10. In *Roll, Jordan, Roll,* Genovese notes the case of Lou Smith, a South Carolina slave whose children had been sold away from her one after the other until at last she poisoned the next baby she bore and vowed she would have no more (497).

11. This "God will provide" uttered by a slave woman eerily echoes my slaveholding great-great-great-grandmother's admonitions to her own descendants. See the preface of this book.

12. See Sanchez-Eppler's illuminating discussion of Jacobs's work in terms of joining the personal and the political.

13. This scene of a Charleston slave auction and a physically exposed, sexually harassed slave woman is reminiscent of *Uncle Tom's Cabin* and other abolitionist texts, and even of a few scenes in some anti–Uncle Tom novels by men, though never in anti–Uncle Tom novels by women.

14. For example, in one poignant scene Other walks past her own white mother, Lady, to Mammy, who pulls Other, not her own black daughter, onto her lap to breast-feed.

15. In the 1960s, Fannie Lou Hamer said: "You [white women] thought you was *more* because you was a woman, and especially a white woman, you had this kind of angel feeling that you were untouchable; . . . but coming to the realization of the thing, her freedom is shackled in chains to mine, and she realizes for the first time that she is not free until I am free" (Palmer 462).

BIBLIOGRAPHY

FICTION

Adams, Nehemiah. *A Southside View of Slavery; or Three Months at the South*. Boston: T. R. Marvin and B. B. Mussey, 1854.

———. *The Sable Cloud: A Southern Tale, with Northern Comments*. Boston: Ticknor and Fields, 1861.

Bacon, Eugenia Jones. *Lyddy: A Tale of the Old South*. New York: Continental Publishing, 1898. Intro. Lucinda H. MacKethan. Athens: University of Georgia, 1998.

Baldwin, Joseph G. *Samuel Hele, Esq*. New York: D. Appleton, 1853.

Bradley, Mary E. *Douglass Farm: A Juvenile Story of Life in Virginia*. New York: D. Appleton, 1858.

[Brown, David]. *The Planter; or, Thirteen Years in the South*. By a Northern Man. Philadelphia: H. Hooker, 1853.

Bruce, Mrs. William Liddell [Andasia Kimbrough Bruce]. New York: Neale Publishing, 1906. *Uncle Tom's Cabin of Today*. Freeport, N. Y.: Books for Library Press, 1972.

Burwell, William M. [William McCreary]. *White Acre vs. Black Acre. A Case at Law*. Richmond, Va.: J. W. Random, 1856.

Butt, Martha Haines. *Antifanaticism; A Tale of the South*. Philadelphia: Lippincott, Grambo, 1853.

Chase, Lucian B. *English Serfdom and American Slavery: or Ourselves—As Others See Us*. New York: H. Long and Brother, 1854.

Cowdin, Mrs. V. G. *Ellen; or, The Fanatic's Daughter*. Mobile, Ala.: S. H. Goetzel, 1860.

Criswell, Robert. *Uncle Tom's Cabin Contrasted with Buckingham Hall, the Planter's Home; or, A Fair View of Both Sides of the Slavery Question*. New York: D. Fanshaw, 1852.

Cutler, Lizzie Petit. *Household Mysteries; A Romance of Southern Life*. New York: C. Appleton, 1856.

Delany, Martin R. *Blake; or, The Huts of America.* 1859–62. Boston: Beacon Press, 1970.

Douglass, Frederick. "The Heroic Slave." In *Autographs for Freedom,* ed. Julia Griffiths. Cleveland: John P. Jewett, 1853.

Eastman, Mary H. *Aunt Phillis' Cabin; or, Southern Life as It Is.* Philadelphia: Lippincott, Grambo, 1852.

[Estes, Matthew]. *Tit for Tat: A Novel by a Lady of New Orleans.* New York: Garret, 1856.

Flanders, Mrs. G. M. *The Ebony Idol, by a Lady of New England.* New York: D. Appleton, 1860.

Gilman, Caroline. *Recollections of a Southern Matron and a New England Bride.* New York: Harper and Brothers, 1838. New York: Harper and Brothers, 1852.

Hale, Sarah Josepha. *Liberia; or, Mr. Peyton's Experiment.* New York: Harper and Brothers, 1853.

———. *Northwood: Life North and South.* Boston: Bowles and Dearborn, 1827. New York: H. Long and Brother, 1852.

Hall, Baynard R. *Frank Freeman's Barber Shop: A Tale.* New York: C. Scribner, 1852.

Harland, Marion. *Alone.* Richmond, Va.: A. Morris, 1854.

Harper, Frances Ellen Watkins. *Iola Leroy; or, Shadows Uplifted.* Philadelphia: Garrigues and Brothers, 1892. Introd. Frances Smith Foster. New York: Oxford University Press, 1988.

Harris, Joel Chandler. *The Chronicles of Aunt Minervy Ann.* New York: Charles Scribner's Sons, 1899.

———. *On the Plantation: A Story of a Georgia Boy's Adventures during the War.* 1892. Athens: University of Georgia Press, 1980.

Hentz, Caroline Lee. *The Planter's Northern Bride: A Novel.* 2 vols. Philadelphia: T.B. Peterson, 1854. Chapel Hill: University of North Carolina Press, 1970.

Herndon, Mary E. *Louise Elton; or, Things Seen and Heard.* Philadelphia: Lippincott, Crambo, 1853.

Hungerford, James W. *The Old Plantation, and What I Gathered There in an Autumn Month.* New York: Harper, 1857.

Ingraham, Joseph Holt. *The Sunny South; or, The Southerner at Home: Embracing Five Years' Experience of a Northern Governess in the Land of the Sugar and the Cotton.* Philadelphia: G. G. Evans, 1860.

Kennedy, John Pendleton. *Swallow Barn.* London: Printed for A.K. Newman and Co., 1832. New York: G. P. Putnam, 1856.

Latimer, Elizabeth Wormeley. *Our Cousin Veronica; or, Scenes and Adventures over the Blue Ridge.* New York: Bunce, 1855.

Little Eva. The Flower of the South. Aunt Mary's Picture Book. New York: Phil. J. Coxans, c. 1853.

Longstreet, Augustus Baldwin. *Georgia Scenes.* New York: Harper and Brothers, 1840. New York: Harper and Brothers, 1897.

[Mathews, Theodore Dehone]. *Old Toney and His Master; or, The Abolitionist and the Land-Pirate, Founded on Facts: A Tale of 1824–1827. By Desmos* (pseud.). Nashville: Southwestern Publishing House, 1861.

McIntosh, Maria Jane. *The Lofty and the Lowly; or, Good in All and None All Good.* 2 vols. New York: D. Appleton, 1853.

Mitchell, Margaret. *Gone with the Wind.* 1936. New York: Warner Books, 1993.

Morrison, Toni. *Beloved.* New York: Alfred A. Knopf, 1987. New York: Signet, 1991.

Neville, Lawrence. *Edith Allen; or, Sketches of Life in Virginia.* Richmond: J. W. Randolph, 1855.

The Olive-Branch; or, White Oak Farm. Philadelphia: J. B. Lippincott, 1857.

Page, John W. *Uncle Robin in His Cabin in Virginia, and Tom without One in Boston.* Richmond: J. W. Randolph, 1853.

Price, Eugenia. *Savannah.* New York: Doubleday, 1983. New York: Berkley, 1984.

Randall, Alice. *The Wind Done Gone.* New York: Houghton Mifflin, 2001.

Randolph, J. Thornton [Charles Jacobs Peterson, pseud.]. *The Cabin and the Parlor; or, Slaves and Masters.* Philadelphia: T. B. Peterson, 1852.

Rush, Caroline E. *The North and South; or, Slavery and Its Contrasts.* Philadelphia: Crissy and Markley, 1852.

Schoolcraft, Mrs. Henry R. [Mary Howard Schoolcraft]. *The Black Gauntlet: A Tale of Plantation Life in South Carolina.* Philadelphia: J. B. Lippincott, 1860.

Simms, William Gilmore. *Woodcraft; or, Hawks about the Dovecote: A Story of the South at the Close of the Revolution.* New York: J. S. Redfield, 1854.

Smith, William L. G. *Life at the South; or, "Uncle Tom's Cabin" as It Is: Being Narratives, Scenes, and Incidents in the Real "Life of the Lowly."* Buffalo, N. Y.: George H. Darby, 1852.

[Smythe, James M.]. *Ethel Somers; or, The Fate of the Union. By a Southerner.* Augusta, Ga.: H. D. Norrell, 1857.

Southworth, Emma Dorothy Eliza Nevitte [E.D.E.N.]. *The Curse of Clifton: A Tale of Expiation and Redemption.* London: Clake, Beeton, 1852.

———. *Virginia and Magdalene.* Philadelphia: A. Hart, 1852.

[Starnes, Ebenezer]. *The Slaveholder Abroad; or, Billy Buck's Visit with His Master, to England.* Philadelphia: J. B. Lippincott Co., 1860.

Stowe, Harriet Beecher. *Uncle Tom's Cabin, or Life among the Lowly.* Boston: John P. Jewett, 1852. Ed. Elizabeth Ammons. Norton Critical Editions. New York: W.W. Norton, 1994.

———. *The Minister's Wooing.* New York: Derby and Jackson, 1859. Cambridge, Mass.: Houghton Mifflin, 1896.

Tademy, Lalita. *Cane River.* New York: Warner Books, 2001.

Thorpe, Thomas B. *The Master's House; or, Scenes Descriptive of Southern Life.* 3rd ed. New York: J. C. Derby, 1855.

Vidi [pseud.]. *Mr. Frank, the Underground Mail-Agent.* Philadelphia: Lippincott, Grambo, 1853.

Wiley, Calvin Henderson. *Utopia; An Early Picture of Life at the South.* Philadelphia: T. B. Petersen, 1852.

Wilson, Augusta Jane Evans. *Beulah.* New York: G. W. Dillingham, 1859.

Wilson, Harriet E. *Our Nig; or, Sketches from the Life of a Free Black, in a Two-Story White House, North. Showing that Slavery's Shadows Fall Even There. By "Our Nig."* Boston: Geo. C. Rand, 1859. New York: Random House, 1983.

Yankee Slave-Dealer; or, An Abolitionist down South: A Tale for the Times. By a Texan. Nashville: Author, 1860.

DIARIES, LETTERS, AND OTHER NONFICTION PRIMARY SOURCES

Bolokitten, Oliver, Esq. [pseud.]. *A Sojourn in the City of Amalgamation, in the Year of Our Lord 18—.* New York: Author, 1835.

Brevard, Keziah Goodwyn Hopkins. *A Plantation Mistress on the Eve of the Civil War: The Diary of Keziah Goodwyn Hopkins Brevard.* Columbia: University of South Carolina Press, 1993.

Bumpus, Fanny Moore Webb. Diary. Southern Historical Collection, University of North Carolina, Chapel Hill.

Carolinian. *Slavery in the Southern States.* Cambridge: John Bartlett, 1852.

Chestnut, Mary Boykin. *A Diary from Dixie.* 1949. Ed. Ben Ames Williams. Foreword by Edmund Wilson. Cambridge: Harvard University Press, 1962.

———. *Mary Chestnut's Civil War.* Ed. C. Vann Woodward. New Haven: Yale University Press, 1981.

Dawson, Sarah Morgan. *A Confederate Girl's Diary.* Boston: Houghton Mifflin, 1913.

Felton, Rebecca Latimer. *Country Life in Georgia, in the Days of My Youth.* Atlanta: Index Printing, 1919.

Fidler, William Perry. *Augusta Evans Wilson.* Tuscaloosa: University of Alabama Press, 1951.

Fitzhugh, George. *Sociology for the South.* Richmond: Morris, 1854.

Fox, Tryphena Blanche. *A Northern Woman in the Plantation South: Letters of Tryphena Blanche Fox, 1856–1876.* Columbia: University of South Carolina Press, 1993.

Grimké, Angelina. "Appeal to the Christian Women of the South." In *The Heath Anthology of American Literature,* vol. 1, ed. Paul Lauter et al. Lexington, Mass.: D. C. Heath, 1990, pp. 1826–34.

Grimké, Sarah. *Letter on Equality of the Sexes.* Boston: I. Knapp, 1838.

Harrison, Constance Cary. *Recollections Grave and Gay.* London: Smith, Elder, 1912.

Hentz, Caroline Lee. Diary. Southern Literary Collection, University of North Carolina, Chapel Hill.

Hurmence, Belinda, ed. *Before Freedom, When I Just Can Remember: Twenty-seven*

Oral Histories of Former South Carolina Slaves. Winston-Salem, N.C.: J. F. Blair, 1989.

Jacobs, Harriet A. *Incidents in the Life of a Slave Girl: Written by Herself.* Cambridge: Harvard University Press, 1987.

Julian of Norwich. *Revelations of Divine Love.* New York: Penguin Books, 1966.

Kemble, Frances Anne. *Journal of a Residence on a Georgian Plantation in 1838–39.* New York: Alfred A. Knopf, 1961. Ed. John A. Scott. Athens: University of Georgia Press, 1984.

Lady in New-York. *The Patent Key to Uncle Tom's Cabin; or, Mrs. Stowe in England.* New York: Pudney and Russell, 1853.

McCord, Louisa S. Review of *Uncle Tom's Cabin* by Harriet Beecher Stowe. *Southern Quarterly Review* 23 (1853), 81:120.

McDonald, Cornelia. *A Diary with Reminiscences of the War and Refugee Life on the Shenandoah Valley.* Nashville: Cullom and Ghertner, 1935.

McIver, Sarah. Diary. Southern Historical Collection, University of North Carolina, Chapel Hill.

Norton, Sara, and Mark A. DeWolfe Howe. *Letters of Charles Eliot Norton, with Biographical Comment.* Boston: Houghton Mifflin, 1913.

Phillips, Wendell. *Speeches, Lectures, and Letters.* Boston: James Redpath, 1863.

Richmond, Legh. *Authentic Narratives—Abridged.* New York: American Tract Society, c. 1850.

Saxon, Elizabeth Lyle. *A Southern Woman's Wartime Reminiscences.* privately printed, 1905.

Shewmake, Susan Cornwall. Diary. Southern Historical Collection, University of North Carolina, Chapel Hill.

Simms, William Gilmore. Review of *A Key to Uncle Tom's Cabin,* by Harriet Beecher Stowe. *Southern Quarterly Review* 7 (1853): 214–54.

Smedes, Susan Dabney. *Memorials of a Southern Planter.* Ed. Fletcher Green. New York: Knopf, 1965.

Stearns, E. J. *Notes on* Uncle Tom's Cabin, *being a Logical Answer to Its Allegations and Inferences against Slavery as an Institution.* Philadephia: Lippincott, Grambo, 1853.

Stone, Kate. *Brockenburn: The Journal of Kate Stone.* Ed. John Q. Anderson. Baton Rouge: Louisiana State University Press, 1955.

Thomas, Ella Gertrude Clanton. Diary. Manuscripts Dept., Duke University.

"*Uncle Tom's Cabin* and Its Opponents." *Eclectic Review* 4 (1852): 717–44.

HISTORY, CRITICISM, AND THEORY

Allen, Theodore. *The Invention of the White Race.* Vol. 1. New York: Verso, 1994.

Ammons, Elizabeth. "Heroines in Uncle Tom's Cabin." *American Literature* 49 (1977): 161–79.

————. "Stowe's Dream of the Mother-Savior: *Uncle Tom's Cabin* and American Women Writers before 1920." In *New Essays on* Uncle Tom's Cabin. New York: Cambridge University Press, 1986.

Bakhtin, M. M. *The Dialogic Imagination: Four Essays by M. M. Bakhtin.* Ed. Michael Holquist. Trans. Caryl Emerson and Michael Holquist. Austin: University of Texas Press, 1981.

Bartlett, Irving H., and C. Glenn Cambor. "The History and Psychodynamics of Southern Womanhood." *Women's Studies* 2 (1974): 11–20.

Baym, Nina. *Woman's Fiction: A Guide to Novels by and about Women in America, 1820–1870.* Ithaca: Cornell University Press, 1978.

Bell, Roseann P., Bettye J. Parker, and Beverly Guy-Sheftell, eds. *Sturdy Black Bridges: Visions of Black Women in Literature.* Garden City, N.Y.: Anchor, 1979.

Bercovitch, Sacvan. *The American Jeremiad.* Madison: University of Wisconsin Press, 1978.

Bleser, Carol, ed. *The Hammonds of Redcliffe.* New York: Oxford University Press, 1981.

————, ed. *In Joy and in Sorrow: Women, Family, and Marriage in the Victorian South, 1830–1900.* New York: Oxford University Press, 1991.

Bloch, Ruth H. "American Feminine Ideals in Transition: The Rise of the Moral Mother, 1785–1815." *Feminist Studies* 4 (June 1978): 100-126

Braxton, Joanne M. *Black Women Writing Autobiography: A Tradition within a Tradition.* Philadelphia: Temple University Press, 1989.

Browne, Margaret. "Southern Reactions to *Uncle Tom's Cabin.*" MA thesis, Duke University, 1994.

Brown, Gillian. *Domestic Individualism: Imagining Self in Nineteenth-Century America.* Los Angeles: University of California Press, 1990.

Bynum, Caroline Walker. *Jesus as Mother: Studies in the Spirituality of the High Middle Ages.* Berkeley: University of California Press, 1982.

Carby, Hazel. " 'On the Threshold of Women's Era': Lynching, Empire, and Sexuality in Black Feminist Theory." In *"Race," Writing, and Difference,* ed. Henry Louis Gates Jr. Chicago: University of Chicago Press, 1986.

————. *Reconstructing Womanhood: The Emergence of the Afro-American Woman Novelist.* New York: Oxford University Press, 1987.

Cash, Wilbur J. *The Mind of the South.* New York: A. A. Knopf, 1941.

Castronovo, Russ. "Incidents in the Life of a White Woman: Economies of Race and Gender in the Antebellum Nation." *American Literary History* 10.2 (Summer 1998): 239–65.

Clinton, Catherine. *The Plantation Mistress: Woman's World in the Old South.* New York: Pantheon Books, 1982.

————. "Sex and Sectional Conflict." In *Taking Off the White Gloves: Southern Women and Women Historians,* ed. Michele Gillespie and Catherine Clinton. Columbia: University of Missouri Press, 1998. 43–63.

————. " 'Southern Dishonor': Flesh, Blood, Race, and Bondage." In *In Joy and in*

Sorrow: Women, Family, and Marriage in the Victorian South, ed. Carol Bleser. New York: Oxford University Press, 1991. 52–68.

———. *Tara Revisited: Women, War, and the Plantation Legend.* New York: Abbeville Press, 1995.

Clinton, Catherine, and Michele Gillespie, eds. *The Devil's Lane: Sex and Race in the Early South.* New York: Oxford University Press, 1997.

Collins, Patricia Hill. "Shifting the Center: Race, Class, and Feminist Theorizing about Motherhood." In *Representations of Motherhood,* ed. Donna Basin et al. New Haven: Yale University Press, 1994.

Cone, James H. "Black Theology: Where We Have Been and a Vision for Where We Are Going." In *Yearning to Breathe Free: Liberation Theologies in the United States,* ed. Mar Peter-Raoul, Linda Rennie Forcey, and Robert Frederick Hunter Jr. Maryknoll, N. Y.: Orbis Books, 1990. 48–60.

———. *God of the Oppressed.* 1975. Maryknoll, N.Y.: Orbis Books, 1997.

Coté, Richard N. *Mary's World: Love, War, and Family Ties in Nineteenth-Century Charleston.* Mount Pleasant, S.C.: Corinthian Books, 2003.

Cowie, Alexander. "The Vogue of the Domestic Novel, 1850–1870." *South Atlantic Quarterly* 41 (October 1942): 420.

Cuenca, Carme Manuel. "An Angel in the Plantation: The Economics of Slavery and the Politics of Literary Domesticity in Caroline Lee Hentz's *The Planter's Northern Bride.*" *Mississippi Quarterly* 51 (Winter 1997–98): 87–104.

Darden, Robert R. *People Get Ready: A New History of Black Gospel Music.* New York: Continuum, 2004.

Davidson, Cathy N. *Revolution and the Word: The Rise of the Novel in America.* New York: Oxford University Press, 1986.

Degler, Carl N. *The Other South: Southern Dissenters in the Nineteenth Century.* New York: Harper and Row, 1974.

Donald, David. "The Pro-Slavery Argument Reconsidered." *Journal of Southern History* 37 (February 1971): 3–18.

Donaldson, Susan V., and Anne Goodwyn Jones. "Haunted Bodies: Rethinking the South through Gender." In *Haunted Bodies: Gender and Southern Texts,* ed. Donaldson and Jones. Charlottesville: University Press of Virginia, 1997. 1–22.

Eaton, Clement. *The Mind of the Old South.* Baton Rouge: Louisiana State University Press, 1964.

Evans, Sara M. "Women." In *The Encyclopedia of Southern History,* ed. David C. Roller and Robert W. Twyman. Baton Rouge: Louisiana State University Press, 1979. 1353–55.

Fox-Genovese, Elizabeth. "Family and Female Identity in the Antebellum South: Sarah Gayle and Her Family." In *In Joy and in Sorrow: Women, Family, and Marriage in the Victorian South, 1830–1900,* ed. Carol Bleser. New York: Oxford University Press, 1991. 15–31.

———. *Within the Plantation Household: Black and White Women of the Old South.* Chapel Hill: University of North Carolina Press, 1988.

Frankenberg, Ruth. "Whiteness and Americanness: Examining Constructions of Race, Culture, and Nation in White Women's Life Narratives." In *Race*, ed. Steven Gregory and Roger Sanjek. New Brunswick, N.J.: Rutgers University Press, 1994. 62–77.

———. *White Women, Race Matters: The Social Construction of Whiteness*. Minneapolis: University of Minnesota Press, 1993.

Franklin, John Hope. *From Slavery to Freedom: A History of Negro Americans*. 3rd ed. New York: Vintage Books, 1969.

Gaines, Francis Pendleton. *The Southern Plantation: A Study in the Development and the Accuracy of a Tradition*. New York: Columbia University Press, 1925.

Gardiner, Jane. "The Assault upon Uncle Tom: Attempts of Pro-Slavery Novelists to Answer *Uncle Tom's Cabin*, 1852–60." *Southern Humanities Review* 12 (1978): 313–24.

Gates, Henry Louis Jr. Introduction to *Our Nig; or, Sketches from the Life of a Free Black, in a Two-Story White House, North. Showing that Slavery's Shadows Fall Even There. By "Our Nig,"* by Harriet E. Wilson. 1859. New York: Random House, 1983.

———, ed. *"Race," Writing, and Difference*. Chicago: University of Chicago Press, 1986.

Genovese, Eugene D. " 'Our Family, White and Black': Family and Household in the Southern Slaveholders' World View." In *In Joy and in Sorrow: Women, Family, and Marriage in the Victorian South, 1830–1900*, ed. Carol Bleser. New York: Oxford University Press, 1991. 69–87.

———. "Toward a Kinder and Gentler America: The Southern Lady in the Greening of the Politics of the Old South." In *In Joy and in Sorrow: Women, Family, and Marriage in the Victorian South,* ed. Carol Bleser. New York: Oxford University Press, 1991. 125–134.

———. *The World the Slaveholders Made: Two Essays in Interpretation*. New York: Pantheon, 1969.

Goddu, Teresa A. *Gothic America: Narrative, History, and Nation*. New York: Columbia University Press, 1997.

Gossett, Thomas F. *Race: The History of an Idea in America*. Dallas: Southern Methodist University Press, 1963.

———. Uncle Tom's Cabin *and American Culture*. Dallas: Southern Methodist University Press, 1985.

Gross, Theodore. Preface to *America in Literature*. Vol. 2. Ed. Gross. New York: Wiley Press, 1978.

Gutierez, Gustavo. *The Power of the Poor in History*. Trans. Robert R. Barr. Maryknoll, N.Y.: Orbis Books, 1984.

———. *A Theology of Liberation: History, Politics, and Salvation*. Ed. and trans. Sister Caridad Inda and John Eagleson. Maryknoll, N.Y.: Orbis Books, 1973.

Gwin, Minrose C. *Black and White Women of the Old South: The Peculiar Sisterhood in American Literature*. Knoxville: University of Tennessee Press, 1985.

Hall, Jacquelyn Dowd. *Revolt against Chivalry: Jessie Daniel Ames and the Women's Campaign against Lynching.* New York: Columbia University Press, 1979.

Haney-Lopez, Ian. *White by Law: The Legal Construction of Race.* New York: New York University Press, 1996.

Harris, Cheryl. "Whiteness as Property." In *Critical Race Theory: The Key Writings that Formed the Movement*, ed. Kimberlé Crenshaw et al. New York: New Press, 1995. 276–91.

Hayne, Barrie. "Yankee in the Patriarchy: T. B. Thorpe's Reply to *Uncle Tom's Cabin.*" *American Quarterly* 20 (1968): 180-95.

Helper, Hinton Rowan. *The Impending Crisis of the South: How to Meet It.* New York: Burdick Brothers, 1857.

Higginbotham, Evelyn Brooks. "African-American Women's History and the Metalanguage of Race." In *Revising the Word and the World: Essays in Feminist Literary Criticism*, ed. VeVe A. Clark, Ruth-Ellen B. Joeres, and Madelon Sprengnether. Chicago: University of Chicago Press, 1993.

hooks, bell. *Black Looks: Race and Representation.* Boston: South End Press, 1992.

———. *Feminist Theory from Margin to Center.* Boston: South End Press, 1984.

———. *Outlaw Culture: Resisting Representations.* New York: Routledge, 1994.

Johnson, Michael P., and James L. Roark. "Strategies of Survival: Free Negro Families and the Problem of Slavery." In *In Joy and in Sorrow: Women, Family, and Marriage in the Victorian South, 1830–1900*, ed. Carol Bleser. New York: Oxford University Press, 1991. 88–102.

Jones, Jane Anne Goodwyn. *Tomorrow Is Another Day: The Woman Writer in the South, 1859–1936.* Baton Rouge: Louisiana University Press, 1981.

Kaplan, Amy. "Manifest Domesticity." *American Literature* 70.1 (September 1998): 581–606.

Kaplan, Amy, and Donald E. Pease, eds. *Cultures of United States Imperialism.* Durham: Duke University Press, 1993.

Kelley, Mary. *Private Woman, Public Stage: Literary Domesticity in Nineteenth-Century America.* New York: Oxford University Press, 1984.

———. "The Sentimentalists: Promise and Betrayal in the Home." *Signs* 4 (Spring 1979): 434-46.

Kreyling, Michael. *Figures of the Hero in Southern Narrative.* Baton Rouge: Louisiana State University Press, 1987.

Lerner, Gerda. *The Creation of American Feminist Consciousness: From the Middle Ages to 1870.* New York: Oxford University Press, 1993.

———. *The Creation of Patriarchy.* New York: Oxford University Press, 1986.

———. *The Grimké Sisters from South Carolina: Pioneers for Women's Rights and Abolition.* New York: Oxford University Press, 1967. New York: Schocken Books, 1971.

Levy, David. "Racial Stereotypes in Antislavery Fiction." *Phylon* 31 (Fall 1970): 265-79.

Lincoln, C. Eric. "The Racial Factor in the Shaping of Religion in America." In *African*

American Religious Thought, ed. Cornel West and Eddie S. Glaude Jr. Louisville, Ky.: Westminster John Knox Press, 2003.

MacKethan, Lucinda H. "Domesticity in Dixie: The Plantation Novel and *Uncle Tom's Cabin*." In *Haunted Bodies: Gender and Southern Texts*, ed. Susan V. Donaldson and Anne Goodwyn Jones. Charlottesville: University Press of Virginia, 1997. 223–42.

Marable, Manning. "Groundings with My Sisters: Patriarchy and the Exploitation of Black Women." In *Black Women's History: Theory and Practice*. Vol. 2. Ed. Darlene Clark Hine. Brooklyn: Carlson Publishing, 1990. 407–46.

Marx, Karl and Friedrich Engles. *The Communist Manifesto*. London: Published for the Communist League, 1848. New York: Washington Square Press, 1965.

McCurry, Stephanie. *Masters of Small Worlds: Yeoman Households, Gender Relations, and the Political Culture of the Antebellum South Carolina Low Country*. New York: Oxford University Press, 1995.

McFague, Sallie. "Mother God." In *Motherhood: Experience, Institution, Theology*, ed. Anne Carr and Elisabeth Schussler Fiorenza. Edinburgh: T and T Clark, 1989. 138–44.

McMillen, Sally Gregory. *Motherhood in the Old South: Pregnancy, Childbirth, and Infant Rearing*. Baton Rouge: Louisiana State University Press, 1990.

Merish, Lori. *Sentimental Materialism: Gender, Commodity Culture, and Nineteenth-Century American Literature*. Durham: Duke University Press, 2000.

Morrison, Toni. *Playing in the Dark: Whiteness and the Literary Imagination*. Cambridge: Harvard University Press, 1992.

Morton, Patricia. *Discovering the Women in Slavery: Emancipating Perspectives on the American Past*. Athens: University of Georgia Press, 1996.

———. *Disfigured Images: The Historical Assault on Afro-American Women*. New York: Greenwood Press, 1991.

Moss, Elizabeth. *Domestic Novelists in the Old South: Defenders of Southern Culture*. Baton Rouge: Louisiana State University Press, 1992.

Nuhrah, Arthur G. "John McDonough: Man of Many Facets." *Louisiana Historical Quarterly* 33 (1950): 125–26.

Osler, Anne Lewis. " 'That Damned Mob': Northern and Southern Women Writers and the Coming of the American Civil War." Ph.D. diss., University of Wisconsin–Madison, 1995.

Paine, Gregory, Ed. *Southern Prose Writers*. Atlanta: American Book Company, 1947.

Painter, Nell Irvin. "Soul Murder and Slavery." Charles Edmondson Historical Lectures. Baylor University, Waco, Tex., 5–6 April 1993.

Palmer, Phyllis Marynick. "White Women/Black Women: The Dualism of Female Identity and Experience in the United States." In *Black Women's History: Theory and Practice*. Vol. 2. Ed. Darlene Clark Hine. Brooklyn: Carlson Publishing, 1990. 447–66.

Papashvily, Helen Waite. *All the Happy Endings*. New York: Harper and Brothers, 1956.

Parish, Peter J. *Slavery: History and Historians*. New York: Harper and Row, 1989.

Perry, Carolyn, and Mary Louise Weaks, eds. *The History of Southern Women's Literature*. Baton Rouge: Louisiana State University Press, 2002.

Railton, Stephen. *Uncle Tom's Cabin and American Culture*. Institute for Advanced Technology in the Humanities, University of Virginia and the Harriet Beecher Stowe Society, Hartford, Conn., 23 November 2003. *http://www.iath.virginia.edu/utc/index2f.html*.

Rich, Adrienne. *Of Woman Born: Motherhood as Experience and Institution*. New York: Bantam, 1977.

Ridgely, J. V. *Nineteenth-Century Southern Literature*. Lexington: University Press of Kentucky, 1980.

Romero, Lora. *Home Fronts: Domesticity and Its Critics in the Antebellum United States*. Durham: Duke University Press, 1997.

Rose, Willie Lee, ed. *A Documentary History of Slavery in North America*. New York: Oxford University Press, 1976.

Rubin, Louis D. Jr., ed. *The History of Southern Literature*. Baton Rouge: Louisiana University Press, 1985.

Samuels, Shirley, ed. *The Culture of Sentiment: Race, Gender, and Sentimentality in Nineteenth-Century America*. New York: Oxford University Press, 1992.

Sanchez-Eppler, Karen. *Touching Liberty: Abolition, Feminism, and the Politics of the Body*. Berkeley: University of California Press, 1993.

Saxton, Alexander. *The Rise and Fall of the White Republic: Class Politics and Mass Culture in Nineteenth-Century America*. New York: Verso, 1990.

Scott, Anne Firor. *The Southern Lady: From Pedestal to Politics, 1830–1930*. Chicago: University of Chicago Press, 1970.

Simpson, Lewis P. *The Dispossessed Garden: Pastoral and History in Southern Literature*. Athens: University of Georgia Press, 1975.

Smith, Karen Manners. "Southern Women Writers' Responses to Uncle Tom's Cabin." In *The History of Southern Women's Literature*, ed. Carolyn Perry and Mary Louise Weaks. Baton Rouge: Louisiana State University Press, 2002.

Smith, Lillian. *Killers of the Dream*. New York: Norton, 1947. New York: Doubleplay, 1961.

Starke, Catherine. *Black Portraitures in American Fiction: Stock Characters, Archetypes, and Individuals*. New York: Basic Books, 1971.

Steckel, Richard H. "Women, Work, and Health under Plantation Slavery in the United States." In *More Than Chattel: Black Women and Slavery in the Americas*, ed. David Barry Gaspar and Darlene Clark Hine. Bloomington: Indiana University Press, 1996. 43–60.

Sterling, Dorothy, ed. *Turning the World Upside Down: The Anti- Slavery Convention of American Women*. New York: Feminist Press, 1987.

————, ed. *We Are Your Sisters: Black Women in the Nineteenth Century.* New York: W.W. Norton, 1984. New York: W. W. Norton, 1997.

Stowe, Charles Edward. *Life of Harriet Beecher Stowe Compiled from Her Letters and Journals.* Boston: Houghton Mifflin, 1890.

Sundquist, Eric, ed. *New Essays on Uncle Tom's Cabin.* New York: Cambridge University Press, 1986.

————. *To Wake the Nations: Race in the Making of American Literature and Culture.* Cambridge: Harvard University Press, 1993.

Takaki, Ronald. *A Different Mirror: A History of Multicultural America.* Boston: Little, Brown, 1993.

————. *Iron Cages: Race and Culture in Nineteenth-Century America.* New York: Oxford University Press, 1990.

Tandy, Jeanette Reid, "Pro-Slavery Propaganda in American Fiction of the Fifties." *South Atlantic Quarterly* 21 (1922): 41–50 (part 1); 170–78 (part 2).

Taylor, William R. *Cavalier and Yankee: The Old South and American National Character.* New York: Braziller, 1963.

Tompkins, Jane. *Sensational Designs: The Cultural Work of American Fiction, 1790–1860.* New York: Oxford University Press, 1985.

————. "*Uncle Tom's Cabin* and the Politics of Literary History." *Glyph* 8 (1981): 79–102.

Tracy, Susan Jean. *In the Master's Eye: Representations of Women, Blacks, and Poor Whites in Antebellum Southern Literature.* Amherst: University of Massachusetts Press, 1995.

Trible, Phillis. *God and the Rhetoric of Sexuality.* Philadelphia: Fortress Press, 1978.

Wacker, Marie-Theres. "God as Mother? On the Meaning of a Biblical God-Symbol for Feminist Theology." In *Motherhood: Experience, Institution, Theology,* ed. Anne Carr and Elizabeth Schussler Fiorenza. Edinburgh: T and T Clark, 1989. 103–11.

Watson, Ritchie Devon Jr. *The Cavalier in Virginia Fiction.* Baton Rouge: Louisiana State University Press, 1985.

Welter, Barbara. "The Cult of True Womanhood: 1820–1860." *American Quarterly* 18 (Summer 1966): 151–74.

————. "The Feminization of American Religion, 1800–1860." In *Dimity Convictions,* Ed. Barbara Welter. Athens: Ohio University Press, 1976.

West, Cornel. *Race Matters.* New York: Vintage Books, 1993.

West, Cornel, and Eddie S. Glaude Jr., eds. *African American Religious Thought.* Louisville, Ky.: Westminster John Knox Press, 2003.

Williams, Delores S. "Womanist Theology: Black Women's Voices." In *Yearning to Breathe Free: Liberation Theologies in the United States,* ed. Mar Peter-Raoul, Linda Rennie Forcey, and Robert Frederick Hunter Jr. Maryknoll, N.Y.: Orbis Books, 1990. 62–69.

Wills, Gary. *'Negro President': Jefferson and the Slave Power.* New York: Houghton Mifflin, 2003.

Wyatt-Brown, Bertram. *Hearts of Darkness: Wellsprings of a Southern Literary Tradition.* Baton Rouge: Louisiana State University Press, 2003.

———. *Honor and Violence in the Old South.* New York: Oxford University Press, 1986.

———. *Lewis Tappan and the Evangelical War against Slavery.* Cleveland: Press of Case Western Reserve University, 1969.

Yellin, Jean Fagan. *The Intricate Knot: Black Figures in American Literature, 1776–1863.* New York: New York University Press, 1972.

———. Introduction to *Incidents in the Life of a Slave Girl. Written By Herself.* Boston: Published for the author, 1861. Cambridge: Harvard University Press, 1987.

INDEX